For David Erdman

who has put all
students of Romantic
literature, including
this one, in his debt

with my best wishes,

Laurence Moldstein

RUINS AND EMPIRE

Young Girls Dancing Around an Obelisk, by Hubert Robert. Courtesy of the Montreal Museum of Fine Arts.

RUINS
AND
EMPIRE

*The Evolution of a Theme
in Augustan and Romantic Literature*

LAURENCE GOLDSTEIN

University of Pittsburgh Press

Published by the University of Pittsburgh Press, Pittsburgh, Pa. 15260

Copyright © 1977, University of Pittsburgh Press
All rights reserved
Feffer and Simons, Inc., London
Manufactured in the United States of America

Library of Congress Cataloging in Publication Data

Goldstein, Laurence, birth date
  Ruins and empire.

  Includes bibliographical references and index.
  1. English literature—18th century—History and criticism. 2. English literature—19th century—History and criticism. 3. Ruins in literature. I. Title.
PR449.R9G6   820'.9   76-50889
ISBN 0-8229-3345-4

Grateful acknowledgment is made for permission to reprint the following:

Lines from *At the End of the Open Road,* copyright © by Louis Simpson. Reprinted by
permission of Wesleyan University Press.

Lines from "Watering the Horse" reprinted from *Silence in the Snowy Fields,* Wesleyan
University Press, © 1962 by Robert Bly.

For Cecil and Helen Goldstein

 About the Author

LAURENCE GOLDSTEIN is Assistant Professor of English at the University of Michigan. A graduate of the University of California, Los Angeles, he received his Ph.D. from Brown University. Abattoir Editions (University of Nebraska at Omaha) will publish his first volume of poems, *Altamira*, in 1978. He is an editor of the *Michigan Quarterly Review*.

 Contents

 Illustrations

Illustrations

 Acknowledgments

THE FIRST POEM about ruins I remember reading is Pablo Neruda's *Alturas de Macchu Picchu,* which I carried with me on a visit to the Inca site and read on the slopes above the Urubamba River. That may have been the origin of this book, and an appropriate one since many of the authors I discuss conceived their work while gazing at the decay they would later memorialize.

A grant from the Horace Rackham School of Graduate Studies of the University of Michigan enabled me to begin work on this project. A fellowship from the Andrew Mellon Foundation provided me with a year at the University of Pittsburgh to bring it to completion.

Chapter one appeared in the *Journal of English and Germanic Philology;* an essay in *ELH, A Journal of English Literary History* made use of material from several chapters. For permission to reprint in a revised form I wish to thank the respective editors.

Special thanks are due to James Boulger and Robert Stilwell for their constant encouragement and their useful comments on the manuscript. Richard C. Boys, Bert Hornback, James Gindin, Radcliffe Squires, John Styan, Barton St. Armand, and R. H. Super each contributed valuable suggestions and stimulated me to broaden the range of discussion by their own wide knowledge of literary history.

And most of all I am grateful to my wife Nancy for her scrupulous and sympathetic reading, and rereading, of the manuscript.

Acknowledgments

 Textual Note

IN THIS BOOK I quote from texts both obscure and celebrated. My guiding principle has been to use editions which are reliable, accessible, and designed to aid consultation. I have retained the editors' orthography in each instance. Editions I quote from extensively are listed below, with the short titles used in text and note citations given in parentheses.

William Blake

Blake: Complete Writings. Ed. Geoffrey Keynes. London: Oxford University Press, 1972.

The Letters of William Blake. Ed. Geoffrey Keynes. Cambridge, Mass.: Harvard University Press, 1968. *(Letters)*

William Cowper

Cowper: Poetry and Prose. Ed. Brian Spiller. Cambridge, Mass.: Harvard University Press, 1968. All citations of Cowper's prose are to this edition *(Prose)*

The Poetical Works of William Cowper. Ed. H. S. Milford. London: Oxford University Press, 1934.

John Dyer and Thomas Parnell

Minor Poets of the Eighteenth Century. Ed. Hugh I'Anson Fausset. London: J. M. Dent, 1930.

Oliver Goldsmith

The Poems of Gray, Collins, and Goldsmith. Ed. Roger Lonsdale. London: Longmans, 1969.

Edmund Spenser

The Works of Edmund Spenser: A Variorum Edition. Ed. Edwin Greenlaw, Charles Grosvenor Osgood, Frederick Morgan Padelford, and

Ray Heffner. 9 vols. Baltimore: The Johns Hopkins University Press, 1932–57.

William and Dorothy Wordsworth

The Letters of William and Dorothy Wordsworth. Ed. Ernest de Selincourt. 2nd ed. 3 vols. Oxford: The Clarendon Press, 1967–70. I. *The Early Years, 1787–1805*, rev. Chester L. Shaver, 1967. II. *The Middle Years, Part 1, 1806–11*, rev. Mary Moorman, 1969. III. *The Middle Years, Part 2, 1812–20*, rev. Mary Moorman and Alan G. Hill, 1970. *(Letters)*

The Poetical Works of William Wordsworth. Ed. Ernest de Selincourt and Helen Darbishire. 5 vols. Oxford: The Clarendon Press, 1940–49. *(PW)*

The Prelude. Ed. Ernest de Selincourt and Helen Darbishire. 2nd ed. Oxford: The Clarendon Press, 1959.

The Prose Works of William Wordsworth. Ed. W. J. B. Owen and Jane Worthington Smyser. 3 vols. Oxford: The Clarendon Press, 1974. *(Prose)*

Edward Young

The Complete Works of the Rev. Edward Young. Ed. John Doran. 2 vols. London: William Tegg, 1854. Except for *Night Thoughts*, which is in volume one, all references are to volume two.

RUINS AND EMPIRE

1 Introduction

THE BROTHER OF RUIN, according to Thomas Warton in *The Pleasures of Melancholy*, is Horror. Horror is a word without precise meaning in our time, but Warton's eighteenth-century contemporaries understood its significance. Ann Radcliffe explained that "terror and horror are so far opposite, that the first expands the soul, and awakens the faculties to a high degree of life; the other contracts, freezes, and nearly annihilates them."[1] In his poem Warton invites this congealing of his faculties by visits to "ruin'd seats" and "solemn glooms / Congenial with my soul." He wishes to mortify his love of the external world, a process readily identifiable to us in the practice of mourning. Here it is civilization that Warton imagines under the aspect of death. He envies the satisfaction of a hermit gloating over the ruins of Persepolis, "the dwellings once of Elegance and Art." Instructed by the fate of Persepolis, the poet annihilates in himself the desire to preserve his thought in material forms. At the conclusion of the poem he retires to live in solitude with his austere muse, Contemplation.

The long verse paragraph describing the ruins of Persepolis has an important place in Warton's poem. Because it occurs toward the end and immediately precedes a renewal of spirit, the ruin scene represents a simulated experience of dying and rising; the worldly self is extinguished and immateriality embraced. Samuel Johnson's *Rasselas* has the same narrative turn in the penultimate chapter, when the Prince's party visits the Egyptian catacombs. Eighteenth-century authors habitually gave monumental ruins the role of antagonist in the drama of human salvation. Ubiquitous in literature as in geographical location, ruins were a means of mortifying in the public those worldly desires which caused the great empires, like Persepolis and Egypt, to decline and fall.

The eighteenth century had an undeniable mania for physical representations of decay. Louis XIV incorporated six hundred col-

3

umns from the ruined Roman city Leptis Magna into Versailles. On a
smaller scale, English noblemen placed classical ruins on their estates,
or, most notorious in this period, constructed new ruins to create
particular effects. The ruin piece in painting and poetry became an
increasingly popular mode throughout the century as archaeologists,
historians, and even casual travelers provided new information about
antiquity. The accumulation of data and opinion enriched the symbolic associations of ruins and impressed them (to adopt the Lockean
terminology of the period) upon the imagination. If the ruinological
texts seem to us now rather slight, this lack is insignificant beside the
fact of repeated attention to ruins which distinguished the age. Artists
and public alike developed an art of seeing which we have not lost,
one that discovers significant patterns of change and decay in everyday scenes and events. The ruin sentiment became a mental construct
capable of universal application and for that reason a determinant of
policy and conduct in a time of expanding empire.

If we set a typical eighteenth-century expression of the ruin sentiment beside one from the classical period we can mark some disturbing complications in the later work. In the second century B.C., Antipater of Sidon recorded a lament for Corinth after it was sacked by the
Roman general, Mummius. Here is the complete poem:

> Where, Corinth, is the glory of thy keep,
> The ancient wealth, the turret-circled steep?
> Where are thy fanes, thy homes? Where all thy wives?
> Where do the myriads of thy people sleep?
>
> Of all thy pride no sign is left today:
> All has war taken, all consumed away.
> Only the halcyons, Ocean's Nêreïd brood,
> Unravished yet, to weep thy downfall stay.[2]

The emotion in Antipater is deep but not broad. The poet catalogues
what is no longer present, and each noun in the list—keep, fanes,
wealth, and so forth—reinforces the same pathetic contrast of past
and present. A poem like Antipater's enacts the process of grief by
tracing the descent of glory from its greatest height, the keep, to the
level wilderness of desolation, "all consumed away." The same
movement of eye and mind occurs in a seventh-century Anglo-Saxon
poem on the sack of Bath in A.D. 577:

> Magnificent rose the fortresses, the lavish swimming halls,
> The profuse and lofty glory of spires, the clangour of armies,
> The drinking-halls crammed with every man's delight,

> Till that was overturned by steadfast fate.
> The broad walls were sundered: the plague-days came:
> The brave men were rapt away by the bereaver,
> Their war-ramparts razed to desolate foundations,
> Their cities crumbled down.[3]

The poet preserves the forms of vitality and power, and then, at the word "Till," re-creates their disintegration by elegiac action.

The poetic structure represents the ambivalent character of historical consciousness itself. In her travelogue through antiquity, *Pleasure of Ruins,* Rose Macaulay remarks, "Ruin is always over-stated; it is part of the ruin-drama staged perpetually in the human imagination, half of whose desire is to build up, while the other half smashes and levels to the earth" (p. 100). The poem is perforce an artifact of civilization, a product of the creative impulse it praises in the ruined city. That very praise becomes a foundation stone for the new city by goading princes and artisans to build something worthy of posterity's regard. The poet performs a vital function by not only urging new light upon nations but embodying it in his own discipline. This bardic assumption prevails in the Renaissance, when, however, it is darkened by the antagonistic forces I examine in my chapter on Spenser's *The Ruines of Time.*

By the eighteenth century the ruin sentiment has adopted a different tone, that of the prophet's scorn for worldly splendor. Here is a passage from a London periodical of 1793, *The Looker-On:*

When we reflect on the sinking fortunes of nations, and the sudden falls of mighty kingdoms, we are impressed with an awful idea of the supreme Disposer, in whose hands a whole nation is but as one man. When we walk upon fields and meadows, where nothing but a few mounds remain to remind us that here, in ancient times, was raised a fortification that withstood the efforts of armies, and reflect that on the same spot where oxen now graze in tranquillity, was once decided the fate of empires;—when we tread upon piles of stones, which once administered to the grandeur of princes, and over-awed the territory round; how can we persist in building our pride upon such transitory foundations, and in sacrificing the repose of our minds for such unstable rewards?[4]

The first sentence encapsulates the principal features of the ruin sentiment in the eighteenth century. It asserts that Providence controls the course of historical events, a belief both comforting and horrifying. Comforting because it endows structure and meaning upon the seemingly random sequence of incidents in time, but horrifying because it insists on a teleology that dooms all of material life as we know it. The cyclical view of history urged by classical writers, one that analogized the rise and fall of empires to the process of organic reproduction, yields to an apocalyptic conception in which all material forms reach an irresistible terminus before the Last Judgment. Nations and individuals share this fate, as the Looker-On dramatizes when he collapses the "whole nation" into "one man" in the first sentence, and later by making the phrase "our pride" support both conditions.

The Looker-On had prepared this linkage in an earlier section of the paper, where he remarks ruefully that "the living faculties are destined here to work with instruments not immortal like themselves, but of frail and perishable natures." The whole matrix of civilization, including the arts and sciences, is forcefully denied essential value in such a conception. When man proposes his schemes he is only building his pride, a phrase that recalls the story of Babel but includes all of human effort throughout history. The cruel conclusion is that if man believes in the supreme Disposer he must assent to the vanity and futility of even his most inspired labors. In the Arab Dream section of *The Prelude*, which I analyze at some length in chapter nine as a culminating expression of the ruin sentiment, Wordsworth utters a similar cry: "Oh! why hath not the Mind / Some element to stamp her image on / In nature somewhat nearer to her own?" (V.45–47). The classical and Anglo-Saxon poets had the comfort of believing that what Antipater calls "the power of song" would prevail over time. As he puts it in a dedicatory poem for a deceased poetess: "So lives her name for ever, nor lies lost / Beneath the shadow of the wings of gloom."[5] But later writers must condemn their art, in exchange for the blessings of immateriality, as one of the "unstable rewards" resting on "transitory foundations."

In the Looker-On's passage, then, Ruin and Horror seem to usurp the very possibility of glory. It is ironic that Christianity, which seized upon the Western imagination in part because it promised a new heaven and new earth, tended to militate against the same eventuality. Millennial thought certainly underlies the utopian optimism of the period, the belief that, in Carl L. Becker's words, "the new heaven had to be located somewhere within the confines of the earthly life, since it was an article of faith that the end of life is life itself, the perfected temporal life of man."[6] But Christianity also added to the classical theme of transience a religious justification of ultimate ruin, what Thomas Browne calls "the necessity of oblivion." When the Enlightenment strove for the secrets of worldly immortality it carried in its quest the seeds of its own disillusionment. The more it built for the future the more it invited punishment by its pride.

A writer who confronts a physical ruin sees human creativity under the aspect of death. His mourning not only records a present fatality but anticipates the destruction of all future places sacred to human happiness. In England, where architects served their apprenticeship by studying classical ruins, the whole visible environment of monuments and buildings became a *memento mori*. The associations of neoclassical architecture with the triumph of barbarism were strong enough to cause Lord Kames, in his *Elements of Criticism* (1762), to argue against the placement of classical ruins in parks and gardens, and to lead a movement toward the Gothic revival. Gothic ruins, he explained, symbolize the triumph of time over art without the uncomfortable suggestion of military conquest.[7] The possibility of being overwhelmed by a hostile army is never far from the English mind during the Augustan and Romantic periods. The Looker-On's comments of 1793 emerge from a historical context that makes his elegiac sentiments more personal in application. In other papers the Looker-On is virulently anti-Jacobin; when he looks on the overthrow of the French monarchy he reports that "the very elements of civilization have been destroyed in a moment, and society itself disbanded" (p. 31). Wherever he walks while contemplating the danger to England's civilization he sees ruins and ruins-to-be.

The inheritance of humanism carries an entail of doom; every high ideal represented by the classical style contains a premonition of reversal. To cite a recent example that attracted much attention in 1971, President Nixon, speaking of the columns of the National Archives Building in Washington, D.C., remarked, "Sometimes when I see those columns I think of seeing them in Greece and Rome, and you see only what is left of great civilizations of the past—as they became wealthy, as they lost their will to live, to improve, they became subject to the decadence that destroys the civilization. The United States is reaching that period."[8] This habit of mind is itself an inheritance from the eighteenth century and most directly from England. The notion that God had chosen England as the specific agent of redemption in the world had been gradually abandoned by all but a few poets and preachers. Following the euphoria of centuries in which England seemed the location of all the graces, this disillusionment, not unlike the current feeling in America, gave way to a despairing acknowledgment that the law of growth and decay might not, probably would not, spare the island of Great Britain and its overseas empire. Thomas Love Peacock asked in *The Genius of the Thames* (1810):

> Cannot the hand of patriot zeal,
> The heart that seeks the public weal,
> The comprehensive mind,

Retard awhile the storms of fate,
That, swift or slow, or soon or late,
Shall hurl to ruin every state,
And leave no trace behind?[9]

The Napoleonic wars lie behind this question, but more significant is the whole tradition of pessimism represented by the Looker-On's passage, which opposes the hand of patriot zeal to the hands of the supreme Disposer.

In this study I provide scenes from the ruin-drama of the Augustan and Romantic periods which exhibit both the descent into gloom and the rescue of the imagination by new light. My aim is not to catalogue or classify the many expressions of the ruin sentiment but to select representative works spanning three centuries which demonstrate how the experience of horror results in renewed loyalty to some enduring symbol of potentiality, be it place, person, or artifact. I devote most attention to those writers who invest immortal longings in some worldly place which they conceive as the site of a new heaven and new earth. This may be a childhood home, as in Goldsmith's case, or the English state, as in Spenser's and Dyer's case, or it might be both, as in Wordsworth's composite ideal of perfection. Each writer positions at the center of his work an analysis of psychohistorical forces, such as luxury and ambition, which endanger the survival of his favored place. The dramatic figures who embody these forces in eighteenth-century literature possess features common to an age of imperial expansion. Defoe's Roxana exemplifies the same desolating power in her society as do Goldsmith's tyrants in a later generation and the historical avatars of "rapine, avarice, expense" that Wordsworth expected to overwhelm his "fearful innocence" (PW, III, 116) in the remote vale of Grasmere.

Wordsworth's poetic career is the one I most desire to illuminate in this book. Wordsworth attempted to locate a ground for his immortal longings

Not in Utopia,—subterranean fields,—
Or some secreted island, Heaven knows where!
But in the very world, which is the world
Of all of us,—the place where, in the end,
We find our happiness, or not at all!   (Prelude, XI.140–44)

Aware of the pitfalls from his reading of ruins literature, he nonetheless persisted in his belief that such a place could be founded and preserved against the forces of change and loss. I trace in some detail how Wordsworth at first rejects the formulaic despair of ruins literature but gradually lapses into those formulas as the landscapes he invested with spiritual faith undergo essential change. The despair of his later years recapitulates the sorrow of his predecessors, but the worldly immortality he sought by continuous effort persists through modern structures of belief, and makes his case worthy of the most extensive study. My final chapter, on Wordsworth's American contemporaries, indicates how laments over the ruin of the last Eden, a significant theme in American literature of the nineteenth century, added a new dimension of horror to the ruin-drama.

Ruin pieces of all kinds derive from an author's response to events and beliefs which may have only a shadowy life in the text. Restoration of the context in which these authors lived and worked, including essential details of their biographies, seems to me a prerequisite for the fullest understanding of their work. This is especially true of Wordsworth, whose art drew so often on contemporary occasions. I accept F. W. Bateson's argument that Wordsworth's individual poems are best understood by analysis which includes his other work and materials from his life and times:

To a greater degree than with any other major English poet his reader needs continuous extraneous assistance—not so much to clear up *minutiae* of interpretation as to understand the whole poetic attitude, what Wordsworth is getting at in the widest sense. . . . We cannot read Wordsworth properly until we have got to know Wordsworth. . . . The determining events of his career and the sources of all that is essential in his poetry were the personal tragedies, the anguished decisions, the half-conscious half-animal terrors and ecstasies, and *not* the discoveries of the intellect.[10]

In other writers as well, one must have recourse to extraneous materials in order to establish a habit of mind, a fixed attitude, an obsession. My method has been to devote each chapter to one or two key texts and trace the influences that press on the writer's conception. I have tried to provide greater coherence between chapters by repetition of phrase and idea, a system of cross-reference that will further illustrate the formulaic structure of the ruin sentiment itself.

I have cited Rose Macaulay's claim that ruin is always overstated. In the ruin-drama preceding our own moment on the stage some writers may have overstated the condition of decay, their own and their cherished place's, and exaggerated also the preservative measures needed to check untimely death. But this is an area in which the facts of life give rhetoric a free hand. Because the human condition remains constant through all changes of historical circumstance, the fundamental horror persists in all meditations on decay. A literary work that suppressed emotion on this subject would not be worth reading. Shakespeare expressed the horror in a mourning poem of unusual concentration and purity, his sonnet 64:

> When I have seen such interchange of state,
> Or state itself confounded to decay;
> Ruin hath taught me thus to ruminate,
> That Time will come and take my love away.
>   This thought is as a death, which cannot choose
>   But weep to have that which it fears to lose.

The literary tradition I survey in this book owes its vitality to the strange death-dance of thought occasioned by ruin. If an exuberant vitality did not characterize these visions they would have become part of the oblivion they beheld, instead of being instructors in their turn.

2 Immortal Longings and
The Ruines of Time

"THERE IS NOTHING strictly immortall, but immortality," Thomas Browne wrote in *Urne Buriall*, meaning of course Christian immortality, "Paradise [that] succeeds the Grave."[1] All other immortalities he regarded as pseudo doctrine, superstition that could be refuted by scriptural and scientific proofs, or by common sense. Against the belief of Aristotle and Pliny that the world itself was immortal he opposed a degenerationist philosophy that deduced from the decay of human morals the imminent destruction of the earthly macrocosm. "The created World is but a small *Parenthesis* in Eternity" (p. 421), he insisted. Believing this, Browne could more easily countenance the discoveries of celestial "corruption" and mutability by contemporary astronomers. Even the heathens, he remarks in *Religio Medici,* understood that whatever was created must be consumed, and he quotes Lucan as evidence: "There yet remaines to th' world one common fire, / Wherein our bones with stars shall make one pyre" (p. 53). As for magicians like Paracelsus who claimed that an individual could perpetuate his body eternally by potable gold, Browne needed only note that the magus himself died at age forty-seven. If Browne were alive today and apprised of advances in cryobiology, transplantation of organs, and genetic adjustments of our life span, he would pose the psalmist's question, whose answer remains the same: "What Man is he that liveth and shall not see Death?"

Cryonics is a modern version of mummification, and the subject of mummies fascinated Browne.[2] Mummification had as its purpose the preservation of the personal identity of the deceased. In magical rites recorded by *The Book of the Dead* the Egyptians sought to maintain forever the physical composition of the mummy, who is made to say, "I shall not decay, I shall not rot, I shall not putrefy, I shall not turn into worms.... I shall have my being, I shall have my being.... My body shall be established. It shall neither become a

11

ruin, nor be destroyed on this earth."[3] This refusal to submit to the proper sentence of God Browne considered impious in the extreme, for the given destiny of dust is dust. John Donne, likewise, preached that "it is *lex*, you were born under that law, upon that condition to die; so it is a rebellious thing not to be content to die, it opposes the Law."[4]

As Donne's language suggests, the author of man's desire for unchristian immortality is Satan, and it is an ever-present theme in seventeenth-century writing that Satan encourages our fear of bodily extinction. "He advanceth the opinion of totall death, and staggereth the immortality of the soul," Browne writes (p. 152). Satan and his spirits convince kings and artists that unless they leave behind monuments they shall entirely die. The enduring presence of such monuments reminded writers like Browne and Donne of Satan's ability to compel wonder and envy. Browne acknowledged the desire for continued life; he knew that the human understanding was easily misled into wholly materialist goals. Many of the errors he attempts to explode in his writings are those the decaying body invents to secure its own perpetuation. In *Religio Medici* and *Pseudodoxia Epidemica* he displays a credulity in some areas that has always been part of his charm, but on certain subjects his skepticism is inflexible: he does not believe in the earthly survival of the soul or the body, in metempsychosis, in transmigration, or in ghostly apparitions of the recently departed (these are Satan's inventions). Earthly souls are "single individuals" and as such ought to yearn for the exact forms of their immortality, which Browne describes as "Christian Annihilation, Extasy, Exolution, Transformation, the Kiss of the Spouse, and Ingression into the Divine Shadow" (p. 422). The soul can pleasure itself by studying these mysteries—it is the mortal body that dotes upon its simulacrum, monumental ruins. Thus the ruins of empire and the perishable body are, in Thomas More's phrase for the latter, "the relics that remain in mankind of old original sin."[5]

We might pause to sympathize with Browne's efforts to compete with so many surrogates of everlasting life. Pyramids and mummies were a remote form of the specter Francis Bacon memorably describes as "that whereunto man's nature doth most aspire; which is immortality or continuance; for to this tendeth generation, and raising of houses and families; to this buildings, foundations and monuments; to this tendeth the desire of memory, fame, and celebration; and in effect, the strength of all other human desires."[6] In England a popular folklore had arisen during the medieval and Renaissance periods that set against Christian orthodoxy a range of white magic in which revivals from the dead (like Thaisa's in *Pericles*), miraculous cures,

Faustian pacts, life-tokens, and legends of the Grail all promised relief from mortal limitations.

Consider the fountain of eternal youth. The Letter of Prester John, which was translated into almost every European language during the Middle Ages, owed some of its popularity to its description of this wonder: "And this water, thus thrice times consumed or drunk, then, as I say, they throw off their age of 100 years and are thus relieved of it, so that without delay they appear to be of the age of thirty or forty years and no more. And so each 100 years they are rejuvenated and are altogether changed."[7] This tall tale, which Browne would have read in Mandeville, is a spiritual first cousin to *The Book of the Dead:* "I shall not decay, I shall not rot." And to other ears the echo is from the Satan of Genesis: "Ye shall not surely die." Browne defends his belief against such blandishments by pursuing them to the graveyard; from that landscape he speaks to the superstitious with elegiac condescension: "To subsist in bones, and be but Pyramidally extant, is a fallacy in duration. Vain ashes, which in the oblivion of names, persons, times, and sexes, have found unto themselves a fruitlesse continuation, and only arise unto late posterity, as Emblemes of mortall vanities; Antidotes against pride, vainglory, and madding vices. Pagan vainglories which thought the world might last for ever, had encouragement for ambition, and finding no *Atropos* unto the immortality of their Names, were never dampt with the necessity of oblivion" (p. 280).

The persistence of ruins, as of mummies, represented the very worst models for human endeavor. Such models perpetuate a hunger for longer and longer life which, as Browne often remarks, makes a person susceptible to Satanic lures: the gullible buy pieces of "mummy" at the apothecary shops where *"Pharaoh* is sold for balsoms" (p. 283) or imagine with the poets that fame will somehow outlast the Last Day. If fame is insufficient, a Renaissance man might be tempted by even more powerful lures. Marlowe's Doctor Faustus, for example, yearns for the magical power of holding mutability in check, of suspending entirely the physical (and moral) laws of the world. "A sound magician is a mighty god," he remarks, not concerned that the god of earthly continuance is the prince of devils. In the political dimension this overreaching makes everyman his own Tamburlaine, perpetrating godless acts in order to stamp his signature on the ruins of time. To the most extreme efforts and the most grandiose monuments Browne responded with a persistent refrain: *"Pyramids, Arches, Obelisks,* were but the irregularities of vain-glory" (p. 285).

Browne had a more limited sympathy in this regard than his

contemporary, Robert Burton, whose attitude toward antiquities partakes always of the sentimental. Like his Anglo-Saxon forebears, Burton summons images of glory to stand behind the ruins. It is impossible to imagine Browne writing in this tone: "Who telling such a tale could keep from tears? Who is so hard, so iron-hearted? . . . Who is he that can sufficiently condole and commiserate these ruins? . . . Where are those 4000 cities of Egypt, those 100 cities in Crete?" and so forth.[8] Browne looks on Egyptian monuments as Melville does on the ruins of Lima, with a metaphysical shudder at the bleached incorruption of ruins that will not obey the law of nature, which is the law of God. Browne was an antiquarian himself, and felt the seductive charm of pagan monuments. He understood that every achievement in preservation represented an alteration in human consciousness that excited aesthetic admiration. Like Donne and Milton, hower, Browne opposed the sentimental transformation of antiquities into purely aesthetic objects of contemplation, a process that Burton's scholarship had already advanced. If the Pyramids came to be considered as anything but, in George Sandys' phrase, "barbarous monuments of prodigality and vaine-glory,"[9] then England might be lured by their sublimity into paganism. A clear line can be drawn here from Browne to Blake, whose work *Jerusalem* attempts to divide what Browne calls "the great Examples of perpetuity" (p. 284), which are Christian, from the barbaric splendor associated in English history with Stonehenge and the serpent-temple at Avebury.

Urne Buriall is Browne's most cogent critique of worldly immortality. Its narrator surveys the several practices of urn burial, mummification, or cremation with the half-sympathetic, half-ironic detachment he employs in other writings for the wildest folklore. His fierce belief in "the necessity of oblivion" makes it impossible for him to discuss the survival of a bone or a tomb without some deflating remark. Throughout the work we are presented with the embarrassment of bodily remains, the salts, ashes, calx, and cinders that "our Forefathers" dwindled into in spite of bold epitaphs and preservatives. Roman urns, like Egyptian mummies, misconceived the destiny of both the body and the soul. Of the body, Browne had written in *Religio Medici*: "I beleeve that our estranged and divided ashes shall unite againe; that our separated dust after so many pilgrimages and transformations into the parts of mineralls, Plants, Animals, Elements, shall at the voyce of God return into their primitive shapes; and joyne againe to make up their primary and predestinate formes" (p. 55). How could the world's glory compare to that miracle? To mourn over ruins, over the decaying and fallen body of matter, would be to engage in false belief and false prophecy.

Browne's radical dualism provides the best starting point for a survey of the ruin sentiment. Though he follows in historical time the greatest meditations on ruins—those of Petrarch, Du Bellay, and Spenser—he sounds the bass note of opposition to those immortal longings which ruins and ruins poets alike memorialized. Each writer who confronts a monument looks for something different: its degree of ravagement, its place in the surrounding landscape, its engraved voice (always a variant of *Et in Arcadia Ego*). Browne probes decayed matter—crania of beasts, mouths of mummies, contents of sepulchral pitchers—to assure himself of the absolute separation of matter and spirit. Browne is not, like some of his ectypes in the next century, a morbid person. He celebrates bodily decay because it is a decomposition not just of flesh but of sin. The body builds ruins in the spirit by the energy of its survival wish, and in the view of Christian moralists these erections of desire and presumption underlie all human sorrow. "Mine inward corruptions have made me mine own Pharaoh, and mine own Egypt," John Donne lamented.[10] Though physical death is not the only escape from this Egypt it is the most effective and permanent. Mummification preserves corruption; monuments honor it. And so Browne concludes *Urne Buriall* by insisting on physical oblivion, glorifying it as a providential finality, for "to live indeed is to be again our selves, which being not only an hope but an evidence in noble beleevers, 'Tis all one to lye in St *Innocents* Church-yard, as in the Sands of *Aegypt:* Ready to be any thing, in the extasie of being ever, and as content with six foot as the Moles of *Adrianus*" (pp. 285–86).

In the work and temperament of Edmund Spenser we come as close as we ever will in English literature to the kind of mummy-making sensibility that Browne deplored. Spenser's complaint of the world's mutability is no mere convention; it carries the kind of desperation and even indignation we associate with modern works like Unamuno's *Tragic Sense of Life,* or Alan Harrington's *The Immortalist.* Spenser writes in a Christian tradition in which the expectation of heaven provides comfort, but he is enough of a materialist and sensualist to be on occasion inconsolable at the thought of what he must lose. He is not unlike his own creation, the shepherd Alcyon in *Daphnaida,* who curses heaven because his mistress, untimely dead, "in pureness Heaven itself did pas" (210). Spenser tried to console himself by dreams of worldly immortality. He loved the beautiful things of this world and believed that they imitated and expressed the soul of heavenly beauty. In his *Hymne of Heavenly Beautie* he credits God's works with enabling "plumes of perfect speculation" (135) to mount toward the Virgin-Queen, Sapience. Spenser writes as if poetic works also were plumes of perfect speculation, preservatives not themselves subject to "degendering" because conceived of the inward eye. His patrons and immediate public shared this faith.

The Ruines of Time was written on command of the Dudley family, who expected from Spenser some lasting remembrance of the family's great poet, Philip Sidney, and of its political champion, the late Earl of Leicester. Both had been patrons of Spenser. The finished poem owes its mastery of subject to Spenser's apprenticeship in the elegiac mode during his undergraduate years. He then translated a sonnet sequence of Joachim Du Bellay, Les Antiquités de Rome, a series of "visions" by the same author, and a sequence by Petrarch—all concerned with mutability. The Ruines of Time is a dream-vision, and begins with the poet's visit to the former site of a thriving English city:

> It chaunced me on day beside the shore
> Of silver streaming Thamesis to bee,
> Nigh where the goodly Verlame stood of yore,
> Of which there now remaines no memorie,
> Nor anie little moniment to see,
> By which the travailer, that fares that way,
> This once was she, may warned be to say.   (1–7)

It was a Renaissance commonplace that the Golden Age left no monuments. Spenser is ambivalent about the desirability of such Saturnian serenity. A lack of monuments argues an unconcern about earthly fame which, in his imagination, was linked to a deficiency of genius and virtue. He was more attracted to the Renaissance belief that the glory preserved by history is the spur to virtue. His complaint about the pyramids in The Ruines of Time (407–13) is not Browne's. Spenser despairs because those monuments are not permanent (like Verulam they will crumble) and because they are dumb. The silence of memorial edifices distressed poets like Spenser, who saw it as a mocking omen of their own fate as artists and learned men. Samuel Daniel's complaint about Stonehenge in Musophilus is typical:

> And whereto serve that wondrous Trophei now,
> That on the goodly Plaine neere Wilton stands?
> That huge dumbe heape, that cannot tell us how,
> Nor what, nor whence it is, nor with whose hands,
> Nor for whose glory, it was set to shew
> How much our pride mocks that of other lands?   (337–42)

Poets "angry with time" (353) urge written history, of which poetry is the noblest medium, as the most efficient preservative and restorative; it disseminates counsel in all ages.

Poetry is the "memorie" of the race, and so it is dramatically imperative that the Princesse who personifies Verulam, and who fills most of Spenser's poem with her lament, convince the poet-narrator by her eloquence. She is pleading, literally, for her life. "Name have I none," she tells him, "nor anie being" until he memorializes her and becomes like her favorite historian, Camden, a "nourice of antiquities." The figure of Verulam, of course, also stands for the Dudley family, which will fade into oblivion unless its memory is secured by the harmony of Spenser's numbers. For this reason the poem is among other things a catalogue of names and deeds whereby images of excellence—Verulam and the Dudleys—are embalmed. Spenser addresses one family member, Anne, daughter of the Earl of Bedford, and asserts of her husband, Ambrose, "Thy lord shall never die, the whiles this verse / Shall live, and surely it shall live for ever: / For ever it shall live, and shall rehearse / His worthie praise" (253–56). As in Shakespeare's sonnets, immortality is secured preeminently by the poet's recognition but also by leaving heirs behind to "ensue those steps" taken by the noble progenitor.

Spenser bows at this last notion but does not elaborate on it; he returns at once to *his* powers of preservation: "Ne may I let thy husbands sister die, / That goodly Ladie, sith she eke did spring / Out of this stocke, and famous familie, / Whose praises I to future age doo sing" (274–77). He adds later that those who have neither art nor any accomplishments that can be celebrated in art are destined for oblivion, a state of nonbeing he clearly looks on as an earthly version of hell. His terrestrial vision, unlike Browne's, is not measured by the grave, but by the number and beauty of human achievements. His favorite structure is the narrative pageant, the succession of noble acts in a sequence. Here the catalogue of names and the claims made for their endurance are like the naming rituals of primitive cultures and represent the same primitive fears that objects will disappear unless they are secured by language. Spenser's strategy does not exclude his own claims, for, as he writes in the "L'Envoy" to his translation of Du Bellay, "Needes must he all eternitie survive, / That can to other give eternall dayes." The ultimate horror Spenser foresees is that his art, like Verulam, may only be, in Wordsworth's phrase, a "Poor earthly casket of immortal verse " (*Prelude*, V.164) that will be annihilated by the otherwise welcome return of the Messiah. Spenser presents a version of this destruction in the first set of emblems that concludes *The Ruines of Time*.

The destruction of virtuous and beautiful forms, then, presents Spenser with an ethical problem that Browne sidestepped throughout his writings. If, as Browne maintained, this world is not a place to live

in but to die in, the early death of a genius or benevolent leader can be
celebrated as his good fortune. Contempt of the world is the armor
Browne wears against evil and untimely death, but Spenser's love of
beauty condemns him, in his dramatic narratives, to a constant anxiety. His eye is always on the butterfly, as in *Muiopotmos,* captured
and destroyed by the envious and ugly spider. The deaths of Leicester, Walsingham, and Sidney secured the power of Spenser's political
enemy, Lord Burghley, in Elizabeth's court; the fox who gained such
eminence in Spenser's beast-fable, *Mother Hubberds Tale,* reigned
victorious in the world of men.

Spenser's vision is tragic—he witnesses and records the inevitable triumph of evil over the best attempts of beauty and grace. Such
is the burden of his (original) sonnet sequence, *Visions of the Worlds
Vanitie,* in which he describes in ascending accents of horror the con-
straint, humiliation or overthrow of powerful and admirable things
by the weak and contemptible. Here, as elsewhere in the *Complaints,*
we see the obverse of Spenser's piety in *The Faerie Queene.* In the latter
work he accepts the premise that "all we have is his [God's]: what he
list doe, he may" (V.ii.41), but where he consistently gives the victory
to heaven's grace in his epic, even when he must distort history to do
so, he does not blink in these shorter poems at the unremitting misfortune handed him by Providence. A tone of indignation is present
beneath the despair, a rebellious anger at the world that God seems to
have devised with such malicious humor. The "ruines tragicall" we
are to learn from are not just in his fancy, they are all around him.
Spenser did not invent the gadfly and the venomous spider—God
did. Similarly the evil men that surround the "kingly birds" of court,
who poison their lives and mock their enterprises, are a perpetual
nemesis to the immortal projects of artist and statesman alike.[11] In
this sense, the age of the Tudors recapitulates that of all declining
empires. *The Ruines of Time* reminds us of *Lamentations* in tone, but
directs us also to the more recent history recorded in Spenser's time
by Camden and others: a great (Roman) civilization leveled by the
enemies of culture, the Scots, Picts, and Anglo-Saxons.

Part of Spenser's intention in describing the ruins of Verulam is a
linking of Roman and English empires. His visual descriptions are
deliberately general when he comes to Verulam's evocation of her
departed glory; the catalogue allows English readers to recognize
their own familiar landscape:

> High towers, faire temples, goodly theaters,
> Strong walls, rich porches, princelie pallaces,
> Large streetes, brave houses, sacred sepulchers,

> Sure gates, sweete gardens, stately galleries,
> Wrought with faire pillours, and fine imageries,
> All those (O pitie) now are turned to dust,
> And overgrown with blacke oblivions rust.   (92–98)

Spenser is writing this poem no earlier than 1590, the date of Leicester's death, and we can assume that his meditation on the fate of empires does not exclude the most sensational event of Spenser's life—the defeat of the Spanish Armada in 1588—and the obvious result of that engagement: the triumph of England over the most powerful political and military force in the Western world at that time. The Spanish court had been for a century the envy of all governments throughout Europe. An Englishman of Spenser's sophistication could not have missed the readjustment in social equilibrium that originated in the Spanish defeat, a change that would have been the subject of conversation and pamphlet in the period just preceding the composition of *The Ruines of Time*.

Spenser had certainly seen in his lifetime the growth of England into worldly power and wealth. As early as 1562 a visiting bishop from abroad had remarked: "Englishmen indulge in pleasures as if they were to die tomorrow, and build as if they were to live forever."[12] Increasing commerce was bringing increasing gold, and the rule of Elizabeth seemed to insure the continuing development of a powerful mercantile nation that would challenge any in modern history. The aggressive commonwealth borrowed much of its rhetoric from metaphysics, and we should not be surprised to see the English state described in this period in terms that the Egyptians might have used in *The Book of the Dead*. The aim of political writings such as Raleigh's *Maxims of State,* Richard Eden's *The Decades of the Newe World,* or Gerard Malynes's *A Treatise on the Canker of Englands Commonwealth,* is to "preserve the State from decay." The state is conventionally compared to a human body, and, depending on the ingenuity of the author, the sickness or wound of the body is allegorized as a deficiency in some vital economic preservative, usually bullion. So long as the body receives transfusions and medicines, we are told, it will never decay or wear out. "Bullion is the very Body and Bloud of Kings," Malynes writes, "Money is but the Medium betweene Subjects and their Kings, Exchange the heavenly Mistery that joynes them together." An increase in bullion or export (it amounts to the same thing) was comparable to an increase in Grace—"Exchange [is] the Light that makes the world to see.... Exchange is the Spirit that quickens all the Body."[13]

The prosperity of England created a kind of heady joy in the land

and the belle-lettristic enthusiasm that marked Elizabeth's court. John Davies, in his worshipful acrostics, *Hymnes of Astraea*, foresaw a new golden age from the "Eternall Virgin, *Goddesse* true":

> R udenesse it selfe she doth refine,
> E ven like an Alcymist divine,
> G rosse times of Iron turning
> I nto the purest forme of gold:
> N ot to corrupt, till heaven waxe old,
> A nd be refin'd with burning.   *(Hymne I)*

If Elizabeth had not been acclaimed so unanimously as the Virgin-Queen, or Sapience, the idol of heaven, she might have been mistaken for Pharaoh, so closely was her will and virtue taken to be the whole life of the state. "If we this Starre once cease to see," Davies wrote of Elizabeth, "No doubt our State will Ship-wrackt be, / And torne and sunke for ever" *(Hymne XXII)*. The reign of Elizabeth marks the real beginning of the sacred history of the English people, which insisted that England was the reborn and blessed nation of Israel, an empire that might last "forever" (until the Second Coming) because it enjoyed the protection of God. Expressions of this belief are to be found everywhere in Elizabethan literature, beginning with Foxe's *Actes and Monuments* and gaining momentum with the Protestant conception of Elizabeth as the redeemer of an elect nation.[14]

But the evident decline of the Spanish empire and the rise of the English would have enforced another moral in a temperament as naturally melancholy as Spenser's—that England's rule would merely repeat Spain's vainglorious century, that the Tudors and their heirs would recapitulate the same imperial pattern that moralists had inferred from the classical histories. Indeed, the European discovery of the New World portended not only infinite wealth but infinite war, as the aggressive mercantile policy recommended by Raleigh and Drake took effect. Because he was out of favor Spenser had a particularly good view of those elements in Elizabeth's court that would exchange honor for gold, dignity for power. He would understand also how the cult of Elizabeth in the English public could be exploited in the interests of a blind cupidity. In its accumulation of goods by colonial expansion, England inevitably faced colonial rebellions, increasing expenses for its military to suppress such uprisings, a resultant taxation at home that would create unrest in its turn, and finally the prospect of continuing wars with other great powers over trade routes and trading privileges. It was not only Greek and Roman history that taught this lesson but England's trouble with Ireland, of which Spenser was soon to be such a close witness.

Spenser foresaw these problems—the final stanza of Verulam's lament is a warning to "who so els that sits in highest seate / Of this worlds glorie" (463–64)—but they would have appeared to his understanding in the tragic guise I have indicated. In Spenser's view there is in nations, as in individuals, a need to objectify the purest and most beautiful impulses of the soul. These impulses have survived the Fall, and if nourished by art and religion can help to rebuild the Adamic world in our imagination and in the external world. The duty of man is to pursue the best models of conduct even knowing the probable futility of his actions. Here Spenser and Browne do share certain beliefs. Neither was secure in his nationalism because they knew history to be a wheel of fortune, but they were secure in the religious teaching that required man to help realize the Good in this world as a way of pleasing God. The Good might be re-created as a city, a garden, or a book, and in its realization scientific and mystical efforts could be mingled.

Browne, whose *Garden of Cyrus* is a significant example of such a synthesis, wrote in *Pseudodoxia Epidemica:* "Our understandings being eclipsed... we must betake our selves to waies of reparation, and depend upon the illumination of our endeavours. For thus we may in some measure repair our primary ruines, and build our selves men again" (p. 120). Spenser and Browne agree that this desire for perfection is an expression of Love, the passionate affection for the Good which sustains the momentum of the soul in creating lasting monuments of its own magnificence (the *type* of monument of course divides them). Thus there is a utopian as well as an apocalyptic strain even in Browne's thinking, and the other side of his Janus face looks toward earthly models of immortal Paradise, "the Prototype and originall of Plantations" (p. 301). It need hardly be said that such models are holding actions merely, Goshens in the midst of Egyptian bondage. The Renaissance is an age of utopian speculation, much of it daydreaming, safely removed, like Robert Burton's model, to a distance "in the midst of the Temperate Zone, or perhaps under the Equator, that Paradise of the world, where the laurel is ever green, &c, where is a perpetual Spring."[15] Browne's perfected terrestrial world, like Burton's, collapses into the New Jerusalem when stared at long enough. Once again the worldly Spenser must be consulted if we seek a serious proposal to extend the noblest human civilization.

Spenser's recommendations for the perfection of Gloriana's empire in the book-length tract, *A Vewe of the Present State of Irelande,* are important as a terminal link in the poet's pursuit of an everlasting Good in history. They mark the authentic limits of his—and his nation's—belief that the imperial model still provided moral foun-

dations for the earthly paradise. The tract is cast as a dialogue between Irenius, an Englishman who, like Spenser, has just returned
from administrative service in Ireland, and a skeptic named Eudoxus.
The dialectical form reflects perfectly Spenser's divided opinions on
the subject of colonial empire. Spenser was a confident utopian so
long as the settlements remained across the seas. When he conjures
such a landscape, as in *The Faerie Queene*, he reverts to the rhetoric of
immortality:

> And shame on you, O men, which boast your strong
> And valiant hearts, in thoughts lesse hard and bold,
> Yet quaile in conquest of that land of gold.
> But this to you, O Britons, most pertaines,
> To whom the right hereof it selfe hath sold;
> The which for sparing litle cost or paines,
> Loose so immortall glory, and so endlesse gaines.   (IV.xi.22)

But when Spenser comes closer to home, Verulam fills his imagination and tempers his enthusiasm. The reality of colonialism is not
"endlesse gaines" but perpetual losses. The recent attempt to suppress
a single Irish rebel, the Earl of Tyrone, had resulted in ominous defeat: "the Quenes treasure spente her people wasted the pore Coun-
trie trobled and the enemye nevertheles broughte into no more
subieccion then he was."[16]

Spenser had gone to Ireland as secretary to Lord Grey of Wilton,
an administrator who used methods of extreme ruthlessness in order
to suppress the rebellion. Spenser presents an idealized version of
Lord Grey's crusade in Book V of *The Faerie Queene*, in which Artegal,
the knight of Justice, comes by his mission most honorably:

> That was to succour a distressed Dame,
> Whom a strong tyrant did unjustly thrall,
> And from the heritage, which she did clame,
> Did with strong hand withhold: *Grantorto* was his name.
>
> Wherefore the Lady, which *Irena* hight,
> Did to the Faery Queene her way addresse,
> To whom complayning her afflicted plight,
> She her besought of gratious redresse.
> That soveraine Queene, that mightie Emperesse,
> Whose glorie is to aide all suppliants pore,
> And of weake Princes to be Patronesse,
> Chose *Artegall* to right her to restore;
> For that to her he seem'd best skild in righteous lore.   (V.i.3–4)

Irena is of course Ireland, but the allegory insists on her identification
with the English colonists, not with the natives. These colonists suffer

from the oppression of Grantorto, most likely a figure of the rebellion and the power which Spenser saw behind the Catholic uprisings, Philip II of Spain. Grantorto prevents Irena from enjoying her rightful "heritage" (rightful by previous conquest) and so deserves the punishment which Artegal is charged to perform. Though Spenser pitied the horrible suffering which Lord Grey inflicted upon the intransigent Irish counties, he nevertheless kept his gaze fixed on a utopian end.

In the *Vewe*, Irenius presents the same hopeful case: "And a governement theareuppon presentlye setled amongest them agreable theareunto they shoulde have byne reduced to perpetuall Civilytie and Contayned in Continuall dewtye" (p. 49). Irenius compares the enforcement of law to "Phisick" which preserves the patient's health indefinitely, but acknowledges that laws imposed regardless of local custom, like medicine administered in ignorance of the disease, invite justifiable resistance; they mortalize not perpetuate the body politic. As Spenser chronicles the history of the Irish wars and looks forward to the inevitable prospect of more and more brutal repression his tone becomes more elegiac and less confident. The Socratic irony of the early part of the dialogue passes into a grim catalogue of weaponry necessary to secure peace by putting the land to the sword. How, asks Eudoxus, can the "ruines" (p. 60) of English occupation—a significant epithet—be rebuilt to secure future and perpetual empire? Irenius is pessimistic. He has seen how the original families who settled in Ireland tend to resist rule from London with an intransigence similar in kind, and sometimes in degree, to the wild Irish. What can be expected in the future but a transformation of a colonial war into a civil war, Anglo-Irish landholder against English soldier? And Spenser is writing this dialogue in a decade of unprecedented droughts in England, when peasants in Oxfordshire and elsewhere were rioting against the queen's justices. What hope is there that the public will support an expensive military expedition and garrisoning of troops in Ireland when they are already protesting they have no bread?

Spenser has entangled himself in two myths of contradictory power. On some occasions he embraces the progressive myth of history, and asks that events like Lord Grey's crusade or Leicester's ill-fated expedition to the Low Countries be envisioned as the vanguard of an enduring (English) civilization rising on the ruins of Spain. But he is also committed, and nowhere more strongly than in the proem to his Irish Book (V) of *The Faerie Queene,* to the belief that the world is quickly declining into "ruinous decay" and that attempts to restore, or even imitate, the Golden Age are the idle dreams of poets ignorant of history. In his writings on Ireland he confronts his public with a pragmatic, irresoluble drama terrifying for Fairyland. If you want glory in this iron age, he says to his Prince, you will have to keep beside you the iron man, Talus, who will flail into submission all civil and colonial dissent. If it serves your conception of the Good that Munster be reduced to civility, you will have to depopulate it by a steady policy of annihilation, as Lord Grey had attempted before his recall.

Spenser would have recognized the unflinching military terrorism he advocated for Ireland as exactly that enforced by the Romans in England, and would not have been slow to comprehend the significance of the analogy. Rome reacted to rebellions by Boadicea and other native leaders precisely as Spenser advised Elizabeth to confront the likes of Tyrone and Desmond, by harsh repression in the interests of a utopian future. Was Ireland, then, an outpost like Verulam whose ruin signaled the irreversible retraction of imperial sway? The future became a bleaker prospect to Spenser as his career frustrations made him less and less sensitive to nuances in civil policy. In 1598, chased out of Ireland by the rebels, he condensed the most savage portions of the *Vewe* into a "Brief Note" on Irish rule whose conclusion is that "till Ireland be famished it can not be subdued" (p. 244). Spenser ends his political career still speaking of the "perpetuall establishment of peace and good government" (p. 241) he imagined for Ireland. Thomas Browne might be quoted at this point for the right note of pathos in regard to Spenser's vainglorious dream that any state could sustain its imperial condition indefinitely.

But Spenser is Browne's equal in that role; he mourned the ruin of Verulam, and he communicated the pathos of all ruin in *The Mutabilitie Cantos* which end his poetic career. The arguments of the "hardy Titanesse" Mutabilitie in that work convey, as one critic puts it, "a sense of the ultimate futility of human action in regard to the general structure of the universe,"[17] and though Dame Nature can justify such futility, as Spenser does in the Gardens of Adonis passage elsewhere in *The Faerie Queene*, she does so by an Olympian perspective on events, a detachment Spenser normally abjures. From a survey of his life, and his *Complaints*, we surmise that Mutabilitie could offer as evidence of her claims the experience of Edmund Spenser in the world—a world in which neither friendship nor love nor empire endured. What did endure were his artistic memorials of this fact, as he knew they would—the body of his imagination embalmed in time, immortal.

3 John Dyer in the Eternal City

THERE HAS NEVER BEEN a rush by critics to confirm Wordsworth's judgment of John Dyer: "In point of *imagination*, and purity of style, I am not sure that he is not superior to any writer in verse since the time of Milton." This was written in 1811, the period of Wordsworth's sonnet on Dyer, *Bard of the Fleece*. His more cautious remark in 1829 that "these three writers, Thomson, Collins, and Dyer, had more poetic imagination than any of their contemporaries [except Pope and Chatterton]" attests to a continuing admiration for Dyer's work which seems to our age misplaced or, more likely, another example of Wordsworth's generous support for those poets who gave him no competition.[1] But in fact Dyer provides one of the clearest and most poignant links between the complex of attitudes surveyed in the previous chapter and the pattern of Wordsworth's own career. Of the eighteenth-century poets Wordsworth praises, Dyer is the one most like himself in the conscious shape he gave to his poetic canon. Dyer too begins with lyrics descriptive of country walks and concludes with a long didactic poem which recommends an elevated pastoralism as a cure for social no less than spiritual ills. There is a likeness also in the pressures of personal history which lead to the major poems. *The Ruins of Rome* and *The Fleece* treat the interlocking themes of ruins, immortality, and empire in a significantly different manner from that of the seventeenth century; they foreshadow in their mixture of voices the elegiac mode Wordsworth pursued with greater success.

Recent scholarship has corrected the often repeated errors of Samuel Johnson's *Life of Dyer*.[2] The poet was born in 1699, in Carmarthenshire, South Wales, son of a solicitor. No anecdotes of Dyer's childhood exist, but we know that he was educated at Westminster school to follow his father's profession. He turned instead to painting and moved to London for tutelage under the popular artist, Jonathan Richardson. He soon became an itinerant painter and wrote some of his finest verse while tramping through Wales. Dyer visited Rome in 1724 and returned the next year. He relapsed into a bohemian life of wandering, sketching, cultivating London acquaintances, and writing occasional verse of little interest. A family inheritance in Hereford-shire caused him to set up housekeeping in a rural area that offered imagery and experience he used for his epic of the Fleece. Shortly after the publication of *The Ruins of Rome* in 1740 Dyer's health began to fail, a circumstance that led him to abandon vigorous field work and enter the church. In 1751 he was offered the parish of Coningsby in Lincolnshire. In this remote, boggy place, far from friends and stimulated in his work on *The Fleece* only by correspondence and occasional visits to London, Dyer grew weaker and more melancholy, but did finish his poem and published it in 1757. Discouraged by public indifference he began to write valedictory verses to each of his friends, and died of consumption in December of the same year.

Dyer's earliest poems are idylls derived from the pastoral tradi-tion, though nothing in this work approaches the social and mythical range of *The Shepheardes Calender* or the Virgilian eclogues which Spenser imitated. What Dyer does communicate is an ecstatic joy received from the sensuous beauty of his native landscape. In *The Country Walk,* for example, he rejoices in the plenitude of lovely sights and sounds, even in the "powerful silence" which the mind and nature share as they interact. He does not invent pageantries or pres-ences where none is perceived. He is willing to fill the forests with the fancied sounds of his beloved's voice, but always stops short of ac-tively creating (or even half-creating) the world in which his pleasure has its source. We understand these hesitations when we are led to his darkest thoughts:

> Some wildly to Parnassus wing,
> And view the fair Castalian spring
>
> . . . .
>
> Some meditate ambition's brow,
> And the black gulf that gapes below:
> Some peep in courts, and there they see
> The sneaking tribe of Flattery.
> But, striking to the ear and eye,
> A nimble deer comes bounding by;
> When rushing from yon rustling spray,
> It made them vanish all away.   (58–59, 72–79)

Ambition, the yearning to be placed at a superior elevation, removes a person from his present landscape; his mind is elsewhere. Because advancement occurs in time, against a deadline of age and death, it opens an abyss, a "black gulf" which Dyer connects imagistically to the "sneaking" serpent of falsehood. The banishment of ambition by the fortunate agency of the deer transforms the stoic theme we expect into a more primitivist experience, a claim for the salvific influence of natural objects and beings. A modern poem by Robert Bly, *Watering the Horse*, uses the same design:

> How strange to think of giving up all ambition.
> Suddenly I see with such clear eyes
> The white flake of snow
> That has just fallen in the horse's mane![3]

In both passages the demonic desire of self-promotion is eclipsed by visual perceptions that create joy. The ego subsides at the preternatural insistence of alien life, otherness.

The Country Walk insists on Dyer's *participation* with beings who gather him into their joy. Thomas Browne, by contrast, seems to derive his pleasure more from the geometrical analogies in material forms and the religious inferences his intelligence can abstract from such analogies than from physical being itself. Throughout *The Garden of Cyrus* nature is valued to the extent it recapitulates the "mystical Mathematicks of the City of Heaven." Browne's eye is on the paradise that succeeds the grave; he wishes to "close the five ports of knowledge" so that his immortal pleasures may commence. To his sublunary eye "the Sunne it self is but the dark *simulachrum*, and light but the shadow of God."[4] Browne yearns to remove himself from the secondary world and ascend to another where the harmony is not subject to alterations by growth and decay.

Dyer's ascent occurs within a landscape to whose powers of joy he sets no limit. The godlike "lusty sun" vitalizes all natural being with an erotic energy, from the welcoming chorus of birdsong it receives at dawn to its loving farewell (it "kisses the streams") as it descends. Milton's bold image of the sun in *On the Morning of Christ's Nativity* stands behind Dyer's usage, but where Milton deliberately turns from the pagan conceit of the sun as nature's "lusty paramour" to lines about nature "Pollute with sinful blame," Dyer insists on his springtime paradise "Where thousand flaming flowers glow; / And every neighbouring hedge I greet, / With honeysuckles smelling sweet." The dawn light on the mountains spreads over the woods as his visionary ecstasy increases. The turning of the earth on its axis allows the deepest penetration of sunlight into matter. Time is the agency of nature's joy, not the sign of her corruption. Like James Thomson's description of the Seasons ("These, as they change, Al-

mighty Father, these / Are but the varied God"), Dyer's poem celebrates the mutability of the Creation. The hyperbolical language he
employs belongs to the rapturous tradition that Wordsworth received
and extended.

Dyer emphasizes the quietness and solitude of his immediate
paradise. Having located a garden place "ever green and young"
Dyer breathes a prayer that we will see become more insistent as the
century advances: "Keep, ye gods, this humble seat, / For ever pleasant, private, neat." The probable occasion of Dyer's anxiety follows:

> See yonder hill, uprising steep,
> Above the river slow and deep:
> It looks from hence a pyramid,
> Beneath a verdant forest hid;
> On whose high top there rises great,
> The mighty remnant of a seat,
> An old green tower, whose batter'd brow
> Frowns upon the vale below.   (120–27)

The pyramid—symbol of social enterprise in the service of
vainglory—is naturalized, hidden beneath trees and greenery. Decaying at the top is a remnant of some previous ambition, but it is not so
much decaying as being encircled and penetrated by the greenness it
sought to displace and rise above. Growing on and around the ruin
are the unhistorical ivy and grass that will soften its frown, heal its
"batter'd brow." The facial metaphor makes explicit the analogy of an
(ambitious) mind and the elevated ruin. Stay away from Parnassus,
Dyer is saying to himself. In the next lines after this passage the
reader (with the tower) is directed, "Look upon that flowery plain . . .
And there behold a bloomy mead, / A silver stream, a willow
shade, / Beneath the shade a fisher stand." The fisherman participates in the verdant world as the poet does; his work is continuous
with it and enhances the pleasures of it. Dyer, like Wordsworth, loves
the rural homes with their "smoke in curling spires" coming out the
chimney (Wordsworth remarks on this in *Tintern Abbey*). Such
homely details are bridges over the "black gulf" that gapes within his
psyche, and he inflates his own cure into a universal panacea. After
this poem of his early twenties the attitudes are set: the architecture
and social landscapes erected beyond the basic needs of man will
crumble or be superseded; the simple home man builds, the fields
and animals he cultivates, represent his own and his country's chief
resources.

We might easily mistake Dyer's country walk for the idealized
pastoral, because he adheres to attitudes and phrasing typical of that

mode. We hear about the "Happy swain, sure happier far / Than lofty kings, and princes are!" We witness the monotonously "fair face" that nature shows to her enthusiast, the scene of happy sheep and "jocund" shepherds, and so on. But despite the artifice of Augustan convention, Dyer successfully seized upon one of the legitimate resources of the Virgilian pastoral—its vivid evocation of animate nature—and staying on this side of allegory he authenticated by modesty of intention and exuberance of technique a lyric mode which insists on the primacy of objects in their own being. Such primacy— the nimble deer is an example—yields to loftier purposes in the Spenserian pastoral, the country estate poem, or the hill poem. In John Denham's *Cooper's Hill* (1655), the appearance of a stag alerts the reader to an approaching allegory. Because hunting was taken to be the pattern of diplomacy and war, and because Denham's survey from Cooper's Hill includes obvious political symbols like Windsor Castle, the stag passage, as Earl R. Wasserman notes, "never allows the reader to overlook the fact that the hunt has a parallel in the world of human affairs." The stag is in fact a figure for the Earl of Strafford.[5] Dyer knows that a poet ambitious for recognition must moralize his landscape in just this way, but in early lyrics like *The Country Walk* he eschews the broader view for the distinct and finely observed details of natural scenery. Anne Finch, after compiling a number of these in *A Nocturnal Reverie* (1713), asserts that the soul, charmed by distinct perceptions, "joys in the inferior world and thinks it like her own." This participation, a different mode from the schematization of nature or from its subordination in the service of allegory, requires the kind of concentration which only a traversal of actual landscape permits.

Dyer labors up Grongar Hill a second time in his famous poem of that name. It is not, in my opinion, a better poem than *The Country Walk*. Its prospect on the landscape below excludes the full sound and texture of things and substitutes a hazy patina of fancy. But this very generalizing tendency, this penchant for distant ocular views graduating into panoramic moral judgments, endeared the poem to its century and gave it an influence out of proportion to its merit. For our purposes we might note that Dyer has excised from this jaunt elements of the landscape that generated joy in the earlier walk. His solitude—without fisherman or gardener, the deer gone, and even the shepherd only mentioned—seems more complete, and he clearly finds the experience disturbing. Without his natural allies he falls prey to internal promptings of the ego, the voices of time. As with other poems of this type, we must heed not what the poet declares for rhetorical effect ("Now, even now, my joys run high"), but the way his attention returns continually to images and thoughts of desola-

Grongar Hill.

Frontispiece to *Grongar Hill*. From *Poems by John Dyer, L. L. B.*, 1761.

tion. *Grongar Hill* is the transitional poem between the unadulterated joy of *The Country Walk* and the continuous gloom of *The Ruins of Rome*.

In the earlier poem the description of the ruined tower is scant, only four lines, and yields immediately to the "flowery plain," the fisherman, and so on. In *Grongar Hill*, a poem two lines longer, the ruin passage extends some eighteen lines, followed promptly by the famous maxim:

> A little rule, a little sway,
> A sunbeam in a winter's day,
> Is all the proud and mighty have
> Between the cradle and the grave.   (89–92)

After this passage Dyer turns to the rivers which in the earlier poem "show with what an easy tide / The moments of the happy glide." Here the phrasing is darkened: "Wave succeeding wave, they go / A various journey to the deep, / Like human life to endless sleep!" The reasons for his increased melancholy cannot be pinpointed exactly, but the principal influence is most likely an artistic one. As a painting student, he would have been taught by his recently acquired mentors the practice of combining ruins and natural scenery to suggest the mixed estate of human life. In their book, *English Taste in Landscape in the Seventeenth Century*, Henry V. S. Ogden and Margaret S. Ogden collect a multitude of examples that chronicle the ruin sentiment in the period just before Dyer's apprenticeship. Ruins were a fashion, if not a mania, shared by painters like Poussin, Claude Lorrain, and Salvator Rosa, treatises on architecture, and even the applied arts and stage-set designs. Ruins, especially viewed at a middle distance towering above sunlit trees or figures, extended a landscape in time as well as space and added an elegiac tone to the pastoral prospect. In an early poem, *An Epistle to a Famous Painter*, Dyer asks his tutor for the art of revealing "Some old building, hid with grass, / Rearing sad its ruin'd face, / Whose columns, friezes, statues, lie, / The grief and wonder of the eye." Ogden and Ogden remark that "pictures of classical ruins were one of the most popular kinds of landscape, probably relatively more popular in the second half of the [seventeenth] century than in the first. The inventories and auction catalogues list over 400 pictures specifically designated as ruin pieces. . . . Probably no other kind of landscape except the prospect was more admired during the second half of the century."[6] The preeminence of ideal landscapes encouraged graphic artists like Dyer to transfer affecting imagery from one medium to another.

In the prospect poem the poet removes himself from the midst of the scene and "paints" the long view spreading before him. When the object is a political commentary, as in *Cooper's Hill*, specific places or buildings can be juxtaposed in a dramatic contrast that guides the reader to abstract conclusions. In the more limited pictorial mode the elevation of the poet tends to produce ethical pronouncements that are literally leveled upon objects from a great height. As he achieved the eminence of a didact and prophet Dyer discovered that the habit of moral dicta became harder and harder to break. This understandably affects the quality of his visual perception. When he mentions the presence of raven, toad, fox, and adder in the ancient tower we know that he does not actually see or experience the life of these beings; the "Fancy" he calls upon at the opening of the poem has invented their existence. He has willed these animals into being so that he may introduce the complaint, the shadow, of the poem. We know from his earlier poem that if he kept his eye on the object he would find in the greening of the tower an emblem of rebirth, but his eye turns inward instead and sees only the stock conventions imbibed from literary and graphic models.

Dyer finds himself in a precarious dilemma. To the extent that he chooses to extend his powers, to gain larger and larger vistas, he may lose contact with the conditions of his most original talent. He cannot sustain joy unless he interacts with natural beings; unless the deer leaps into view his philosophic eye strains aimlessly. By temperament he did not care for vast conceptions, a fact that helps to explain his ambivalent treatment when they became his subject matter. His letters and journals show a fascination with gossip and fact, but only a cautionary interest in the grand ideas of his time. He prefers not to bid his free soul expatiate in the skies, like Pope's ideal man in *Windsor Forest* (252), or speculate on historical epochs, or on theories of government. For this reason he correctly perceives that the Miltonic spur of fame may threaten him with spiritual death. "Knowledge is much to be priz'd, but peace of mind more," he commented in a meditation during this period.[7] And in *An Epistle To A Friend in Town* (1729), he argues, echoing *The Country Walk*, that extraordinary effort, intellectual or moral, is senseless:

> Then glide on my moments, the few that I have,
> Sweet-shaded, and quiet, and even,
> While gently the body descends to the grave,
> And the spirit arises to heaven.

On the manuscript Dyer wrote a defense of his position: "I am far from grief, while I think I do my utmost, that in this life I am thought contemptible, and pass away with my talents unexerted. It is soon to be forgotten and over, and another state will succeed."[8]

And yet, Dyer is an artist and like most artists feels the necessity of immersing himself in the destructive element. In him, as in Wordsworth, there exists a "paramount impulse not to be withstood" (*Prelude*, I.240), a passion to use and not bury the talent that God has given him. *Grongar Hill* was a testing of the deep, and his satisfaction with that poem provided encouragement. He realized that his inner resources were capacious, that they could consummate some glorious project, though at the expense of his peace of mind. Readers familiar with *The Prelude* will recognize in Dyer's vacillation the fretting of Book I, in which Wordsworth at one moment feels "goadings on" to high endeavor (142), and the next is tempted "to stray about / Voluptuously through fields and rural walks, / And ask no record of the hours" (250–52). Dyer's decision to visit Rome in 1724 shows him determined to make use of the hours, and to make war with them, for the Eternal City represented the utmost magnification of temporal decay in the world.

Dyer went abroad, most probably, at the advice of Richardson, who would have wanted the novice to study the Italian canvases in person and partake of the Italian light. His first letters from Europe show him homesick; his later poems and letters display an accumulating and deepening melancholy that found only occasional relief in his artistic studies. He had more than one reason to dislike Rome. He did not get along with the Italian people, whom he considered reserved and deceitful; he was disappointed in the Italian landscape, whose mountains and rivers he considered inferior to those of Wales in every particular; he despised the Catholic religion and pageantries; and he contracted malaria from the air of the Campagna. A poem addressed to his friend, Martha Fouke Samson, known to her admirers as Clio, suggests a more fundamental despair:

> Nothing, alas, where'er I walk,
> Nothing but fear and sorrow talk;
> Where'er I walk, from bound to bound,
> Nothing but ruin spreads around,
>
> Or busts that seem from graves to rise,
> Or statues stern, with sightless eyes,
> Cold Death's pale people:—Oh! for love,
> Angelic Clio, these remove!   (*To Clio, From Rome*)

Rome is a landscape where, as Horace Walpole put it, the memory sees more than the eyes. Inward and outward impressions alike accelerated in Dyer the psychic conflict already described.

Rome is preeminently the city of history, and as such inspires a unique horror because its titanic and enveloping forms, which Dyer emphasizes more than any of his contemporaries, usurp the creative faculties and give them only ruin to dwell upon or re-create. The Pantheon replaces the forest scene in Dyer's imagination as "of this our world / Majestic emblem" (*Ruins of Rome*, 180). What does this mean if not that all ambitious plans (as Dyer once suspected), all poems, paintings, buildings, and civilization itself constitute so much vainglory to be ruined in time, before or during the last conflagration? To face the extinction of future achievement, at age twenty-four, opens a vista of such blank futility that early visions of innocent joy may be permanently blasted. In a poem titled *Written at Ocriculum, in Italy, 1725* Dyer makes his first accommodation to a new religious faith, a submission to an all-powerful being whom he gratefully describes as having an essence "where matter has no share."

The poem begins with the speaker standing before "ivy-grown remains / Of once a city populous and proud." He is painting the ruins, "studious to excel, /Of praise and fame ambitious." As in *The Ruins of Rome*, the decayed structures seem to occupy the entire foreground, increasing their symbolic character ominously. When a shadowy "seer" takes form in front of him, the speaker does not know whether it appears from the ruins "or awful rose before the mental eye." The seer rebukes him for his folly in believing that art is immortal. Only a "vain, mistaken man" fails to heed the lesson of the adjacent ruins—time sweeps away everything: "thee, and these thy painting, and thy lyre." *But* "there remains another path" whereon his soul ("great, immortal gift") can lead him, the path of perfect wisdom. The seer makes it clear that man is a contemptible creature, but "as far as nature weak may imitate," he ought to fill his life with good deeds in order that he may hope for heaven. Later poems modify this craven response, but it persists in all of Dyer's compositions. Looking ahead to one of his last works, *On the Destruction of Lisbon, 1756*, we see the fact of ruins strike him with the same unnerving horror as at Ocriculum:

> One moment overturns the toils of man,
> And humbles greatness: Lisbon sinks in dust.
> Earthquakes, and floods, and fires, and falling towers,
> Thunder among the scatter'd crowds! Rich, poor,
> Young, old, slave, peasant, prince, unheeded, fly,
> From the swift rage of death, and strive to grasp
> At wretchedness! When I consider these;
> When I consider scenes of ancient times,
> Ruins on ruins, thrones on buried thrones;

And walk on earth as on a globe of graves;
When the high heavens I view, and there behold
Planets, stars, comets, worlds innumerous,
To splendour rising, and from splendour fall'n;
My spirits shrink within me: what is man!
How poor a worm!—but, when I meditate
His boundless cogitations, high desires;
And th'infinite Creator, all in all,
Gracious and wise;—each gloomy fear retires,
And heaven's eternal light revives my soul.

This change in the use of ruins—from a shadow of nature's brilliance in the early work to these morbid appeals to an angry God in which ruins become the emblem not only of his body but of his art—accounts for Dyer's ready acceptance of any ideology that promised exaltation of the spirit. The sight of ruins draws him into a downward reverie that culminates in extreme mortification—"how poor a worm" is a typical expression. Desperately he fights his way out of his self-created pit in order to affirm some uplifting principle. The Ocriculum and Lisbon poems conclude on a note of Christian orthodoxy; other works crescendo in praise of Liberty, Commerce, Rural Virtue, whatever abiding ideal the fancy can invent to contradict the eye. This mechanical structure makes Dyer a lesser artist but a compelling personality nonetheless. Ruins poetry, like all art that taps the roots of horror, often bypasses the complex intellectual structure we praise in the highest art and affects us by the stark painting of our fear, complete with a defensive posture that we recognize as our own best effort to stave off the horror. The Ocriculum poem is just such a work: private, unsatisfactory as a verbal construct, but effective as an evocation of Dyer's first traumatic experience of history.

Dyer returned to England in 1725 with abundant notes for a lengthy mediation. *The Ruins of Rome* opens with an abrupt dismissal of his previous work: "Enough of Grongar, and the shady dales / Of winding Towy." He wishes a wider view, to "soar a loftier flight": Rome and not Wales, empire not nature, art not superstition ("Merlin's fabled haunt"). Of Grongar Hill he sang "inglorious" but the praise he expects for championing the contempt-of-world theme is one he might share with Du Bellay, Spenser, and the Claude of *Roman Edifices in Ruins*. Rome is a landscape of decay and death but it is not mute; it speaks in all languages in all centuries. It has achieved an immortality of reference in its very decomposition, for artists can remodel its glory to serve themselves. An author who "treads on classic ground"[9] participates by necessity in an international tradition

of concern, of historical scholarship and elegiac conventions. His justification for choosing the Matter of Rome lies in the confidence he
places in his own creative powers, his ability to restore what has
passed, to hypothesize where there is mystery, and to find meaning
in the pathetic contrasts that meet him at every turn. For this reason
the prospect, with its sense of detachment, its emphasis on the
mind's power to enumerate even where objects are not acutely
visualized, becomes the structural mode of *The Ruins of Rome* from the
first paragraph. As Ralph Cohen has pointed out, historical retrospection, including the kind of detailed articulation of scene we find in
Dyer's poem, belongs to the "perceptual reconsideration" forced
upon writers of the time by scientific instruments like the microscope
and telescope, and, more pertinent to Dyer's case, the continuing
excavation of antiquities throughout the world.[10] As Walpole's remark indicates, however, a prospect or panorama of Rome stimulates, or more precisely, *fills* the memory with voices—Dyer is
haunted by voices throughout the poem—which proclaim the futility
of those ambitions by which a civilized person lives and works.

Dyer is determined to be pleased by the sublime aspect of vanished pomp. His artist's eye enjoys the statuary and bas-reliefs, the
sunsets, the color of the woods, the mixture of light and shade. When
several of these effects appear in one prospect he experiences an
intense pleasure: "The solemn scene / Elates the soul." We know also
from his letters that we are not dealing with a chronic melancholic:

I am not a little warmed, and I have a great deal of poetry in my head when I
scramble among the hills of ruins, or as I pass through the arches along the
Sacred Way. There is a certain charm that follows the sweep of time, and I
can't help thinking the triumphal arches more beautiful now than ever they
were. There is a certain greenness, with many other colours, and a certain
disjointedness and moulder among the stones, something so pleasing in their
weeds and tufts of myrtle, and something in the altogether so greatly wild,
that mingling with art, and blotting out the traces of disagreeable squares and
angles, adds certain beauties that could not be before imagined, which is the
cause of surprise that no modern building can give.[11]

In the poem his appreciative and painterly descriptions lend themselves to a more sinister interpretation than perhaps he intended. In
early passages the soft and sensuous adjectives which load his Miltonic style establish his own aestheticism, but toward the end of the
poem they act as instruments of invective against Roman degeneration into effeteness. In one passage (beginning with line 74), for
example, he fondles the "Cerulean ophite, and the flowery vein / Of

orient jasper," and takes pleasure in the vases bossed with "Floras and Chloes of delicious mould." But in the passage beginning "Dissolved in ease and soft delights they lie" (470), he attributes the fall of Rome to the same weakness for "flowery bowers," "beauteous stones," and voluptuous figures that characterizes his own taste. His belief that undisciplined sensuality threatens the survival of civilization becomes a rod to chasten himself and may account for his melodramatic resolve to write a more patriotic, socially useful poetry. He has discovered in Rome another reason for detaching himself from the "inferior world" that once sustained him.

The sense that he embodies the very ruin that overtook Rome must have made Dyer more susceptible to melancholy sensations. His Rome, like Hawthorne's in *The Marble Faun*, seems to exude violence and death from every side. Often the "charm that follows the sweep of time" is usurped by emotions more in keeping with his experience at Ocriculum:

> The pilgrim oft
> At dead of night, 'mid his oraison hears
> Aghast the voice of time, disparting towers,
> Tumbling all precipitate down-dashed,
> Rattling around, loud thundering to the moon...
>
> . . . .
>
> The sunk ground startles me with dreadful chasm,
> Breathing forth darkness from the vast profound
> Of aisles and halls, within the mountain's womb. (38–42, 57–59)

Throughout the poem "terrific, monstrous shapes" (91), the swollen forms of the ruin-on-the-hill in *Grongar Hill* transform the landscape into a fearful necropolis which quite simply represents the demonic past from which he can no longer be distracted by pastoral agency. The increased ghastliness of ruins in Dyer's Italian writings belongs to a more romantic or Gothic tradition, less easy to define in literature than in painting. A draughtsman manipulates the viewer's emotions in obvious ways: by moving the ruin piece to the foreground, setting it amid a violent conflict of light and shadow, drawing out its lines by erratic or arabesque angles and curves, and so forth. A poet relies more on the historicity of scene, and details of what the ruin was in its prime. By sudden shifts in time the poet discovers the horror of time.

In Allen Tate's *Ode to the Confederate Dead*, for example, the poet's vision collapses from the "orient of the thick-and-fast," the Confederate victories, to the immediately perceived and culminating image of the serpent, "sentinel of the grave who counts us all." In *East Coker*

T. S. Eliot shifts within a single paragraph from the recalled vision of noble ancestors "dancing around the bonfire" to "dung and death." These poets recall the past to life by vision, only to lose it in the fiercer despair occasioned by their reveries. Tate and Eliot, like Spenser in *The Ruines of Time*, confront only the barest memorial of what they re-create in their imagination. The more gigantic the structures that stimulate the meditation the more vertiginous and horrific is the response, so that spatial and temporal elements combine to threaten or overwhelm the viewer. As Dyer walks amid the ruins he emphasizes their size as a means of accounting for the amplitude of his horror:

> Amid the towery ruins, huge, supreme,
> The enormous amphitheatre behold,
> Mountainous pile! o'er whose capacious womb
> Pours the broad firmament its varied light;
> While from the central floor the seats ascend
> Round above round, slow-widening to the verge,
> A circuit vast and high; nor less had held
> Imperial Rome and her attendant realms,
> When, drunk with rule, she willed the fierce delight,
> And oped the gloomy caverns.   (146–55)

The reader follows the poet's eye upward, "slow-widening," then suddenly plunges to the underworld of beasts, "tyrants of the wilds" waiting to inflict death. Though it spirals upward, the Roman Colosseum takes on its essential meaning as a moral descent into violence. The phrasing is similar when Dyer describes the Romans building their temples: "From depth to depth in darkening error fallen" (96). Like his contemporary, Samuel Bowden, who confessed that at Stonehenge he descended into history, "lost in the Circle of devouring Days,"[12] Dyer stares into the Circle of the Colosseum as into a maelstrom. At other times he feels that all of Rome is a "capacious womb," inorganic, lithoid, and that his traversal of this landscape carries him deeper and deeper toward the horror of nonbeing.

In Spenser's adaptation of Du Bellay's sonnet sequence on the Roman antiquities we find the same participation with decomposition and death. Du Bellay's metaphors are remorselessly spatial. The corpse of Rome climbs out of his tomb when summoned by the poet's magical power of reconstruction, but it is clear from the entire sequence that this greeting by the spirit is only a prelude to his triumphant capture of the poet's imagination. The poet is led, as he will lead the reader, down into the deep abysses of Rome's departed glory. Time-consciousness is not unlike vampirism, in which the victims yearn to infect others.

Needless to say, this mode should be distinguished from the most admired descriptions of Italy previous to Dyer, those of Joseph Addison and James Thomson. In Thomson's long didactic poem, *Liberty* (1735), the figure of Liberty mechanically laments the collapse of Roman virtue into slavery, superstition, and "unambitious want." Rarely during its 3400 lines does Thomson stray from his political theme to consider the medium (time) of the changes he chronicles. And Joseph Addison, in his verse *Letter from Italy* and the prose travelogue, *Remarks on Several Parts of Italy*, is complacently at home with Roman antiquities. They recall Virgil and Rafael, they speak to him of law and liberty, they suggest pertinent Latin verses which he memorized in boyhood. He confesses "terror" at the size of the Colosseum, but when he extends the cause to the multitudes once in attendance, and then blithely turns to other matters, we recognize the debased idiom of the Sublime. Dyer can certainly be charged at times with unconvincing high notes but not, I think, with insincerity. His broodings about "all devouring Time, / Here sitting on his throne of ruins hoar" (352) recur in writings of all kind throughout his life. At one point in *The Ruins of Rome* he conveys the anxiety of his obsession by breaking off a passage of dismal forebodings by an ejaculation: "Enough—the plaint disdain" (398). He emphatically did not subscribe to the cult of ruins we associate with neoclassical taste. He would not, like his fellow georgic poet, Richard Jago (in *Edge-Hill*), approve the erection of ruins in a garden nor like Horace Walpole construct a Gothic mansion in order to further haunt his imagination. Dyer is the opposite of a Humanist; he desires no synthesis of pagan and Christian, but rather is frightened by the voice of time into an enthusiastic embrace of the unruined future.

Roman ruins, types of the pyramid, resist natural piety; they cause the ambitious artist to consult vanity as a model for conduct. It is no accident that in *The Ruins of Rome* Dyer describes Julius Caesar in terms he used previously for his own poetic flight: "he soars in thought / Above all height." Caesar is the presiding genius of Rome; his ambiguous example, at the head of a catalogue of Roman patriots, spurs the young Dyer—who obviously needs some goading—to enter the lists:

> Me now, of these
> Deep-musing, high ambitious thoughts inflame
> Greatly to serve my country, distant land,
> And build me virtuous fame; nor shall the dust
> Of these fallen piles with shew of sad decay
> Avert the good resolve, mean argument,
> The fate alone of matter.   (127–33)

As in Spenser's case, the comparison of Roman to English empire, explicit in all elegies of this type, enables the poet to discover his vocation in society. He must honestly insist on the melancholy lesson of ruins but must move beyond their "mean argument" to a moral statement, a warning, to his fellow citizens. This reconstituted ambition allows Dyer an exit from the city's depths. As he retraces his steps the clash of monstrous forms fades into a "diapason" which he can turn to political purposes. He had precedents for this in polemical poems of the neoclassical period that used either British ruins (Stonehenge, despoiled abbeys) or the Roman model as arguments for change and innovation, as warnings of the inevitable degeneration that follows upon the authoritarian model of Caesar and king.

For example, when William III returned from signing the Treaty of Ryswick in 1697, ending nine years of war with France, plans (and engravings and poems) were made to welcome him in the style of a Roman emperor, complete with the erection of triumphal arches and obelisks. But a contemporary poem, *Advice to a Painter*, insisted on the negative aspect of this imperial analogy: "What Hand, what Skill can form the Artful Piece, / To paint our Ruins in a proper Dress?" Within the context of pictorial recommendations the poem urges a reformation of political opinion. In the foreground the king is "seated on the Throne, / Spite of all Laws, himself observing none" and behind him "the Ruins of a sinking State."[13] This is a Tory complaint, but the Whigs took their turn at pressing the Roman analogy whenever the monarch seemed to grow too ambitious.

By Dyer's time, it must be emphasized, the authority of a Caesar himself was not the compelling problem it had been. The Bill of Rights in 1689, whatever its other failings, did proclaim a national intention to keep rulers like the Tudors, Stuarts, or Oliver Cromwell from dividing the country into passionate antagonism. By the time of Queen Anne (1702–1714) the specter of totalitarian rule summoned by Hobbes seemed already distant, and the retiring nature of Anne herself contributed to the diminishing fear of royal oppression. What did not disappear was anxiety about *Caesarism*, ambition either naked or disguised that could effect the same abridgment of liberty and law that weakened Rome ("Her power it selfe against it selfe did arme," wrote Du Bellay). Queen Anne was succeeded by George I, a king ignorant of his adopted country's language and culture, easily persuaded into corruption. The ensuing fragmentation of political loyalties, and the abundant conspiracies of Whig and Tory leaders, caused English writers more than a little confusion. Neither the court nor Parliament, as single bodies, deserved consistent praise because each could be swayed by smooth tongues into ruinous policies. All forms of ambition had to stand at the bar.

Roman history offered Dyer and his contemporaries one suitable model for their own literary ambition: the figure of Cicero declaiming against Catiline. Thanks to the rhetorical powers of Cicero and Sallust the name of Catiline is synonymous with ambition. At least since William Shippen's influential poem, *Faction Display'd* (1704), the use of the Catiline conspiracy to characterize either Whig or Tory plots to usurp power had become a standard analogy in English poetry. Dyer contributes to this tradition in a verse paragraph of *The Ruins of Rome* which ties together the pomp of ancient Egypt, the Catiline conspiracy, and the theme of English liberty. Cicero secured immortality for himself, Dyer notes, and for the highest Roman virtues by making himself a bulwark against which "ambition sinks her crest." The madness of Catiline is put down by the discipline, the skill in letters, represented by the great orator. Dyer may have been influenced by Pope's essay on Letters in *The Guardian* (1713), which likewise cited Cicero: "This silent Art of speaking by Letters . . . is much beyond that of the *Egyptians,* who cou'd preserve their Mummies for ten Centuries. This preserves the Works of the Immortal part of Man, so as to make the Dead still useful to the Living. To this we are beholden for the works of *Demosthenes* and *Cicero.*"[14]

Dyer seems not to have specific national issues in mind but he significantly ends his passage with praise of Cecil, Raleigh, Walsingham, and Drake. He joins the side of "equal laws," which commits him, as he well knows, to the ongoing and progressive remolding of constitutional privilege. A commitment of this magnitude, though it delivered him from doubts about the ethical role of ambition, imposed a burden of literary responsibility. He was ill-prepared, temperamentally and intellectually, to speak against the Catilines of his day; he knew enough to pass that enterprise to others. His resolve to leave behind him a significant, extended work that would in its unique way preserve the state from decay and destruction testifies to his essential strength of character. A gifted poet like Dyer feels always the temptation to "glide on my moments." Before the specter of imperial decay he may, like Verlaine's finicky Roman, withdraw from what is doomed:

> Je suis l'Empire à la fin de la décadence,
> Qui regarde passer les grands Barbares blancs
> En composant des acrostiches indolents
> D'un style d'or où la langueur du soleil danse.   *(Langueur)*

Dyer, like Pope, withdrew in person to private retirement, but only to afford himself a better purchase on matters of national destiny.

Dyer had begun his trip to Italy as a "sacred search / Of ancient arts." The seer at Ocriculum unnerved him temporarily, but his pilgrimage to Virgil's humble tenement, reported at length in The Ruins of Rome, validated the high motives of his journey. He embraces the change in his poetic vision as a patriotic duty. There are no more country walks after The Ruins of Rome is published, but Dyer undertakes something of more importance to English literary history—he chooses in The Fleece to "attune the old Arcadian reed" so that it pipes a system of political theory adaptable to the democratic opportunities of his age. It is a salvation of pastor more than flock. By extending his attention to the rural poor Dyer does finally achieve the prospect, the range and dignity, of the Wordsworthian mode.

4 The Fleece and the World's Great Age

WRITERS HAVE long been fascinated by the inability of human beings to believe in the fact of their own death. "All men think all men mortal but themselves," Edward Young remarked in *Night Thoughts* (I.424), a sentiment Freud explored at length in his *Reflections upon War and Death*, and one which has been demonstrated convincingly in experimental studies. If we understand this defense mechanism—and here our private thoughts speak more eloquently than external testimony—we may comprehend the paradox surveyed earlier in the work of Edmund Spenser: that a recognition of the inevitable ruin of empires does not preclude a belief in the continued survival of one's own empire. Psychologists refer to this as "the rule of self-exception,"[1] a habit of mind whose features remain identical from age to age. Former empire-states, the argument runs, dwindled and perished because some element in the social compound became impure; if the perfect formula could be synthesized the nation would preserve its equilibrium. Policy must respond to the danger signals provided by artists—"the antennae of the race," Ezra Pound calls them—in order to make the fine adjustments requisite for survival.

An eighteenth-century reader would expect such prescriptions from a poem like *The Ruins of Rome*. As a newly mantled didactic poet John Dyer would be looked to for useful analogies of ancient and modern empires. Dyer obligingly offered his readers a diagnosis in the conclusion of the poem:

> Vain end of human strength, of human skill,
> Conquest, and triumph, and domain, and pomp,
> And ease and luxury! O luxury,
> Bane of elated life, of affluent states,
> What dreary change, what ruin is not thine?
> How doth thy bowl intoxicate the mind!
> To the soft entrance of thy rosy cave
> How dost thou lure the fortunate and great!

43

Dreadful attraction! while behind thee gapes
The unfathomable gulf where Asshur lies
O'erwhelmed, forgotten; and high-boasting Cham;
And Elam's haughty pomp; and beauteous Greece;
And the great queen of earth, imperial Rome.   (533-45)

Rome, according to Dyer, became the victim of her own success; she perished by the surfeit of goods accumulated as her due reward for strength and skill. So long as empire is motivated by "proud desire / Of boundless sway, and feverish thirst of gold" (454-55) so long will it remain virile, orderly, and the possessor of "proud security." But the quest for gold must remain pure; when it degenerates into a quest for ease, when gold is alchemized into the leaden riots of hedonism, then the national will becomes soft, a prey for vandals. Dyer's analysis, it need hardly be said, appears reductive and jejeune beside those of Gibbon and Burke later in the century. But he is as faithful to the urgencies of his own political climate, the aftermath of the Glorious Revolution, as they are to the significantly different world of the American Revolution and the colonial policies of Hastings and Clive. Gibbon's warnings about the dangers of arbitrary power and corruption are foreshadowed in Dyer's poem—which Gibbon must have read—and of course the theme of luxury receives its definitive commentary in *The Decline and Fall of the Roman Empire*.

England emerged from the civil and international wars of the seventeenth century in an ideal position to exploit the resources of remote lands. When Queen Anne assumed the throne in 1702 the machinery of panegyric lay ready to make the obvious comparison to Elizabeth, to link Anne's reign to one associated by Renaissance poets with an age of colonial aggrandizement. "Queens have to me been always fortunate," Britannia proclaims in one poem, "E'er since my *English Phoenix* rul'd the State, /Who made my people rich, my Country great." Another poem states the case more directly:

ANNE, like her Great Progenitor, sings Praise:
Like her she Conquers, and like her she Prays;
Like her she Graces and Protects the Throne,
And counts the Lands Prosperity her own:
Like her, *and long like her*, be Bless'd her Reign,
Crown'd with new Conquests, and more Fleets from *Spain*. [2]

The comparison of Elizabeth and Anne foundered, however, on the debate over Caesarism, for the power even of an Elizabeth seemed in retrospect a mortal danger to the commonwealth. England's neoclassical writers wanted their country to be both rich *and* free, a novel combination that would, they hoped, preserve the everlasting power of crown and country alike. When Gibbon later in the century wrote that "under the mild and generous influence of liberty, the Roman empire might have remained invincible and immortal,"[3] he sounded a note of warning to king and party that counseled restraint of ambition. Pope, likewise, praised Caesar Augustus in the advertisement to his *Epistle to Augustus* for carrying out the royal responsibility: "the Increase of an *Absolute Empire.*" But his adaptation of Horace's poem contains a contemporary note: "to make the Poem entirely English, I was willing to add one or two of those [qualities] which contribute to the Happiness of a *Free People*, and are more consistent with the Welfare of *our Neighbours.*" The exact prescription for a working harmony of parts eluded Pope, in part because the new age of commercial expansion brought into ascendancy a class of people which offended his taste. Many intellectuals, like Pope, were uncomfortable with the implications of their sincere desire for a commercial empire. The tyranny of things over men, endemic in nations where trade thrives, constitutes the worst bane of luxury, and such tyranny can prosper under any form of civil authority.

After the publication and success of *The Ruins of Rome*, Dyer gave much thought to the advantages and liabilities of empire, the destructive influence of luxury, the proper occupations of king and common man. The literature of political economy which we know he studied insists that these problems are interrelated and that national survival depends upon their harmonious resolution. Plato's *Republic* can serve as a useful paradigm. In that work Socrates demonstrates to his students that a self-contained pastoral state which eschews luxury possesses the greatest equilibrium ("justice"), and therefore resists decay most efficiently. Socrates grants the necessity of trade as a conduit of needed products into the community. Exchange requires local manufacturing and a class of merchants and shopkeepers whose business is the transvaluation of matter into goods which satisfy artificial cravings. Socrates further grants that the mass of citizens will succumb to the appetitive pleasure of material goods. Socrates elaborates on this point in a passage directed at the distempers of Athens:

Some people, it seems, will not be satisfied to live in [a] simple way; they must have couches and tables and furniture of all sorts; and delicacies too, perfumes, unguents, courtesans, sweetmeats, all in plentiful variety. And besides, we must not limit ourselves now to those bare necessaries of house and clothes and shoes; we shall have to set going the arts of embroidery and painting, and collect rich materials, like gold and ivory.... Then we must once more enlarge our community. The healthy one will not be big enough now; it must be swollen up with a multitude of callings not ministering to any bare necessity.

The republic can resist the destabilizing effect of luxury only by the subjugation of the "inferior multitude . . . by the desires and wisdom of the superior few."[4] These few philosopher-kings must be taught subjects—music, mathematics—which best wean the mind from material things and lend to each consciousness models of ideal harmony and order.

Almost all subsequent utopias follow Plato's recommendations for a simple life in which no caste increases its material needs intemperately. A work like *The Fleece*, concerned with "the high business of the public good" (II.493), had to reconcile the universal principles of utopian thought with the particular economic realities of eighteenth-century England. Dyer's response is a carefully calculated pastoral which attempts in a serious way to relocate the moral center of civilization. He does this, as Wordsworth does a half century later, by insisting on the literal meaning of an allegorical mode. When Dyer apostrophizes the king as a shepherd, in a poem devoted to the manufacture of wool, and asks that he keep watch over rural occupations, the wit and point of the suggestion must be distinguished from similar compliments in the conventional idyll. Dyer does not allegorize entirely; he means what he says. In *The Ruins of Rome* he made it clear that Rome prospered because its greatest leaders came from the land:

> From the plough
> Rose her dictators; fought, o'ercame, returned,
> Yes, to the plough returned, and hailed their peers;
> For then no private pomp, no household state,
> The public only swelled the generous breast.
> Who has not heard the Fabian heroes sung?
> Dentatus' scars, or Mutius' flaming hand?
> How Manlius saved the capitol? the choice
> Of steady Regulus? As yet they stood,
> Simple of life; as yet seducing wealth
> Was unexplored, and shame of poverty
> Yet unimagined—Shine not all the fields
> With various fruitage? murmur not the brooks
> Along the flowery valleys? They, content,
> Feasted at Nature's hand, indelicate,
> Blithe, in their easy taste; and only sought
> To know their duties.   (425–41)

He repeats this sentiment in Book III of *The Fleece*. His insistence flows from a revised version of Plato's advocacy of philosopher-kings. If a king is to rule England, he says, or if the guardians "whom public voice approves" are to shape policy and construct laws to preserve the state from decay, then they must have at least *some* knowledge of the industry which all Europe acknowledged to be the foundation of English wealth and the promise of its continuing eminence. Shepherds cannot tend their sheep by benevolence alone; they must know how to counteract danger, how to recognize diseases and prepare cures, how to increase nutritious grasses and fence off harmful ones. In this inversion of Platonic idealism the forms of the Good are visible, not invisible. Not metaphysical subjects but the rankest and most common require study, and Dyer in effect rubs his reader's nose in the different soils of England as a means of transferring the wisdom necessary for enlightened statecraft. The "indelicate" rural dictators of early Rome—vulgar, in love with the commonplace—are the tutelary spirits of *The Fleece*. English rulers are asked to be only philosophic enough to understand the methods and smooth the way of sheep raisers and merchants, into whose hands Dyer delivers the destiny of England.

Dyer's fusion of pastoral poem and commercial tract reflected the Whig strategy to undermine not only monarchial power but the *mortmain* of influence passed down through the great families. An essential Whig concern was the proper stewardship of England and from this concern the merchant emerged as an exemplary culture hero for a strife-torn nation. Under Walpole and Chatham, merchants, especially the directors of great chartered companies like the East India and South Seas, became the proponents of peace, or so it seemed to writers like Dyer. Trade undoes princely jealousies, they argued, because it insists on international cooperation. The art of peace would stimulate all other arts, most significantly agriculture and crafts. A thriving trade insured employment and provided moral purpose for the lower classes, who otherwise would be a burden or danger to the state. Trade helped to define national identity and national pride. Merchants, then, composed a patriotic body with a common interest in self-preservation; there was no integrating tendency in English life that merchants did not foster, contribute to, or approve. In the most impassioned arguments for the merchant's status, such as Glover's *London: or the Progress of Commerce* and Lillo's domestic tragedy, *The London Merchant*, the merchant was deliberately conceived with the virtues that low-looking poets had previously granted to the farmer and shepherd. Detailed study of his role

in the manufacture and distribution of a product like wool thus became a feasible addition to the traditional georgic.

Dyer devoted minute attention to all aspects of his subject in
imitation of Virgil but received considerably less praise. "He spoke
slightingly of Dyer's 'Fleece'—'The subject, Sir, cannot be made poetical. How can a man write poetically of serges and druggets?' "⁵ Dr.
Johnson's is the most familiar criticism of Dyer, one that Wordsworth
repeated in a letter to Lady Beaumont: "The character of Dyer, as a
patriot, a citizen, and a tender-hearted friend of humanity was, in
some respects, injurious to him as a poet, and has induced him to
dwell, in his poem, upon processes which, however important in
themselves, were unsusceptible of being poetically treated" (Letters, II, 521). Poetic decorum has altered considerably since Wordsworth's time, not enough to bring The Fleece back into favor but
enough to give the modern age a greater sympathy with Dyer's intentions. In America, especially, the muse still resides where Whitman
put her, "install'd amid the kitchen ware." American poetry, in Louis
Simpson's definition, "must have / A stomach that can digest /
Rubber, coal, uranium, moons, poems."⁶ Why not serges and
druggets, then, or the subjects James Grainger proposed for poetic
treatment in the eighteenth century:

> Shall the Muse celebrate the deep dark mould
> With clay or gravel mix'd?
> . . . .
> Of composts shall the Muse didain to sing
> Nor soil her heavenly plumes?⁷

The didactic poets of the century descended the hierarchy of poetic
subjects because they possessed information the country urgently
needed for its survival. Verse was a popular medium in which the
spiritual dimension of commercial subjects might be fruitfully explored. Poems like Cyder, The Fleece, The Sugar Cane, and The Hop-
Garden assume an ignorance of practical matters in the English public;
contemporary accounts suggest that poets were not wrong in such
assumptions.

The intellectual rot began at the top. George II, reigning monarch
during the composition of The Fleece, inherited a Hanoverian stolid-
ness of imagination from his father. A man of narrow vision, one who
loved parades and military spectacles more than statecraft, George II
was satirized continuously for his cynical dispersion of court ap-
pointments and his low tastes. Pope's depictions of Colly Cibber and
Queen Dulness in The Dunciad have a way of turning into satires on

George II and Caroline. Their well-documented follies, in Pope's nightmare vision, have the power to summon Chaos and Old Night to reclaim the minds and hearts of true-born Englishmen. Dyer's standards were not so severe as Pope's, but neither was his judgment of the crown any higher. Caesar Augustus had no more familiarity with the plow than George; he did at least have Virgil to inform him of its use. Though in some part of his psyche Dyer aspired to the same post, the vice and stupidity that characterized George's reign, preserved for us in the fluent wit of his subjects' belles-lettres, must have discouraged Dyer even as he composed.

The level below this royal shepherd presented a condition hardly less disturbing. The eighteenth century saw an increasing transfer of wealth and land from the old aristocratic families to a new bourgeoisie whose urban orientation bred a vulgarized notion of rural economy and practice. These new landowners had to be instructed in the resources of their estates. Not just the new but the old gentry required these poetic almanacs, for the old rich were if anything more stupid, a danger to England's preeminence as a secure bastion of liberty and order. Daniel Defoe comments:

The weakness of the parts, the defect of the understanding, and the want of erudition, which is so much the fashion among our gentry has been the true if not the chief reason of their present poverty and bad circumstances, lessening their estates and ruining their fortunes.

Their want of learning being the cause of their luxury and extravagance, and that luxury reducing them into a readyness of being corrupted, brib'd, and drawn in by partyes to espouse those interests for money which at other times they would abhorr, and which are ruinous to their country's liberties and to their posterity.

In *The Compleat English Gentleman*, from which this quotation is taken, Defoe argued against the archaic study of "dead languages" in English schools and proposed reforms that would emphasize applied knowledge. "The Knowledge of things, not words, make a scholar," he wrote.[8] Defoe is characteristically practical in his recommendations. Like Locke and other reformers, Defoe argued that the gentleman would be a less ruinous influence on the social body if he knew less Greek and Aramaic, and more arithmetic, geography, ethics, civil and common law. In the same spirit Dyer embarked on a project he called "The Commercial Map," which was designed as a visual guide to the resources and industries of England, with suggestions for developments in regions which currently lay idle. The map would promulgate information on minerals, plants, animals, rivers, the location of mines and orchards, and any other data of commercial

interest pertinent to each locality. Anticipating the negative response
he would get from either the crown or any of the great families, he
dedicated the project "to the truly noble; and to the promoters of
most great works, the merchants of England; and to all manufactur-
ers, traders, and men of honest industry."[9]

Dyer's reformed pastoralism is an appropriate mode in light of
the progressive ideals he adopted after his return from Rome. The
wool trade in England, he insists repeatedly in *The Fleece*, was not
essentially a luxury trade, like silk or lace, but benefited all classes
worldwide. After surveying the higher-grade cloths of Belgium, India, and China, he comments:

> Nor do their toils and products furnish more
> Than gauds and dresses, of fantastic web,
> To the luxurious: but our kinder toils
> Give clothing to necessity; keep warm
> The unhappy wanderer, on the mountain wild
> Benighted, while the tempest beats around.   (III.373–78)

At its origin in the fields, the wool industry required the virtues of
gentleness, concern, and devotion; its later stages of spinning, weav-
ing, and dyeing could be justifiably described as arts; and its trade
overseas extended the community Dyer valued in cottage industry to
a "mighty brotherhood" (III.540) of international cooperation and aid.
The wool trade served, as it expressed, the whole emotional and
intellectual life of mankind. Even the energetic competition between
nations for resources and markets could be imagined, at best, as part
of the *concordia discors* necessary for human existence. Like Blake's
Looms of Jerusalem, Dyer's machines weave a continuous atmosphere of peace as well as a product. His conception conforms in its
essentials also to Plato's model in *The Republic*: "a pattern set up in the
heavens for one who desires to see it and, seeing it, [finds] it in
himself. But whether it exists anywhere or ever will exist is no matter;
for this is the only commonwealth in whose politics [the highest type
of person] can ever take part" (pp. 319–20). His ultimate model is the
pastoralism of the New Testament, adapted to the altered needs of
eighteenth-century England. Because Christian charity and piety
would advance in the train of English trade, he could legitimately
claim divine inspiration for his georgic. It would, like all prophecy,
compel the noblest into true understanding.

Bonamy Dobrée describes *The Fleece* as "in many ways the
greatest patriotic poem in the language, bursting with the energy
which characterized the country."[10] Even a brief discussion of the

poem must attend first to its exuberant praise of homeland and the reasons for such praise. Dyer assumes throughout that England is a paradise uniquely bequeathed ideal conditions for the most reward-ing and noble enterprises. Fortunate in men ("our Lockes, our New-tons, and our Miltons"), in rivers and soil, even in climate, England possesses boundless potential for growth. He describes how the in-cessant rains nourish the grasses and timber which guarantee En-gland's fortune; he praises the natural harbors which are God-given to promote her trade. England has no gold mines to distract and enervate her populace, no volcanos to rain death upon it nor deserts to weary it. Physical nature, in England, offers a fair contest. In his role of didact, Dyer appraises the countryside with a stern eye, not for the joy it gives but for the tangible fruits it yields: "Tis art and toil / Gives Nature value, multiplies her stores, / Varies, improves, creates" (II.183–85). Edward Young expresses a similarly practical view of nature in *Imperium Pelagi:*

> Britain! behold the world's wide face;
> Not cover'd half with solid space,
> Three parts are fluid: empire of the Sea!
> And why? For commerce. Ocean streams
> For that, through all his various names:
> And if for commerce, Ocean flows for thee.[11]

Poets like Dyer, Young, and the Pope of *Windsor Forest* imagined the use of nature to be an essential part of its divinely appointed purpose. An accelerated manipulation of natural materials was part of the pas-toral vision, a shared community of effort that would preserve the nation, enrich it, and finally bring into being a "mighty brotherhood" of Christian souls. An equivalent vision in America is that of Whit-man's *Song of the Broad-Axe,* in which the shapes created by the sweep of the axe (shapes of houses, ships, railroads, etc.) are described in the conclusion of the poem as "Shapes of Democracy . . . / Shapes of the friends and home-givers of the whole earth, / Shapes bracing the earth and braced with the whole earth."

The elements of nature rightly viewed are medicine for "the vigorous frame and lofty heart of man" (I.154). Self-improvement through active labor corresponds to God's original plan for Adam in the paradisaical garden, as Milton described it. The punishment for abandoning virtue, for losing the strength and skill Dyer praised in the Romans, is chronicled in the ruins Dyer surveys throughout the poem. "Wild nature back returns," overcoming the remains of "Ne-glected Trade" (IV.65–66). The green forces he praised as they infil-

trated the ruins in *The Country Walk* he now associates with the ruin of
human hopes entire, rich and poor alike. As in *The Ruins of Rome*, the
panorama of history, empire after empire, enforces gloom on the
poet.

Dyer's pessimism derives from two principal literary sources.
One is the chief influence on *The Fleece*, James Thomson's *Britannia*
(1729). Thomson, like Dyer, tries to keep trade and conquest apart
in his imperial enthusiasm, but he acknowledges in the poem that
there has never been a case in history where kings achieved one
without wanting the other. His proclamations to Britannia to "extend
your Reign from Shore to Shore" carry therefore a melancholy recognition that he is almost certainly wishing upon his country not only
the peaceful war of commerce but the bloody warfare of conquest and
colonization. If this were not true, Thomson's lapse into the ruin
sentiment could not be explained,

> For should the sliding Fabrick once give way,
> Soon slacken'd quite, and past Recovery broke,
> It gathers Ruin as it rolls along,
> Steep-rushing down to that devouring Gulph,
> Where many a mighty Empire buried lies.
> And should the big redundant Flood of Trade,
> In which ten thousand Labours join
> Their several Currents, till the boundless Tide
> Rolls in a radiant Deluge o'er the Land,
> Should this bright Stream, the least inflected, point
> Its Course another way, o'er other Lands
> The various Treasure would resistless pour,
> Ne'er to be won again; its antient Tract
> Left a vile Channel, desolate, and dead,
> With all around a miserable Waste.   (213–27)[12]

In the cycle of empires England has the current good fortune to receive the inflected tide of commercial prosperity. By an analogy of
England and Egypt which immediately follows this passage, Thomson does two things. First, he pleads that England seize the opportunity (from France, it is understood), and avert the danger of losing its
colonies by attrition or carelessness. And second, Thomson makes it
clear that England will in the nature of history itself lose the "radiant
Deluge" that now overwhelms it. The term "Deluge" contains an
ambiguity Thomson does not neglect, for the word was popularly
linked by English writers to any divine act with destructive consequences. Here, as in passages I shall study later, culminating in

Wordsworth's dream of the Arab rider, biblical images of deluge and waste are related to government policies affecting national destiny.

The warnings of contemporary economists were a second source of Dyer's anxiety. Joseph Schumpeter remarks of the period just preceding the Hanovers that "complaints about... decay of English power were so frequent as to constitute a most interesting phenomenon of political psychology.... Parallel with them went complaints about a wholly imaginary economic decay."[13] Schumpeter is not entirely just to the complainants. There were constant market fluctuations caused by fashion (Defoe applies these to the wool trade in his *Plan of English Commerce*), and considerable instability in revenues due to the imperial wars. Ruin is always overstated, by economists no less than poets. Arguably, an activity like the slave trade would not have been tolerated by the English government and public had they not been alarmed by forecasts of doom. Dyer's temperamental melancholy would have made him uncommonly alert to warnings that interference in the freest trade, even of human beings, would accelerate the (imaginary) decline of English power and wealth.

Dyer warns of foreign competition in *The Fleece* but his obsessive repetition of the ruin sentiment seems to be motivated less by threats from abroad than from undefined fears of internal decay. The enemy seems not to be France or Holland but time, the time required for any system to run down through entropy. The dilemma is that of *homo econimus:* Time is money; how shall one spend it? Hoarding or wasting, building monuments or doing nothing at all? Because commercial profits can buy time as well as goods, the consumption of both by the leisure class seemed to give it an advantage over the pastoral state. If the luxurious possess a more intense experience of time because of trade, then how can the supporters of a commercial empire discourage even a surfeit of consumption? The public understood the Roman analogy well enough but would not act upon it until presented with a competitive alternative to its pursuit of privilege. To the question, "How shall one spend it?" the answer frequently returned was "in excess, in vice." Bernard Mandeville's *The Grumbling Hive* urged the English populace to follow an obviously Roman example:

> Then leave complaints: fools only strive
> To make a great an honest hive.
> To enjoy the world's conveniences,
> Be famed in war, yet live in ease,
> Without great vices is a vain
> Utopia seated in the Brain.
> Fraud, luxury, and pride must live,
> While we the benefits receive.   (409–16)

Mandeville, to do him justice, points to the positive side of the Roman heritage, for he warns that the vices he obliges must be lopped and bound before they can, like the crooked vine which yields the richest wine, be turned to their most productive use. But even the poets who seem in retrospect most busy in lopping and binding, like Pope, countenanced the spirit of excess. "PROVIDENCE is justified in giving Wealth to be squandered in this manner," Pope remarks in the "Argument" of the *Epistle to Burlington*, "since it is dispersed to the Poor and Laborious part of mankind."

Pope detests Timon's "civil Pride" in the epistle because of Timon's bad taste, not because of any essential flaw in his moral character: "I curse such lavish cost, and little skill, / And swear no Day was ever passed so ill" (167–68). Pope recognizes the perverted impulses of the artist in Timon, a failed artist because he lacks discipline ("skill") and good sense. Every system, Pope argues, requires builders and makers, but it must guarantee that those who have skill are honored and preserved in time, for it is preservation that enriches—gives value to—civilized life. In his own day Pope's modest grotto at Twickenham reproached the bloated vanity of Timon, but the economy of his moral vision demanded a verbal statement of superior durability. Pope survives because his taste and skill, wreaked upon the hapless Timon, guarantee the preservation of virtues that excess like Timon's threatens. For this reason Pope must imagine the oblivion that comes of Timon's pride; he must forcefully deny this "artist" immortality:

> Another age shall see the golden Ear
> Imbrown the Slope, and nod on the Parterre,
> Deep Harvests bury all his pride has plann'd,
> And laughing Ceres re-assume the land.   (173–76)

The pastoralist has but one arrow to use against worldly pride and ambition, but that single shot cannot miss. Dyer's ultimate and irrefutable critique of luxury, like Pope's, is his demonstration that time, in the long view, is intolerant of courts and cities, of civil pride, and that it cherishes the pastoral virtues as it does the poets who applaud them. Pastoral civilizations represent time in their icons, according to Erwin Panofsky, "by symbols of universal power and infinite fertility, but not by symbols of decay and destruction."[14] Pastoral time, the cycles of laughing Ceres, becomes Dyer's muse. The "sacred charge" (II.516) assigned him by this muse is the promulgation of one overwhelming truth: "o'er all [shall] prevail the shepherd's stores" (II.410). Or as he puts it elsewhere in *The Fleece*:

> Lo! the revolving course of mighty Time,
> Who loftiness abases, tumbles down
> Olympus' brow, and lifts the lowly vale.
> Where is the majesty of ancient Rome,
> The throng of heroes in her splendid streets,
> The snowy vest of peace, or purple robe,
> Slow trailed triumphal? Where the Attic fleece,
> And Tarentine, in warmest littered cotes,
> Or sunny meadows, clothed with costly care?
> All in the solitude of ruin lost,
> War's horrid carnage, vain ambition's dust.   (II.328–38)

Here again is the fate of Timon, imagined in the succession of empires. It is also the fate of Dyer's own aspirations to live with his more celebrated contemporaries on Parnassus. Olympus' brow echoes the mountain-tower's "batter'd brow" in *The Country Walk*. Both are ruined eminences placed beyond reach, and for good reason. Dyer did not have to wait for Dr. Johnson's contempt; his lowly choice of subject for *The Fleece* made him a curiosity among his London acquaintances during his lifetime. He looks forward to England's reformation, when the lowly vale will be lifted and the vale's poet with it.

And so Dyer sides not with the consumers but the producers of his nation's wealth. One shepherd reminds another in the interpolated eclogue of Book I, "Dream not . . . our occupation mean" (670). The shepherd rises in spiritual eminence above the privileged ranks and even above royalty because the shepherd is true master of the rites of timelessness, true master of nature's fruits and nature's joy. The festival dance that concludes Book I, like the spousal song that ends Book IV ("T'is [Britannia's] delight / To fold the world with harmony"), guides the reader as effectively from "infectious luxury" (II.462) as the shepherd leads his flock from tedded hay or marsh grass. In Dyer's version of these timeless festivities "we think the golden age again returned" (I.606).

Dyer's scheme is praiseworthy but its internal contradictions are obvious. Like James Thomson, Dyer is loyal to irreconcilable myths: that of the pastoral Golden Age and that of the progress of empire.[15] When Ovid imagined Arcadia as the period prior to the birth of Jupiter he paid tribute to the absolute separation between the pastoral and the imperial which Dyer seems to imply by his opposition of Olympus and the lowly vale. Jupiter is the god of rulers and empires, the agent of radical change. In Ovid he is the light-bringer, Jupiter Lucetius, and endows mankind with those arts and sciences which give it the power to dream new dreams. But a pastoral economy cannot sustain radical change without inviting into itself the luxurious (albeit civilizing) pleasures that ultimately weaken its resistance to anarchy and conquest. The shepherds in Book I of *The Fleece* locate the desire for change in the city, as convention dictates, and mock the city's power and its people. But Dyer himself ends by praising the new manufacturing cities of Birmingham and Manchester, and calling for more urban hegemony. He strongly criticizes "infectious luxury" but elsewhere in the poem turns on critics like himself:

> To censure Trade,
> Or hold her busy people in contempt,
> Let none presume. The dignity, and grace,
> And weal of human life, their fountains owe
> To seeming imperfections, to vain wants,
> Or real exigencies.   (II.618–23)

Dyer sneaks the "vain wants" into this passage as an admission that Ceres would have a long wait before reassuming the land. Dyer knows he is in the midst of a dilemma, but he postpones its resolution. In his own age poverty was too close to common life (including his own) to sanction a reactionary stand against trade or luxury. The original draft of *The Fleece* has several very direct attacks upon the rich, necessarily excised in a final version which had to flatter vain wants. There could be no question of retaining a passage like this:

> Cast your affluence
> Down to comparison with anxious want,
> And meagre penury: behold the poor,
> Whose fireless hearth prepares them no repast;
> For whom no vine the purple cluster hangs,
> To cheer their heart; no corn unfolds its ear;
> Nor shade from heat, nor shelter from the storm,
> Can they demand; beneath the boundless sky
> No property appears which they can claim:
> No thing so small that poverty can say,
> See, this is mine.[16]

Dyer obviously cannot argue for the timeless joy of shepherds *and* include such grim details of country life. He must sacrifice the immediate interests of the poor to the long range advantages of trade. Dyer assumes that as the arts and sciences improve they will heal the worst disabilities of the peasantry. In this sense, also, time provides salvation by revealing, year by year, the secrets of "nature's vast machine" (I.320). Dyer must hope that as man's artful control over the "machine" (and machines) increases, the wealth and well-being of even the poor will be enhanced. According to the myth of progress the people will then be in a position secure enough to rediscover the pastoral values at the source of their wealth.

History did not sustain Dyer's hopes. By the time of Goldsmith's *The Deserted Village* and Crabbe's tales, Dyer's epic attempt to re-vitalize the pastoral appeared evasive of bedrock realities. In the Victorian period, when the wool industry metamorphosed into a fac-tory system of notorious disharmony, Dyer's reputation as a humanitarian reached its nadir. "He wrote," said Wordsworth in 1814, "at a time when machinery was first beginning to be intro-duced, and his benevolent heart prompted him to augur from it noth-ing but good" (PW, V, 469).[17] And yet one could argue that Dyer foresaw the harrowing fate of England's flock and that he forecast the conditions of his country's eclipse by the use of the ruin sentiment throughout *The Fleece*. In the very opening of the poem he directs our eye to Stonehenge in a verse paragraph that closes a discussion of English landscape with a lingering glance at "that hill / Vesuvius, where the bowers of Bacchus rose, / And Herculanean and Pompeian domes" (64–66). The fateful analogy of Italy recurs as a leitmotif in phrase and figure; it coexists with and shadows the most expansive and optimistic prospects.

Like his Renaissance forebears, however, Dyer prefers to yearn westward in space rather than forward in time. Book IV concludes with a celebration of the faraway places in which England's dreams of freedom and order will be renewed and made perfect. Britain has made the West an "asylum of mankind" (512), a retreat for the op-pressed. Not the paradise that succeeds the grave but "the happy regions" (532) to which Englishmen could actually journey lure his imagination. In moving westward the traveler escaped from historical time; there were no ruins in America. Dyer envisions the travelers as merchants who rightfully inherit, as they extend, the pastoral experi-ence of timelessness. He also anchors his vision in commercial realities: the West possesses the gold of Ophir, it offers opportunity for new industry and increasing wealth. To secure dominion over her colonies England must send emigrants "happy in those arts, / That join the politics of trade and war" (IV.553–54). Before England can diffuse her bounty, France and Spain, no less than the recalcitrant Indians, must be defeated wherever they resist. *The Fleece* is a great patriotic poem partly because its bass note throughout is "Rule, Britannia"; it does not flinch at recommending the mailed fist as a means to "mighty brotherhood."

We should not fault Dyer for his evasion of contradictions that

Spenser and Wordsworth, though greater artists, resolved with no greater success. National destiny is an unsolved riddle to which every artist has some kind of answer, some response that amounts to a rule of self-exception. The future may invalidate their ideas but not their texts, and so by a species of patriotism they arrive at the immortality they once construed for their homeland. The only prognosis a prophet's own time affords is its reception of his instruction. Mark Akenside declared "that he would regulate his opinion of the reigning taste by the fate of Dyer's *Fleece;* for if that were ill-received, he should not think it any longer reasonable to expect fame from excellence."[18] In fact, the poem found virtually no audience and never reached a second edition. Let us at least give Dyer credit for hearing the mockery of his own muse. His last known poem is included in a letter of 1757 to an old friend. It records a vision purified of Dyer's ambitious fancy, a haunting by monstrous forms never expelled from his imagination:

> Content thee, Harper, whose plain busy life
> Is all beneficence; nor hope to hear
> Thy name within our numbers: they're the proud,
> The rich and powerful, that the Muses sing,
> Croesus or Caesar. He has long been razed
> From Fame's memorials, long ago in dust
> Been trod beneath the feet of many an age,
> Who gave the world the life-sustaining plough.
> Men lead not now their lives by moral rules;
> Long has the shrine of virtue been destroyed,
> 'Tis now an hoary ruin. Pride, and whim,
> And vice, with all her train, in antic shapes,
> Are perched on every altar: round me run
> From one to one, with bead and bended knee,
> And kiss their shrines as fashion gives the law—
> Fashion, whom you so singularly spurn,
> You, who employ the poor, and hundreds feed!
> Go; feed your poor; and, in this iron age,
> Leaden or wooden, learn to bear contempt.[19]

5 Roxana and Empire

Every wise woman buildeth her house: but the foolish plucketh it down with her hands.
—*Proverbs 14:1*

IN EVERY AGE the creative imagination links the "bone-house" or bodily structure with larger figures of containment: houses, castles, cities, national boundaries. The artists who take these metaphorical connections most seriously, who rejoice in the harmony of man and thing implied by such bonding, are also most susceptible to the pessimism and horror occasioned by the fact of degeneration. "O man, thy kingdom is departing from thee," Edward Young cries in *Night Thoughts* (II.411). Implied in Young's construction of the problem, however, is a solution which offers solace to the dualist: the soul can hold itself aloof and consider the body's decay without necessarily participating in it. The soul owes its integrity to the body's sacrifice, to a deliberate discipline of appetites, including the craving for self-perpetuation. The ruin of the soul presents a drama that can and must be distinguished from the fate of matter on any scale.

Political economy, as we have seen, partakes of the moral ambiguities of personal salvation. A nation's frontiers may be imagined as its body, and the imperial desire to extend those frontiers, to magnify national glory by accumulating property, as its governing will. Eighteenth-century writers freely admit to the spiritual ills that accompany physical growth—some, like Mandeville, insist on them. They justify these ills by invoking natural law, of which survival is the preeminent virtue. As necessity diminished, they hoped, prosperity, and from it charity, would effect a harmonious liaison of the "Desire of Distinction" (as Pope called it[1]) with spiritual needs. So ran the conventional wisdom. Did writers believe it as well as profess it? The examples of Dyer and Thomson suggest that the burden of hope was preferable to the misery of *not* believing in a utopian future. Still, as every expansion of commercial and colonial empire created a new class of victims, even the devout questioned how many more sacrifices of the soul to the body's well-being, all justified in the name of imperial sway, a nation could sustain before it dissolved as a moral entity.

A passage from *The Fleece* illustrates the dilemma:

> On Guinea's sultry strand, the drapery light
> Of Manchester or Norwich is bestowed
> For clear transparent gums and ductile wax
> And snow-white ivory; yet the valued trade,
> Along this barbarous coast, in telling wounds
> The generous heart, the sale of wretched slaves;
> Slaves by their tribes condemned, exchanging death
> For life-long servitude; severe exchange!
> These till our fertile colonies, which yield
> The sugar-cane, and the Tobago-leaf,
> And various new productions, that invite
> Increasing navies to their crowded wharfs.
>   But let the man, whose rough tempestuous hours
> In this adventurous traffic are involved,
> With just humanity of heart pursue
> The gainful commerce: wickedness is blind:
> Their sable chieftains may in future times
> Burst their frail bonds, and vengeance execute
> On cruel unrelenting pride of heart
> And avarice. There are ills to come of crimes.   (IV.189–208)

Dyer assumes throughout *The Fleece* that trade in the world hive enhances and propagates spiritual values; without trade only "barbarity / And brutal ignorance" (IV.228–29) exist. The slave trade, then, presents a complex moral problem, for even if their own tribes condemned these slaves to death, the injustice and oppression of the sentence is perpetuated by the very traders and planters who preserve English civilization. To stauncher Christians like William Cowper and Samuel Johnson the slave trade was a moral abomination pure and simple, but Dyer's eye, as in this passage, looks beyond the "severe exchange" into the far distance of the "fertile colonies" whose produce swells the English treasury and whose pastoral arts contribute at whatever cost to the moral regeneration of the world.[2] The slave traders may therefore continue their traffic but they should treat their victims more charitably. The "just humanity" Dyer urges on them, we notice also, has the fear of retaliation as its explicit rationale.

In Dyer's view, servitude, like poverty, belonged to the misfortunes of the social body which increasing trade would repair in time. To abstain from the slave trade, or any trade, would damage the "mighty brotherhood" he imagined as the end result of mercantile policies. His naive devotion to the public good prevented him from analyzing the implications of his beliefs. In the face of moral contradictions he collapsed utilitarian means into ends; he recommended, simply, the policies which seemed to guarantee immunity from decay. He may be England's chief patriot, as Dobrée suggests, but he is hardly her most rigorous moralist.

Of Dyer's contemporaries that title could go to Daniel Defoe, whose fiction, reportage, and didactic verse demonstrate a fervor, a thoroughness and range, remarkable even in an age which favored the literature of instruction. Defoe's authority derives from his insistence that every thought and action, as every law and policy, produce irreversible results, and that the man of letters must chronicle and scrutinize these results, in their unique contexts, in order to guide the public understanding. An abstract dictum like "Luxury is baneful" misleads the public because it makes no distinction between the hardworking craftsman who uses some of his profit to purchase lace, Timon's extravagance, and a king who increases taxes merely to aggrandize his collection of foreign wines or jewels. Defoe devotes his art to the minute particulars of economy, individual and national, because he shares Dyer's belief in the value of information; he is, however, a moral (and financial) bookkeeper of greater genius.

Defoe's writings assume that individual and national conditions are analogous, and that like Socrates in *The Republic* he can use one model to illuminate the other. Political commentary has the advantage, Socrates claims, of exhibiting principles "in larger proportions, easier to make out."[3] Defoe chose this perspective in *The Consolidator, Jure Divino,* and *History of the Union*—massive, ambitious documents now unread by any but Defoe scholars. In the last decade of his life he applied the opposite lens and wrote those "histories" of individual fortunes that guarantee his immortality. A character study serves truth, he insisted, so long as the "cause and consequence" of the protagonist's actions have universal application and are not "the Chimera of a scribbling Head." Individuals like Robinson Crusoe, Moll Flanders, or Roxana embody aspects of the national character, so that their fates educate the public in civil policy. "Things seem to appear more lively to the Understanding and to make a stronger Impression upon the Mind," Defoe wrote, "when they are insinuated under the Cover of some Symbol or Allegory, especially where the Moral is good, and the Application obvious and easy."[4] Defoe called his fictions "parables" and "moral Romances" and clearly intended them to be read in the same spirit as his political tracts and for the same benefits. They belong to the gallery of national types Defoe collected all his life, beginning with *The True-Born Englishman* (1701) and extending to one of his last works, *The Compleat English Gentleman* (1729).

Roxana or *The Fortunate Mistress* (1724), Defoe's last important novel, is the character study most pertinent to the argument I wish to develop. The Lady Roxana illustrates in her behavior the spiritual decay Defoe believed to be overtaking the nation. "I am a Memorial to all that shall read my Story," she warns, "a standing Monument of the Madness and Distraction which Pride and Infatuations from Hell runs us into; how ill our Passions guide us; and how dangerously we act, when we follow the Dictates of an ambitious Mind."[5] *Roxana* is a confessional narrative, constructed around a series of choices by the narrator, each of which leads directly and often immediately to a consequence from which another choice arises. The episodic structure, mitigated in ways I shall discuss, represents her life as a sequence of events in her entire control. This point must be emphasized because it is precisely Defoe's control of the allegory in *Roxana* that advances the art of this history beyond an earlier effort like *Moll Flanders*. Ian Watt rightly complains of Moll that "It is [her] freedom from the probable psychological and social consequences of everything she does which is the central implausibility of her character."[6] By contrast Defoe prefaces each important stage of Roxana's chronicle with an argument of principles, within Roxana's mind or between Roxana and her servant and alter ego, Amy. The substance of these arguments pertains to problems that policy makers resolve daily on a national scale: the uses of wealth, the limits of liberty, and the like. The common excuse for all of Roxana's behavior is the avoidance of "Ruin," the word she uses consciously and often. Like contemporary economists her prescription for avoiding the ruin of her material wealth is unambiguous, an increase in trade. As she is a whore, this amounts to a simple multiplication of patrons. She neglects the ruin of her soul because, like Dyer, she cannot bear to divide body from soul in the midst of prosperity. The unpredictable connections between one ruin and another, however, compose the lessons of this parable, the epitaph (to use Roxana's repentant metaphor) essential to public salvation.

The first fourteen years of Roxana's life are passed over in two pages of text, but we accumulate important points nevertheless. We learn that Roxana's father was shrewd enough to insure his family's prosperity before emigrating to England, that "he had his door continually thronged with miserable objects of the poor starving creatures who at that time fled hither [from France] for shelter" and that her father's business sense enabled Roxana to obtain a genteel upbringing: "I wanted neither Wit, Beauty, or Money. In this Manner I set out into the World, having all the Advantages that any Young Woman cou'd desire, to recommend me to others, and form a Prospect of happy Living to myself" (p. 7). Defoe has set a scene, that of the princess in the pleasure garden, that will reappear in Roxana's adult imagination. After the ruin of her fortune her ambition will be to climb as far from poverty and impotence as possible, to become the princess-figure again, "to have the entire Possession of one of the most accomplished Princes in the World" (p. 68), to be the mistress of Charles II, the Countess of Wintselheim, the "Queen of Whores" (p. 82). Childhood happiness would not suffice to motivate such ambition; it is the shocking *contrast* between that happiness and the distress of her first marriage that sets her character. The brewer she weds is a symbolic figure of that foppish ignorance Defoe detested and warned against in all his writings. As a representative of the commercial community he threatens England with the same injuries he wreaks on Roxana. "He was the Foundation of my Ruin" (p. 7), she remarks, because his extravagance, harmless in lovers whose business sense is acute, drains the treasury her father endowed on her. Roxana is powerless to help herself; as her husband spends and spends "I saw my Ruin hastening on" (p. 11), a demonic pursuit that recurs in the last section of the novel when Roxana's castaway daughter (bearing her own original name) "haunts" and "hunts" her.

The allegorical significance of this first incident must be emphasized further. Defoe establishes Roxana on the first page as a child of London, a willing emblem of the great city. Like Dreiser's Carrie, whom Roxana resembles in many ways, the young emigrant thrives in a landscape whose social customs are constantly modified by economic changes. Roxana brings an exceptional beauty to the city, a desirable quality that she will later recognize as the "Great Article that supported my Interest" (p. 105). Defoe attributed to beauty the ruin of all mankind, for, as he never tires of repeating in his works, the story of Genesis can be best understood as Satan's perversion of God's generous desire to form human creatures in imitation of the angels:

Eve you may suppose was a perfect beauty, if ever such a thing may be supposed in the human frame; her figure being so extraordinary was the groundwork of Satan's project.... he saw plainly, that if he could but ruin her, he should easily make a devil of her, to ruin her husband and draw him into any gulf of mischief, were it ever so black and dreadful, that she should first fall into herself.[7]

The Fall may occur wherever beauty is flattered and courted, wherever it is valued so highly that the possessor may exchange it at her own inflated price. Defoe locates the temptation in the city because gainful commerce has more influence there in determining standards of moral acceptability.

Society's protection against the destructive power of beauty is the institution of marriage, which confines and domesticates the appetites which beauty stirs into rebellion against right reason. Roxana marries early and produces a large family. The money which she and her husband possess in excess of their needs goes (in part) toward the purchase of luxury items, a wise choice in Defoe's opinion. Luxuries are an investment, easily converted back into cash. And also because linked to the aesthetic pleasure of luxury objects are sublimated sexual instincts that further reconcile the Old Adam (and Eve) to their civilized existence. Werner Sombart comments that "it is our sexual life that lies at the root of our desire to refine and multiply the means of stimulating our senses, for sensuous pleasure and erotic pleasure are essentially the same. . . . For this reason we find luxury in the ascendant wherever wealth begins to accumulate and the sexuality of a nation is freely expressed."[8] Because Roxana craves luxury items later in the novel from avarice and vanity only, we should not overlook her domesticated affection for them in the halcyon phase of her marriage. Enclosed in a warm household with five children and devoted servants, the plate and jewels, pictures and ornaments, cabinets, and pier glasses all share Roxana's satisfaction with life; her pleasure overflows to include them in her being.

When Roxana's husband proves incompetent in the world of trade, they wisely unload the brewery and move away from London to consolidate their fortunes. He becomes more and more improvident, and Roxana sees her ruin hastening toward her when their articles of luxury begin to dwindle. One by one these intermediary surrogates of the "Great Article" disappear. When her husband abandons her and she must sell all these items for bread, she cannot accommodate herself to the uncivilized state, "stripp'd, and naked" (p. 17) any more than Lear on the heath. Roxana recovers her archetypal identity by going the way of her valuables; she transforms herself into a luxury item and achieves unbounded liberty.

The first step of this transformation comes when Roxana, reduced to direst want, is rescued by her landlord, who makes it clear, however, that he expects favors in return. Roxana and Amy conduct an argument on the justice of his demands. Amy argues that necessity returns Roxana to a state of nature in which ethics themselves are a ruinous burden. She ought to oblige the landlord for his charity by sharing his bed. Roxana finally agrees. To preserve her body from starvation, "[I] ruin'd my Soul from a Principle of Gratitude, and gave myself up to the Devil, to shew myself grateful to my benefactor" (p. 38). Defoe forces this melodramatic compromise in order to raise the same questions we have examined in larger historical contexts. Amy argues that Satan wills the death of the *body*; his malign agency engineers the misfortunes that bring ruin on the symbolic household of the brewer. The landlord "brought you out of the Devil's Clutches; brought you out of the blackest Misery that ever poor Lady was reduc'd to" (p. 37). The landlord, a jeweler by profession, has the business sense, the resolution and perseverance which characterized Roxana's father; he is the "Complete English Tradesman" whom Defoe hailed elsewhere as the finest gentleman in the land.

And yet to secure this ministering angel Roxana must commit adultery, she must admit to herself that social and religious laws may be freely suspended in order to effect some future good in the body. Her assumption that the Devil desires to ruin the *soul* represents an orthodox belief that she must shed as soon as she enters the world of trade. The dilemma here is not unlike Dyer's on the slave trade. Dyer settles for Amy's solution, which Defoe's readers usually endorse as well.[9] The problem with Amy's argument, we gradually discover, is that in essence it makes security the preeminent value in a universe of moral relativism. It not only excuses more severe vices like murder, it tends to insist on them. By the law of cause and consequence Roxana's self-transformation leads to her ultimate participation in murder, a murder actively committed by her Talus, Amy, but implicit in her desire throughout to secure her accumulated fortune from decay.

The landlord, true to his bargain, fills Roxana's household again with luxury goods, restores her garden from its wilderness state, and, we infer, capitalizes on the renewed sexuality that such metaphors suggest. As her material fortunes wax, Roxana's spiritual condition worsens. In one scene she tears the clothes off Amy and thrusts her into bed with the landlord: "This is enough to convince any-body that I did not think him my husband, and that I had cast off all Principle, and all Modesty, and had effectually stifled Conscience" (p. 46). From this point moral anarchism accompanies her progress exponentially. Of her affair with the next lover, a French prince, she remarks, "as it was all irresistable, so it was all lawful" (p. 69). Roxana's sense of privilege, as she grows older, owes less to money and more to vanity. Like Eve she looks on herself through the eyes and words of her admirers and this narcissism breeds a "Corruption" (p. 65) in her soul that increases in proportion to the stasis of her bodily beauty. The fame pertaining to her beauty, a fame she hopes to sustain by this autobiography, contrasts to the "insignificant, unthinking Life" of her first husband, whom she discovers by chance later in her career. "When he was gone," she comments, "[he] would leave no Remembrance behind him that ever he was here" (p. 95), a certain oblivion that Roxana, no less than Spenser, finds depressing. Even this statement by Roxana suggests the power of Satan over her, since Defoe credits Satan with persuading mankind to the necessity of worldly memorials. In *The Political History of the Devil*, for example, Defoe asserts that Satan built Stonehenge for the ancient Britons and that he works upon modern Britons by promising them fame for their crimes.[10]

"The desire of bettering our condition," wrote Adam Smith, "is a desire which though generally calm and dispassionate, comes with us from the womb, and never leaves us till we go into the grave."[11] Roxana's desire is far from dispassionate. Despite heavenly warnings from a storm at sea, she refuses to repent of her crimes: "with our return to life, our wicked Taste of Life return'd, and we were both the same as before, if not worse" (p. 128). The society around Roxana reinforces her narcissism, which in turn strengthens her malignant will. She evolves into the instrument and symbol of a caste whose lust for power is expressed by cruelty, self-serving exhibitionism, and waste. Certainly Roxana receives no instruction in self-control from her betters. The Restoration setting makes this something of a historical novel but Defoe's readers would not miss the contemporary flavor of his satire on unscrupulous financiers, merchants, money-lenders, and nobility. The South Sea Bubble had burst in 1720. Robert Walpole, first as chancellor of the exchequer and then as prime minister, had begun to alter the tone of English life in a way that kept Augustan satirists busy for two generations. Pope used Walpole's estate at Houghton as a model for Timon's monstrosity. John Gay employed the Walpole spoils system, in *The Beggar's Opera*, for the ultimate example of the power of commerce: a government for sale to intriguers and hired hands. When Roxana enters the *haut monde* of balls and gaming, titles and privilege, she falls most appallingly under the sway both of external despots (king and court) and the internal despotism her vanity exerts on her thoughts and actions. She acts more and more from the need for applause, a servitude she herself deplores even as she secures its power. She is from the beginning "the vainest Creature upon Earth" (p. 62), at the beck and call of those potentates who, like the prince, value her as a disposable concubine.

Defoe gives Roxana one last chance before her catastrophe. The Dutch merchant who saves her fortune from a scheming Jew proposes marriage to her. Though she respects and perhaps loves him, she refuses because the status of a wife decreases a woman's value and destroys her security, as Roxana discovered by her marriage to the brewer. She prefers absolute liberty as a means of bettering her condition. The astounded merchant, ignorant of her past, replies within a context that indicates Defoe's sympathy: "Dear Madam, you argue for Liberty at the same time that you restrain yourself from that Liberty, which God and Nature has directed you to take; and to supply the Deficiency, propose a vicious Liberty, which is neither honourable or religious" (p. 157). Defoe has embodied in Roxana the willful egotism he deplored in the whole populace a quarter century earlier:

> Their Liberty and Property's so dear,
> They scorn their Laws or Governors to fear:
> So bugbear'd with the name of Slavery,
> They can't submit to their own Liberty
> *Restraint from Ill is Freedom to the Wise;*
> *But* Englishmen do all Restraint despise.[12]

Roxana's refusal to heed the merchant's advice precedes her great success at court where she attracts the notice of among others a maid-servant from her retinue who is also her daughter. For Susan no less than for Amy this queen of whores has been the "wicked Example" (p. 126) of ruthless struggling for advantage. Susan also wishes to better her condition, she also yearns for liberty, and her claims upon Roxana represent to some extent those of the Great Beast, the multitude, upon the rich and powerful.

If Roxana's love of liberty is vicious, so too is her practice of restraint. Throughout the novel she hoards her fortune. She accepts gifts and enjoys them but she cannot spend her capital any more than she can constrain her liberty by a commitment of love. She uses her sexuality as provender to pay off debts of gratitude and dispenses some charity, but not until she amasses a capital sum whose interest will support her handsomely does she think of renouncing her sinful life. In these scenes Defoe makes Roxana the most monstrous creature in his fiction. Of one rich lord who woos her, she writes: "He then turn'd his Discourse to the Subject of Love, a Point so ridiculous to me, without the main thing, I mean the Money, that I had no Patience to hear him" (p. 183). The lord is accepted as a lover on a strictly pecuniary basis, valued by her only in terms of his gifts. Significantly, he misuses her sexually in ways that Defoe does not make explicit but which clearly demonstrate the contempt of self and the destructive nature of sensual enjoyment that unrestrained liberty

makes inevitable. Later, Roxana writes, "I was frequently visited . . .
by some others" (p. 208). "Some others" is all the identity they have.

Roxana is the eternal Eve. She prevails because she embodies (to
her lovers) the timelessness that is an essential aspect of the Garden
vision. Roxana never seems to grow old; her features do not significantly undergo the ruin of time. In one poignant scene the prince
takes out a handkerchief to wipe away Roxana's tears, and then hesi-
tates. Roxana chides him for fearing he might spoil her makeup and
shows him that her clear, rosy complexion owes nothing to paint. He,
like all her lovers, is profoundly impressed by her natural youthful-
ness. Like Adam, the prince willingly joins Roxana in the "gulf of
mischief" to which her beauty attracts all men. She remarks that:

> I cou'd not but reflect upon the Brutallity and blindness of Mankind; that
> because Nature had given me a good Skin, and some agreeable Features,
> should suffer that Beauty to be such a Bait to Appetite, as to do such sordid,
> unaccountable things, to obtain the Possession of it.   (Pp. 74–75)

Roxana achieves power over men by nature's gift. Her scheming self-
interest, however, makes this attraction a demonic parody of the
animal magnetism exerted in the traditional pastoral of, say, Dyer's
The Country Walk. In that poem the deer chases away ambition; Roxana rouses it as she embodies it. Her good capitalist soul yearns continually for more expansive and more expensive property, and to the
extent it symbolizes the will of the English empire her avaricious soul
endangers all of the king's dependencies:

> Nature has left *this Tincture in the Blood,*
> That all Men *would be* Tyrants if they cou'd:
> If they forebear their Neighbours to devour,
> 'Tis not for want of *Will,* but want of *Power.*
>   (*Jure Divino,* Introduction)

The scenes of Roxana at court represent the clearest phase of Defoe's
political allegory. Here we see the courtesan-tyrant in all her Augustan splendor, Pope's "whole Sex of Queens! / Pow'r all their end, but
Beauty all their means."[13]

The name Roxana—given to the Fortunate Mistress one evening
as she dances in Turkish costumes for the court—has appropriate
antecedents in the Oriental queens of heroic drama. Roxolana is the
name of Solyman's mistress in William D'Avenant's *The Siege of
Rhodes* (1656), and Roxana the name of Alexander the Great's whore
in Nathaniel Lee's immensely popular *The Rival Queens* (1677).[14] In

both plays Roxana represents the "jealous, bloody, and ambitious" (*RQ*, II.i.62) lust for power of which the tyrants are masculine symbols. "Empire grows often high / By rules of cruelty" (IV.iii.342–43), Solyman tells Roxolana, and Alexander, the "Immortal Image" of the imperial spirit, exults:

> Sure I was formed for war, eternal war;
> All, all are Alexander's enemies,
> Which I could tame. Yes, the rebellious world
> Should feel my wrath.   (IV.ii.91–94)

Just as Alexander boasts of setting Persepolis on fire, Roxana claims she could "tear . . . all the world to pieces" (IV.i.117–18) to achieve her mad desires. Both are characters "for whose desire all Earth should be too little" (III.i.117); their rabid dissatisfaction with life destroys the innocent, and ultimately themselves.

Both Solyman and Alexander, as convention dictates, own the power of love over their tyrannical souls. In D'Avenant's transparent allegory, Ianthe, the virtuous lady from the West, charms the Oriental warlord, who tells her, "I am content it should recorded be, / That, when I vanquisht Rhodes, you conquer'd me" (V.vi.210–11). The isle of Rhodes, like England in the seventeenth century, is perpetually in danger of attack from a hostile emperor, and its English defenders fear that oblivion may follow defeat. A Sicilian duke gives this fear voice:

> Sink not the western kingdoms in our loss?
> Will not the Austrian eagle moult her wings,
> That long hath hover'd o'er the Gallick-Kings?
> Whose lillies too will wither when we fade;
> And th'English lyon shrink into a shade.   (I.i.50–54)

Ianthe preserves the island from ruin by confronting Solyman with model conduct, with temperance, loyalty, and self-control. Unlike Roxolana, who is always "guilty of excess" (III.i.223) Ianthe is the spirit of moderation. The Roxana figure in these plays corrupts both love and policy by whipping them to extremes; she is the "queen of devils" (*RQ*, V.i.122) because her passions perpetuate Satan's power of destruction. She shares the immortal longings that drive Alexander to secure his fame by irreversible acts of military brutality. "Eternal gazers lasting troubles make" (II.i.417), Alexander says in one play, and in the other Ianthe echoes, "In tracing human story we shall find / The cruel more successful than the kind" (V.vi.133–34). In De-

foe's tale, Roxana's ambition carries the same dangers as her ancestors', and her presence at the king's court, as a symbolic figure,
threatens the course of empire. Her immoderate eroticism, linked as it
is to avarice and finally murder, has the power to transform London
into Babylon (the setting of Lee's play) and like her namesake "ruin
all that's right and reasonable" (RQ, I.i.55).

Defoe's Roxana decides to abdicate her thralldom, withdraw
from London high society and live with a Quaker woman of simple
piety. Roxana desires one thing from her retirement, to recapture the
guiltless satisfaction, the peace of mind, she enjoyed before her first
ruin. Matrimony, once described by the Dutch merchant as the union
most approved by God and nature, now beckons with the attractive-
ness it possessed in her juvenile years. The Dutch merchant, rediscovered in London, still ignorant of her notorious adventures, offers
once again to secure her in the pleasure garden preserved by memory. Roxana has been a homeless wanderer for years, "as to me, every
Place was alike" (p. 248). Her marriage to the merchant appears, for a
few pages, to satisfy a spiritual craving very much like homesickness.
But the injured Susan, Roxana's second self, provides an object lesson in the demonic cycles of experience. "The most secret Crimes are,
by the most unforseen Accidents, brought to light and discover'd" (p.
297), Roxana ruefully remarks. Her own crimes seal off the innocent
past; they prevent the reunion of mother and daughter and leave
Roxana defenseless against "the Blast of Heaven" which follows her
into the final paragraph of the novel. The past which now haunts
Roxana, like that which haunted Dyer, takes hideous shapes: "the
most frightful and terrible things imaginable: Nothing but Apparitions of Devils and Monsters. . . . I was Hag-ridden with Frights, and
terrible things, form'd meerly in the Imagination" (p. 264).

Roxana's nightmares provide the best argument against her pursuit of selfish pleasures; they express the "desires, terrible in their
untamed lawlessness" for which Plato prescribed enduring social
controls in The Republic (p. 297). Roxana, however, must go the limit;
she insures a quiet retirement as ruthlessly as she achieved notoriety.
She cunningly deploys the innocent Quaker as a palace guard to keep
the persistent Susan from learning the truth, and meanwhile attempts to formulate a final conquest of the "She-Devil" (p. 301), the
"plague" (p. 302), the "hound" (p. 317), the "demon" (p. 280)—her
daughter—that insists on Roxana's acknowledgment. The murder of
Susan brings Roxana's character close to the Gothic villainy of romantic fiction. Coleridge clarifies the connection in his marginalia for Robinson Crusoe, remarks pertinent to Roxana's obsessive fear of ruin:

When once the mind, in despite of the remonstrating conscience, has abandoned its free power to a haunting impulse or idea, then whatever tends to give depth and vividness to this idea or indefinite imagination increases *its* despotism, and in the same proportion renders the reason and free will ineffectual. Now fearful calamities, sufferings, horrors, and hair-breadth escapes will have this effect far more than even sensual pleasure and prosperous incidents. Hence the evil consequences of sin in such cases, instead of retracting and deterring the sinner, goad him on to his destruction.[15]

Though Roxana's life is calculated, episode by episode, her very choices are fated because of her obsession; Coleridge articulates this paradox as the "tyranny of the sinner's own evil imagination which he has voluntarily chosen as his master."

If Roxana is a moral Caesar, Amy is the executive arm of her tyranny. She is the agent of benevolence and murder alike, and because Roxana has communicated her obsessions to Amy they become equals in guilt. At one point Roxana remarks, "Amy effected all afterwards [the murder of Susan], without my Knowledge, for which I gave her my hearty Curse, tho' I cou'd do little more; for to have fall'n upon Amy, had been to have murther'd myself" (p. 302). Amy resembles the agents of moral damnation in later Gothic novels, apprentices like Matilda in Lewis's *The Monk,* who are always ready to offer Satan's arguments. When Ambrosio murders Elvira in that novel, for example, Matilda justifies the act in familiar terms: "She represented, that He had only availed himself of the rights which Nature allows to every one, those of self-preservation."[16]

It is not *The Monk,* however, but *Melmoth the Wanderer,* published a century after Defoe's novel, which draws together the themes I have discussed into a "moral Romance" of the highest quality. In this work of Charles Maturin, Melmoth is a human being who has sold his soul to the Devil in order to gain enduring power over others. He has terrorized humanity, driving people to despair and madness for two centuries. But we learn that all these years he has sought someone to exchange fates with him, the only way he may be released from his immortality. Melmoth's desire for eternal life arises from a detestation of his body as a natural (mutable) thing. He extends this contempt to all other bodies, and under the pressure of his obsession, to all other souls. Upon them he wishes a universal ruin:

Perish to all the world, perhaps beyond the period of its existence, but live to me in darkness and in corruption! Preserve all the exquisite modulation of your forms, all the indestructible brilliancy of your coloring—but preserve it for me alone! me, the single pulseless, eyeless, heartless embracer of an unfertile bride—the brooder over the dark and unproductive nest of eternal sterility.[17]

This is Adam speaking from the bottom of the gulf of mischief, and not Adam only but each person and each political body. "The Imagination of the Heart of Man is Evil and only Evil, and that Continually," Defoe wrote, echoing God's conclusion in Genesis 6:5.[18] Now as then man deserves to be wracked by deluge, but in the meantime the innocence that remains must be protected from moral contamination. It may not be too farfetched to compare even the island in *Melmoth the Wanderer*, where Imalee lives in peace and security, to that which Ianthe preserves in D'Avenant's play: a symbolic England which tryants and rabid imperialists like Solyman, Alexander, or, in their Jungian form of the Shadow, Melmoth and Satan endanger by their insatiable and destructive appetites.

Roxana's intentions seem more modest, but they belong to the same order as later figures in the Gothic mold. She has transformed herself into a dragon, a "Man-Woman" (p. 171), who generates corruption by her association with gold. Behind Roxana's fornications we always glimpse the Whore of Babylon from Revelation, who achieves her imperial power when "the merchants of the earth are waxed rich through the abundance of her delicacies" (18:3). Roxana's confession is a warning to the republic whose values she endangers, a cautionary plea for understanding no less than forgiveness. Her tale, however, owes its consequence not to the apocalyptic rhetoric of a character like Melmoth but to the realistic detail which informs her melancholy narrative. The popular success of this moral exemplum might have surprised even Defoe. At the end of his own century a critic wrote in *The Monthly Review* that "few novels are better known than the story of the Lewd Roxana"[19] and nothing has changed in human nature since then that would render its parabolic force less instructive. As Defoe's last significant literary work, *Roxana* belongs with his century's greatest histories, of persons and nations alike.

6 Graveyard Literature: The Politics of Melancholy

Fundamentals: Edward Young

DEFOE'S CRITIQUE of Roxana permits the moderate pursuit of material goals while disapproving the insatiable lust that leads to antisocial activity, to crime. But there existed in the eighteenth century a more stringent critique of worldliness than Defoe's, one that moralists pressed in numbers large enough to justify their own self-conception as the spokesmen of the age. I refer to the Christian writings which so often took the form of somber meditations in the graveyard. These works applied Thomas Browne's criterion of the grave to daily aspirations and endeavors, to commerce and politics alike. To the most absolute of the Christian writers not what man does but what he is causes the ruin of his ambitions. In *Night Thoughts*, for example, Edward Young criticizes Lorenzo, the unfortunate auditor of his "monumental sigh" (VII.832), for holding life too dear. Young preaches to him that materialism, hedonism, atheism, and deism are self-destroying beliefs, and puts forward as his fundamental proof the corpse of his daughter, Narcissa. She has followed his wife and son-in-law into death, and they will be followed in turn by Young and Lorenzo. The fate of matter, Young warns, cancels its value.

Though the label is not a favored one, "graveyard literature" accurately describes a religious mode preoccupied with human remains and their final destination. In its narrowest usage the term applies to works with prescribed machinery—yew trees, screech owls, mouldering tombstones—and lacks the flexibility of most literary labels. Young provides a broader description of the mode in his early poem, *The Last Day* (1713):

> In hopes of glory to be quite involved!
> To smile at death, to long to be dissolved!
> From our decays a pleasure to receive,
> And kindle into transport at a grave! (I.222–25)

73

The transport may convey a contemplative poet almost anywhere, but his thoughts return constantly to their originating landscape. Graveyard literature is an antipastoral mode, a systematic critique of pagan delight. *Night Thoughts* may be set in Young's house and garden, but illustrators of the poem in England and the Continent more often showed Young burying his daughter or walking sorrowfully among graves. In the most important sense their depictions are faithful not only to Young's work but to the other-worldly spirit of all eschatological literature.

The popularity of such literature during the early and middle part of the eighteenth century can scarcely be overestimated. Books of religious instruction were the largest class of published material during Defoe's and Young's lifetime, and the most favored of these described the four last things: Death, Judgment, Heaven, and Hell. Defoe's own writings on the plague and spiritualism contributed to the subject, but more popular than his semiauthentic fictions were sermons and handbooks of future prospects. A representative list would include Jeremy Taylor's *Holy Living* and *Holy Dying*, William Sherlock's *Practical Discourses Concerning Death*, Charles Drelincourt's *The Christian's Defense Against the Fear of Death*, John Shower's *Serious Reflections on Time and Eternity*, and John Bunyan's writings on the same themes. Lucretius and Horace were much read and translated in this period, intensifying the kinship of Roman and Englishman claimed by Renaissance humanists. Amy Reed comments that "the essential resemblance between the general mood of thoughtful Englishmen at the end of the seventeenth century and of many Romans at the close of the Republic was . . . not fanciful. . . . Political unsettlement of the times . . . drove men of sensitive and refined natures into seclusion. The solitary way of life was a symptom of the despair over the welfare of the state. . . . The dissolution of religious belief awoke a deeper interest in ultimate questions of existence . . . and the destiny of the human soul."[1] I have indicated how this psychic mechanism operated in John Dyer's *The Ruins of Rome,* but Dyer's career does not encompass the range of imaginative responses we refer to as the ruin sentiment. When he broadened his outward prospect, he narrowed his view of inward corruption. The authors cited above chose instead to expand their inward gaze, and by meditation on self-ruin guide their countrymen into a commonwealth more fruitful than the Indies.

Like Dyer in *The Ruins of Rome,* these writers move ruin into the foreground of their works in order to inspire terror, but unlike him they prefer to describe psycho-spiritual states rather than colossal stonework or natural disasters. The Fall, in particular, is a popular subject, for it antedates all ruin in history and is the cause of it. The

Fall is universal in application and its effects (such as death) of compelling human interest in every generation. Furthermore, the Fall is a catastrophe that has a cure, a resolution, so that no matter how deep into the abyss a writer leads his reader there is always a final ascent, laborious or swift, into a place without mutability. Terror itself came to be associated with redemption; as John Dennis wrote, "Let any man shew me where Terror is mov'd to a Heighth, and I will shew him that that place requires the Belief of a God, and particular Providence."[2] The increasing popularity of the Sublime as a rhetorical mode, grounded at least since Milton in the Christian drama, nourished the public appetite for eschatological terrors. Eighteenth-century readers were glad to be frightened into piety and willingly stared at horrors for the good of their souls.

These writers begin, as we might expect, at the end. A typical argument proceeds in the following way. Death is the "King of Terrors" and like other kings he threatens each small "kingdom," the individual person. Donne to the contrary, each man is an island, a decaying Albion endangered daily by an omnipotent force, for Death in his quotidian manifestation is Time. Man releases himself from terror by submission to the necessity of his own bodily ruin. He must preserve and extend the soul's immortal hopes by identifying his will with the power of time over his person. Human resistance to time takes the various forms of worldly immortality, and therefore these writers argue against worldly achievements with unremitting fervor. Drelincourt recounts the basis of man's vain obsession: "We flatter ourselves in our Hearts, that Man should look upon us as so many little Gods. We suffer ourselves to be deceived by the flattering insinuations of our corrupted Flesh, by the artificious Suggestions of the old Serpent, that whispers to us, as to our first Parents, 'You shall not die!' "[3] And Young, in *Night Thoughts*, supplies the social implications of this deception:

> 'Tis immortality your nature solves;
> 'Tis immortality deciphers man,
> And opens all the mysteries of his make.
> Without it, half his instincts are a riddle;
> Without it, all his virtues are a dream.
> His very crimes attest his dignity.
> His sateless thirst of pleasure, gold, and fame,
> Declares him born for blessings infinite:
> What less than infinite makes unabsurd
> Passions, which all on earth but more inflames?
> Fierce passions, so mismeasured to this scene,
> Stretch'd out, like eagles' wings, beyond our nest,

Far, far beyond the worth of all below,
For earth too large, presage a nobler flight,
And evidence our title to the skies.   (VII.506–20)

Young perceives no advantage in condemning the insatiable ambitions that Providence has placed in the human breast. He applauds
them for offering man the potentiality of salvation. The Christian
afterlife offers very obvious rewards for the meek, but writers like
Young appeal to the powerful and passionate. They condemn the
world-shakers, the Roxanas and Alexanders, not for their immortal
longings but for the theater of actions they choose for their self-
transformation into deities.

In history, the argument continues, we make ourselves into gods
by means of Fame; in Eternity by means of Glory. The worldly body is
perpetuated by legend, Spenser's "memorie," as a name only, or as a
painted portrait. Some artists recommend this form of immortality
from self-interest. Thomas Flatman, for example, gives the conceit a
characteristic point when he writes in *On the Noble Art of Painting*,
"Strange rarity! which canst the body save / From the coarse usage in
a sullen grave, / Yet never make it mummy!"[4] A writer like Young,
however, insists that this vicarious perpetuation demeans its subject;
we become in time the shadow not even of our selves but of our
observed appearance (painting) or of our corruptible history. Glory, by
contrast, perpetuates the self unsubdued to its element, the self
which our highest understanding (reason) frames in its most exalted
mood. Heaven perpetuates our bodily (Adamic) form as Fame cannot, and therefore the immortality that we ought to embrace is Christian, not secular.

In order to emphasize the glorious body to be gained, these
writers devalue the worldly body we will lose. They often dwell upon
the loathsome vegetable carcass that imprisons the soul. Richard Bax-
ter, in his poem, *Man*, advises "Go see an open'd Corps, and that will
shew / What Garbage, Filth, and Dung are hid within, / What thy vile
Body is, thou there maist know."[5] Bishop Porteus, in *Death*, affirms
that "God never made a creature / But what was good. He made a
living Soul, / *The wretched mortal* was the work of Man."[6] The
Adamic body was prepared as a palace for the living God, Drelincourt
argues, "but Sin that is a kind of infectious leprosy, hath insinuated
itself and disfigured it; it hath entered the Skin, corrupted the Blood,
disordered the Spirits, it is crept into the Joynts and Marrow, and
hath spread its venom in such a manner that there is none of our
members but is an instrument of iniquity and unrighteousness."[7]

William Blake would not call it sin but he describes in *The Book of Los* the same horrifying formation of our "white Polypus" (plate IV.57) in this fallen universe. The King of Terrors can be welcomed if his empire consists only of garbage and filth, if he is the agent of our true liberation and not our destruction.

By the same logic the natural world is devalued in graveyard literature. God designed nature, as he did the human body, in perfect lineaments. But the Fall infected nature as well. William Cowper remarks that a vengeful God "Doom'd [nature] as insufficient for his praise" (*The Task*, V.565). Nature ought to be studied for the clues it provides to God's intentions in the Creation, but not as an active spiritual force in itself. Having no grace of its own, nature cannot extend salvation to the human soul. Even the most Edenic of rural scenes, we are told again and again, is paradisaical only to the cows and birds that inhabit it and lack the reason to know their distinction in the chain of being. According to the graveyard writers, man asserts his Christian humanity by imagining natural landscape as, in their word, a "monitor" of his own death. If he were to yield to an aesthetic experience of nature he would sacrifice his highest pleasure, the ecstatic vision of eternity's interpenetration into time, for a barren appreciation of formal symmetry and color. Because eternity exists in the future, beyond the grave, man receives supernatural intimations by first acknowledging death's presence and authority in everyday life. By summoning the thought of death at every moment, we measure our gradual victory over Satan, over the winter of change and loss he introduced into the world.

The imagination, then, must be trained to redeem the instantaneous perception, the "straw-like trifles on life's common stream" (*Night Thoughts*, II.78) by alchemizing it into a monitor of mortality. "This, the blest art of turning all to gold," says Young (II.85). God, whom Young praises as a "great ECONOMIST" (IX.1089), rewards such imaginative conversions by "immense revenue! every moment pays" (II.88). The largest bonus of course is not the common reminders of death but "Our day of dissolution!—name it right; / 'Tis our great pay-day" (III.501–02). Young's financial metaphors attempt to match Roxana on her own ground. She passionately accumulates wealth; he insists that real wealth comes only by spending and becoming spent. Since "life's a debtor to the grave" (III.472), the increase of worldly goods only impoverishes the possessor. We earn worldly fortune by ecstatic perceptions of all animate nature as in essence a graveyard. Young's contemporary, Robert Blair, describes this sentiment in *The Grave:*

What is this world?
What but a spacious burial-field unwall'd,
Strew'd with death's spoils, the spoils of animals
Savage and tame, and full of dead men's bones!
The very turf on which we tread once lived;
And we that live must lend our carcases
To cover our own offspring: in their turns
They too must cover theirs.—'Tis here all meet!   (483–90)[8]

To see nature as a universe of death is to achieve an eminence over it, in Young's words to "mount upward on a strong desire, / Borne, like Elijah, in a car of fire" (*Last Day*, I.220–21). That prophetic transport is itself evidence of man's immortality.

When Blair and Young imagine the natural world as a compost they compare it, unsurprisingly, with ruined empires. The failure to perpetuate imperial kingdoms enforces the lesson Young preaches in *Night Thoughts* to each reader: "O man, thy kingdom is departing from thee" (II.411). Just as man's bodily energies alchemize life into death, an art of dying that belongs to each unit in the social body, so in the macrocosm of the state "each Moment has its sickle" (I.193). There has never existed an empire since the Fall which did not engineer its own ruin simply by using up all the energies which nourished it. Thus Young can term all of history Babylon, uniting the biblical associations of sin with a historical ruin. History, like our adult selves, is mostly ruins already, and the goal of our remaining lifetime should be the yearning forward to our ruin's completion, a consummation devoutly wished and ecstatically recounted by all writers of this mode. "Haste, then, and wheel away a shatter'd world, / Ye slow-revolving seasons!" Cowper writes in *The Task* (VI.823–24), and Young concludes *Night Thoughts:*

> When, like a taper, all these suns expire;
> When TIME, like him of Gaza, in his wrath,
> Plucking the pillars that support the world,
> In NATURE'S ample ruins lies entomb'd;
> And MIDNIGHT, universal Midnight, reigns.   (IX.2430–34)

The huge, dissolving presences of time that terrified Dyer in Rome are gleefully imagined by Young in their final, apocalyptic forms. Like Samson he rejoices in his own overwhelming.

There is no writer of the graveyard tradition more fond of apocalyptic scenes than Young. His imagination kindles when he dramatizes acts of annihilation or the casualties of terrific force and power. Because he believed that man's "crimes attest his dignity"

Young felt as much at home in heroic drama as in Christian homily.
Young's tyrants, like Busiris in his play of that name (1713), possess
the "sateless thirst of pleasure, gold, and fame" which he praised in
Night Thoughts as an index of the Christian spirit and which he evi-
denced in his own devious career. A pious writer who also views the
court as a theater for his ambition will find congenial the conventions
of heroic drama which transfer absolute power from heavenly to
worldly ruler. Busiris, king of Egypt, compels thousands of slaves to
build monuments of lasting glory for him, no matter how great the
toll of human life. From his eminence over the captive throng Busiris
thunders at those who question his sovereign will:

> Collected in myself, I'll stand alone,
> And hurl my thunder, though I shake my throne:
> Like Death, a solitary king I'll reign
> O'er silent subjects, and a desert plain;
> Ere brook their pride, I'll spread a general doom,
> And every step shall be from tomb to tomb.   (P. 145)

Though Busiris is supposed to remind us of Satan, the resemblance is
more to Jehovah threatening a general doom to the cities of the plain.
That Young's Egypt deliberately recalls eighteenth-century England,
especially in its recent acquisition of a "still-growing empire" (p. 144),
confirms the reader's suspicion that Young intends the all-powerful
Busiris as a model for the new king, George I. George will have to
continue the European and colonial wars, and, as we shall see, this
will require an enthusiasm for war. Busiris's last words are not just
bombast but a clear warning to the king that must guide the fortunes
of an aggressive mercantile nation:

>   In after-ages,
> Who war or build shall build or war from me;
> Grow great in each as my example fires.
> 'Tis I of art the future wonders raise;
> I fight the future battles of the world.—
> Great Jove, I come! Egypt, thou art forsaken;
> Asia's impoverish'd by my sinking glories;
> And the world lessens, when Busiris falls. (*Dies.*)   (P. 185)

    Busiris has its moments but the requirements of heroic drama,
especially the love plots, hampered Young's imagination. In *The Last
Day* his talent for earth-shaking scenes had found its most perfect
subject, and after some unsuccessful plays and satires he returned to
the same well for his *Night Thoughts*. In his eschatological work he

is more free to describe how "final Ruin fiercely drives / Her Ploughshare o'er Creation!" (*NT*, IX.167–68). Long before Blake, who illustrated the *Night Thoughts*, Young achieved a marriage of Christ and Satan based on their common attribute of terrifying power. Or perhaps Nimrod rather than Satan, for it is the insatiable desire to "build or war" that Young, as an artist and an English citizen, finds most compelling.

It would be difficult to read through all of Young's works and not feel the author's passionate sympathy for figures of great power, his exultation in their willingness to remold the world in their own image. "The God of the 'Night Thoughts' is simply Young himself, 'writ large,'" George Eliot shrewdly remarked,[9] for it clearly is Young who wishes to inflict damage upon a world he considers a hindrance to his eagles' wings. One who believes that death is man's greatest boon usually projects outward the fate he wishes on himself. Freud has given the classic formulation to this mechanism:

Even where [the death instinct] emerges without any sexual purpose, in the blindest fury of destructiveness, we cannot fail to recognize that the satisfaction of the instinct is accompanied by an extraordinarily high degree of narcissistic enjoyment, owing to its presenting the ego with a fulfillment of the latter's old wishes for omnipotence. The instinct of destruction, moderated and tamed, and, as it were, inhibited in its aim, must, when it is directed toward objects, provide the ego with the satisfaction of its vital needs and with control over nature.[10]

Freud has only put into different language Young's own observations, though of course Young would insist that the objects of his (and God's) wrath deserve the annihilation he visits upon them.

Young's religious attitudes have rather obvious political implications. He himself insisted on their application; as he wrote one influential lord, "divinity promotes / True politics, and crowns the statesman's praise" (p. 73). Young's political opinions have been a subject of attention, and contempt, since Samuel Johnson's *Life of Young*. His fundamental credo is that power must be constantly exercised by those in high positions: "'Tis Power's supreme prerogative to stamp / On others' minds an image of its own" (p. 62). Though he condemned Busiris for abuses of power, he believed that his own king and counselors ought to have virtually unlimited authority in order to prevent the Catholic dragon (France) from destroying his homeland. In his *Reflections on the Public Situation of the Kingdom*, a poem written after *Night Thoughts* and originally printed as its conclu-

sion, Young urges the Duke of Newcastle to break through the hesitations of the court, which he depicts as bonds of duty preventing
English politicians from increasing the nation's military capacity.
"Are there Samsons that can burst them all?" he asks the Duke, "Yes;
and great minds that stand in need of none" (p. 69). Young himself
aspires to be one of these, a divinely inspired Samson who dares (in
his art) to bring down the enemy's temples everywhere.

He advises the Hanovers throughout his career to follow his lead.
Britannia's own moral corruptions upset him but external threats
rouse his fiercest rhetoric. In a poem like his *Sea-Piece* (1733) he concludes on a note of military triumph:

> Let George the Just chastise the vain.
> Thou, who dost curb the rebel Main,
> To mount the shore when boiling billows rave!
> Bid George repel a bolder tide,
> The boundless swell of Gallic pride,
> And check Ambition's overwhelming wave.　　　　　(P. 51)

"Ambition's overwhelming wave" is not just a deluge that threatens
the island of England, but a Satanic force that must be conquered
everywhere—in the Americas, Asia, and Africa as well as on the
Continent. The pursuit of such slaughter would be morally question-
able if Britain were not "high favour'd of indulgent Heaven! /
Nature's anointed empress of the deep" (p. 66). But heaven *is* indulgent, God wants George to overwhelm all of his enemies and not
himself be overwhelmed. When Young turns to the subject of warfare, in his *Reflections*, his imagination kindles, for nothing pleases
him like worldly rehearsals for Armageddon:

> O what illustrious images arise!
> Embattled round me blaze the pomps of war.
> By sea, by land, at home, in foreign climes,
> What full-blown laurels on our fathers' brows!
> Ye radiant trophies and imperial spoils!
> Ye scenes, astonishing to modern sight!
> Let me at least enjoy you in a dream.
> Why vanish? Stay, ye godlike strangers, stay!　　　　　(P. 65)

In fact, such combative and militaristic images did stay with him in his
imagination to the end of his life, and when transferred to manuscript
they became an important contribution to the literature of English
imperialism.

A Quiet Retreat: Parnell and Hervey

Graveyard literature arises from the powerful fear of being orphaned by God, of being exiled in the flesh and prevented by the flesh from experiencing eternity. Graveyard literature actively reaches to heaven by passionate meditation. A favorite biblical passage of these writers is St. Paul's admonition that when we are at home in the body we are absent from the Lord, but when we are absent from the body, we are present with the Lord (II Cor.5:7–9). In order to bring the soul to its heavenly home the poet willfully removes himself from worldly experience. He must journey to the landscape closest to the frontier of heaven. The ominous stillness of the graveyard, the embrace of darkness, the solitude—these intentionally deny the importance of those incidents, the movements and resolutions, which narrative fiction and verse require. The ending, the blank wall of death, lures the questing poet. In the graveyard the blank wall is like a membrane, through which supernatural intimations pass by an osmosis of the poetic imagination. "How *thin* is the partition between this world and another," James Hervey writes in *Meditations Among the Tombs*[11]; his task is to look through the door and like any other travel writer report the foreign prospect to his reader.

An elementary but significant example of the graveyard mode is Thomas Parnell's *A Night Piece on Death* (1721). The poem opens on what seems a Faustian note: the dissatisfied speaker puts aside the books he is studying and complains:

> Their books from wisdom widely stray,
> Or point at best the longest way.
> I'll seek a readier path and go
> Where wisdom's surely taught below.

Goethe's scholar desires a consummate happiness in mortal life and journeys throughout the world to seek it before he attains his goal in the service of his community, but this scholar descends instead into a graveyard. The external darkness nourishes insight, as in most meditations of this genre. The sun, though it is God's handiwork, has the malign effect of lighting and making attractive the material objects which must be put by for wisdom to be attained. "Let Indians, and the gay, like Indians . . . the sun adore," writes Young:

> Darkness has more divinity for me:
> It strikes thought inward; it drives back the soul
> To settle on herself, our point supreme!
> There lies our theatre; there sits our judge.

> Darkness the curtain drops o'er life's dull scene;
> 'Tis the kind hand of Providence stretch'd out
> 'Twixt man and vanity; 'tis Reason's reign,
> And Virtue's too; these tutelary shades
> Are man's asylum from the tainted throng.   (NT, V.126–36)

As darkness strengthens piety and virtue it quiets the ambitious ego. Cowper writes in a letter that "self is a subject of inscrutable misery and mischief, and can never be studied to so much advantage as in the dark" (*Prose*, p. 745).[12] Parnell's night journey leads him to a landscape in which all motion has ceased, even "the slumbering breeze forgets to breathe." The graves ("solemn heaps of fate") are illuminated by the stars and moon, a conventional tableau in graveyard writing. Young also alludes to "the ghastly ruins of the mouldering tomb" symbolically lighted by the heavens (*NT*, IV.690). This landscape is perfectly static; it approximates death. Now Parnell's imagination makes a leap. As the poet gazes, "the bursting earth unveils the shades!" Ecstatic, the poet pleads for mortal time to cease entirely: "Ye tolling clocks, no time resound / O'er the long lake and midnight ground." The personified figure of Death arises and delivers the wisdom sought by the poet:

> Death's but a path that must be trod,
> If man would ever pass to God;
> A port of calms, a state of ease
> From the rough rage of swelling seas.

The journey to the graveyard fulfills the desire for spiritual "asylum" that pilgrims sought in the Americas, or gentlemen in country estates. The graveyard writers sympathized with all withdrawals or retirements from the appetitive world of Babylon, but they reminded their readers, by a favored metaphor, that such asylums are only "inns" offering temporary retreat from the discomforts of foreign travel. An inn can never be a home, nor should any worldly surrogate cheat the instinct for heaven-haven. In real life, however, there existed even for melancholy poets a middle state between the ephemeral conveniences of an inn and heaven. These writers tended to settle in comfortable parishes whose pastoral economy, highly ritualized and conventional, could not help but become a value in itself. Their terrestrial asylum imitates the chief virtues of Paradise, which are a freedom from anxiety and an unqualified adoration of the Father-King whose reciprocal love brings unending joy. The rural landscape to which the pious flee becomes a spiritual center whose disturbance by the forces of change offends the holy spirit. The con-

servative character of all graveyard writing owes much to this desire
to be left alone. How can these authors interest themselves in questions of progress and reform when their whole aspiration is, in Sherlock's words, "to mortify all Remains of Love and Affection for this
World; to withdraw ourselves as much as may be from the Conversation of it; to use it very sparingly and with great Indifferency"?[13]

We observe the political implications of this philosophy in the
work of James Hervey (1714–1758). After an Oxford education, during
which he studied with John Wesley, Hervey spent most of his life in
the remote curacies of Biddeford and Weston Favell, in Hampshire. In
1746 he published his most famous works, *Meditations Among the
Tombs* and *Reflections on a Flower Garden, and a Descant on Creation*.
Other works in the same vein, including his *Contemplations*, appeared
the next year. An early biographer suggests Hervey's personality
when he remarks approvingly that "he had no taste for amusements
or converse of the world" and that "he was grieved and dejected
whenever the hours of social intercourse were polluted by mirth."[14]
Like Young, who covered the windows of his college rooms and piled
up skulls and bones around him when studying or composing, Hervey felt himself a stranger in a world of mutability. As *Night Thoughts*
grew from Young's affection for his daughter, the original of Narcissa, Hervey's fondness for a female parishioner who died young
seems to have initiated the *Meditations*.

Hervey's prose works adhere faithfully to the conventions of
graveyard writing. He wanders among the graves and discourses on
the folly of ambition. An unusual tension exists in his work, however,
represented by his divided devotion to botany and astronomy, the
mutable and immutable. In his most characteristic discourse he contrasts the two conditions to point the conventional moral. When he
summons the thought of a covenanting God, for example, he imagines him emblematically in the heavenly bodies, which unlike sublunary bodies are fixed and unalterable in their movements. "While
mighty cities are overwhelmed with ruin," he writes, "and their very
names lost in oblivion; while *vast empires* are swept from their foundations... while *all terrestrial* things are subject to vicissitude and
fluctuating in uncertainty, *these* are permanent in their duration." (p.
340). Like Young, Hervey is a connoisseur of imperial decay. Blake
emphasized this aspect of his vision in his water color illustration of
the *Meditations* (ca. 1810) in which all of history is revealed to Hervey,
as to Adam in *Paradise Lost*. As Blake looked to Hervey, Hervey
looked to Dyer as a forerunner of his own historical imagination.
When he mentions the Egyptian pyramids in *Reflections on a Flower
Garden* he remarks. "I know not any performance, in which the *tran-*

sitory nature of these most *durable* monuments of human grandeur, is hinted with such a modest air of instruction; or their hideous ruin described in such a pomp of pleasing horror; as in a small, but solemn, picturesque, and majestic poem, entitled The Ruins of Rome" (pp. 181–82). He then quotes Dyer's lines about the destructive "voice of time" that I have discussed in chapter three.

Hervey's tribute to Dyer, a ruin piece of his own, reveals the tension in his philosophy most clearly. "Amidst these views of general ruin," he writes, "here is our refuge; this is our consolation; *we know that our Redeemer liveth*" (p. 182). Knowledge which is itself a refuge, however, is best sustained in a place of refuge, away from the influence of worldly change. Though Hervey would deny perfection to this world, he does believe that a community distant enough from the temptations of everyday commerce may be reasonably regarded as a simulacrum of the paradise to come. Wherever knowledge of the Redeemer can be held in integrity, that place, that shelter or inn, is a remnant of God's kingdom. "Here *safety* dwells," he writes of his Hampshire retreat, "here I may, without disturbance, commune with my own heart; and learn that best of sciences, to *know myself*. Here the soul may rally her dissipated powers, and grace recover its native energy" (p. 232).

Because his retreat belongs to the soul's province, his remote locality is a landscape like the graveyard itself, a state of ease abutting the partition between life and eternity. The greatest horror Hervey can imagine is the interpenetration of Satanic agency into this spiritual place. And in 1745 the rebellion mounted by Prince Charles Edward appeared to divines like Hervey as precisely that horror. The Catholic forces rising against the king seemed the very embodiment of that ambitious and destructive world that Hervey tried to escape by leaving London for the country. The solitude his soul demanded for its integrity was threatened and not until the battle of Culloden was the danger removed. Hervey's remarks after the battle need to be quoted in full because they anticipate in important ways the responses of Goldsmith and Wordsworth to similar threats of forcible intrusion:

Who then can be sufficiently thankful for the gracious interposition of Providence, which has not only averted the impending ruin, but turned it, with aggravated confusion, on the authors of our troubles?

   Methinks, every thing *valuable* which I possess, every thing *charming* which I behold, conspire to enhance this ever-memorable event. To this it is owing that I can ramble unmolested along the vale of private life, and taste all the innocent satisfactions of a *contemplative* retirement. Had rebellion suc-

ceeded in her detestable designs, instead of walking with security and com-
placence in these flowery paths, I might have met the *assassin* with his *dagger*,
or have been obliged to abandon my habitation, and "embrace the rock for a
shelter." Farewell then, ye fragrant shades, seats of meditation and calm
repose! I should have been driven from your loved retreats, to make way for
some barbarous, some *insulting victor*. Farewell then, ye pleasing toils, and
wholesome amusements of my rural hours; I should no more have reared the
tender flower to the sun; no more have taught the espalier to expand her
boughs; nor have fetched any longer from my kitchen-garden, the purest
supplies of health.   (Pp. 226–27)

Hervey has toned down his contempt of the world. He displays tender affection for real objects of desire, for the fair forms of plants and
flowers, for the seats and shades of his local walks. Once cast out of
his garden he would return to the state of necessity and undergo the
spiritual and moral humiliations that overtook Roxana.

The identification Hervey makes of his soul and his locality extends to the island of England as well. In *Contemplations on the Starry
Heavens* Hervey associates King George II with "the King immortal
and invisible" (p. 342) or Christ himself. Rebellion against one represents rebellion against the other. George has acted the Redeemer's
role in his conquest of the Catholic dragon, and Hervey pursues the
analogy by warning his readers that their rebellion against God endangers George as well. He describes how the prodigal sons of English families riot in the cities, defile the Sabbath, abase themselves
before luxury, take the Lord's name in vain, and banish God from
their conversation. Linked to these abominations are the "carnal diversions" (p. 269) which Hervey, in a fine passage, describes as
will-o-the-wisps, fiery eidolons which impersonate angelic guides
but are actually Satanic lures. He warns that God is displeased by the
faithlessness of Britain and may be planning a "second deluge" that
would bring "universal desolation" (p. 274). His fears that England
might join the company of ruined empires are very much connected
to the recent rebellion, just as his qualms about his local refuge belong
to a larger patriotism. "May we turn from all ungodliness," he prays
for his countrymen, "before wrath come upon us to the uttermost,
before iniquity prove our ruin" (p. 272).

The iniquity of the Jews, in the biblical account, resulted in their
subjugation by Babylon and later by Rome. The Jews could not advance in spirit and so the new light of Christ's teaching could not
break in upon their darkness. Writers like Hervey foresaw a danger of
exactly this kind for the English, God's new chosen people. In the
concluding passage of *Night Thoughts*, Young imagined Samson as a
figure of redemptive time, a foretype of the Messiah. But the common

identification of a strong and pious Albion with Samson, popularized in Milton's *Areopagitica*, had its sinister side as well. England's self-indulgence and sensuality might bring it low in the short run, as Samson lost power and hope together when the "carnal diversions" of Delilah overcame him. In his fallen state, "Eyeless in Gaza at the mill with slaves" (*Samson Agonistes*, 41) Samson prefigures England's own subjugation by an evil oppressor. For this reason Hervey is justified in seeing the excesses of London as a threat to the preservation of his innocent refuge. The participation of the court, including King George, in vice and corruption, seemed to strengthen the power of Babylon over the English spirit, so much so that some writers of Hervey's time began to wonder if the Gallic tide had not been designated by God as his punishment of the profligate English.

The Example of Cowper

The corruption of political life had important results in the tradition of religious literature. Writers in verse and prose had long agreed that the king in his spiritual body represents the dominion of the Good Shepherd over his flock. Whenever a poet like Young conceives of heaven it is usually as a glorified court, "the bright palace of the lord of day." This had been a standard analogy since the Middle Ages.[15] The moral degeneration of the royal office, however, forced poets to find some other "place" or landscape as a focus of concentration for their meditations on paradise. The retirement myth, associated with royalism in poetry since the defeat of the king's party in the Civil War, and robust even into the generation of Hervey and Young, took on an antiroyalist appearance as the century progressed. When Cowper excoriates the sins of the town in his long poem, *Retirement*, and affirms that retreat to a country asylum allows a person "to serve the Sov'reign we were born t' obey" (50) he is not referring to the Hanovers.[16] Increasingly, poets turned to their own experience for the forms of devotion. Childhood events and feelings, particularly, had the recommendation of Jesus as foretypes of celestial joy.

Such backward excursions in one sense violated the logic of graveyard literature, which devalued the past, individual and social, and condemned nostalgia as a heathen yearning for a recoverable perfection in the body. Young emphasizes the debilitating dangers of nostalgia most clearly. In *Night Thoughts* he describes the horror which "hauntings" by ghosts of the past add to everyday life. He justifies backward looks only as monitors of decay, a lesson in the futility of worldly affections:

Must I then forward only look for Death?
Backward I turn mine eye, and find him there.
Man is a self-survivor every year.
Man, like a stream, is in perpetual flow.
Death's a destroyer of quotidian prey.
My youth, my noon-tide, his; my yesterday;
The bold invader shares the present hour.
Each moment on the former shuts the grave.   (V.709–16)

If the "bold invader" has seized most of the kingdom already, then
the wise man will yearn toward his Redeemer, death's assassin, and
not uselessly toward that part of his self which can never be recon-
quered. Other poets, however, discovered a religious use for the
happy childhood or young manhood. As a foretype of the pleasure to
come these could be summoned, fondled in memory, and then dis-
patched back into darkness with the rumination that such joy will be
recaptured in a finer and more permanent tone after death. The
danger in this, according to Young, is that fancy cherishes the recalled
scene for its own beauty and sets it up as a rival god.

On this issue Young fought a losing battle, however. As religious
verse became more personal and subjective, the memories of individual poets served increasingly to suggest dreamscapes of perfect
happiness. Without disputing death's claim on his past, without
wishing for the return .of childhood joy in this lifetime, a poet like
Blair could still praise the intensity of past experience:

Oh! then the longest summer's day
Seem'd too, too much in haste: still the full heart
Had not imparted half! 'twas happiness
Too exquisite to last. Of joys departed,
Not to return, how painful the remembrance.   (Grave, 106–10)

A step beyond this is the spellbound fascination with the past that
gains its force by a loss of active belief in the afterlife. Common to all
of these views is the longing for some perfect place or state of being
whose lineaments are known, known in one's own pulse and not
from speculations and recorded visions of others. The past, like the
future, can be an asylum from the chaotic and distrubing present. It is
changeless, and in recollection infinite, offering to each person a
virtually unlimited succession of complex and beguiling images.
Without the possibility of recurrence, however, without some sense
of continuity between childhood and adult life, such memories stimulate pain equal to their pleasure.

William Cowper is the best example of this syndrome, and of the relation between nostalgia and the ruin sentiment. Cowper always remembered his childhood, until the death of his mother when he was six, as a period of radiant happiness. Even in old age he could write: "I can truly say that not a week passes, (perhaps I might with equal veracity say a day) in which I do not think of her" (*Prose*, p. 724). The loss of his mother upset his confidence and very likely introduced the intense despair of achieving happiness in any form that dogged him throughout his life. In the autobiographical poem, *On the Receipt of my Mother's Picture out of Norfolk*, he reflects upon his early years, and by "Elysian reverie / A momentary dream" he cherishes images of home. Following a description of his mother's burial he writes:

> Thy maidens griev'd themselves at my concern,
> Oft gave me promise of a quick return.
> What ardently I wish'd, I long believ'd,
> And, disappointed still, was still deceiv'd;
> By disappointment every day beguil'd,
> Dupe of *to-morrow* even from a child.
> Thus many a sad to-morrow came and went,
> Till, all my stock of infant sorrow spent,
> I learn'd at last submission to my lot;
> But, though I less deplor'd thee, ne'er forgot.   (36–45)

As a "dupe of *to-morrow*" Cowper traversed the entire spectrum of eschatological possibilities. At one period of his life he considered himself immortal and believed he would never die. Losing that faith he became obsessed with death, but ecstatic visions persuaded him that his immortal soul would be preserved. Then he lost his belief in an afterlife altogether, regained it, but with the provision that his soul was damned throughout eternity. At each stage he found that the memory of his childhood served his belief. As a model of perfect joy it suggested the asylum he desired above all things; as an inaccessible ruin it emblematized his soul's hopeless alienation from grace.

It is a commonplace of psychology that the early loss of a maternal figure enforces on a child materialist conclusions that no subsequent doctrine can entirely remove. Cowper at a very young age became obsessed with the theme of degeneration in time. He imagined his own life to be a recapitulation in small of the course of history since the Fall. God had proclaimed doom on the whole world, and Cowper could not help personalizing His wrath so that it appeared, the more so the older Cowper became, a vendetta against the poet himself. Moments of redemption, when salvation seemed possible, took the semblance of his childhood, as in a famous dream when he is

comforted by a four-year-old child. A more enduring redemption was
the chaste community of feeling he established with Mary Unwin
later in life; this he compared always to the comforting dependency
and love he had experienced with his mother.

But these were remissions of a constitutional melancholy.
Cowper's typical attitudes are expressed in his unfinished poem,
Yardley Oak. Written after *The Task*, in 1791, it was interrupted by his
translation of Homer and not published until 1806. The poem opens
with his visit to an aged but still living oak. The reflections which
follow make implicitly an identification that is stated explicitly toward the end:

> Thou, like myself, hast stage by state attain'd
> Life's wintry bourn; thou, after many years,
> I after few; but few or many prove
> A span in retrospect; for I can touch
> With my least finger's end my own decease
> And with extended thumb my natal hour,
> And hadst thou also skill in measurement
> As I, the past would seem as short to thee.   (144–51)

The comparison of man's life to a tree is common in Cowper's poetry,
but instead of being the Romantic symbol of endurance and organic
vitality the tree is presented at the beginning or end of a natural cycle.
Cowper reminds himself on these occasions of mutability, the condition of all things in nature: "Change is the diet, on which all
subsist / Created changeable, and change at last / Destroys them"
(72–74). Even to begin living is to begin dying; the energy of change
flows in one direction only:

> Nature's threads,
> Fine passing thought, ev'n in her coarsest works,
> Delight in agitation, yet sustain
> The force that agitates, not unimpair'd,
> But, worn by frequent impulse, to the cause
> Of their best tone their dissolution owe.   (80–85)

Hervey echoes this sentiment when he writes of blood that "the crim-
son fluid, which distributes health, is impregnated with the seeds of
death" (p. 63). The flowering of this death in his arbors fascinates
Cowper, who employs trees as other poets use ruins or tombs. Living
as he did in rural scenery for most of his life, this had the effect of
converting all greenery into monitors, a daily prospect of death. In his
lyrics we see a compulsive return to such vistas:

My fugitive years are all hasting away,
And I must ere long lie as lowly as they,
With a turf on my breast, and a stone at my head,
Ere another such grove shall arise in its stead.

'Tis a sight to engage me, if any thing can,
To muse on the perishing pleasures of man;
Though his life be a dream, his enjoyments, I see,
Have a being less durable even than he.   *(The Poplar Field)*

Green as the bay-tree, ever green,
With its new foliage on,
The gay, the thoughtless, have I seen;
I pass'd—and they were gone.

Read, ye that run, the awful truth
With which I charge my page;
A worm is in the bud of youth,
And at the root of age.   *(Stanzas, Dec. 21, 1787)*

   Which shall longest brave the sky,
Storm and frost? these oaks or I?
Pass an age or two away,
I must moulder and decay,
But the years that crumble me
Shall invigorate the tree,
Spread the branch, dilate its size,
Lift its summit to the skies.   *(Inscription for a Stone)*

Cowper loves natural things but never loses sight of their share in
man's fate. Because he associated the forms of nature with his own
childhood experience of them, the sight of such forms in adult life is
often a balm for his spirit. Working in his garden, tending his pet
hares, birds, and fish, or walking through the artificial wilderness at
Weston he could recapture the unthinking joys of the past. But the
same trees which brought pleasure by their association with childhood could also metamorphose, by a freak of his fancy, into Yardley
Oak, a *memento mori*.

    When Cowper imagines Adam in *Yardley Oak* he sees him just
before the expulsion which begins the cycles of history. The poem
breaks off at that still moment before change and loss reign, a moment Cowper must have associated with the prelapsarian joys of his
own Eden, Berkhamstead. Writing to a friend about those early days,
he said, "There was neither tree, nor gate, nor stile, in all that country, to which I did not feel a relation." But after his father's death,
while he was at Westminster School, his relation was severed: "Then,

and not till then, I felt for the first time that I and my native place were disunited for ever" (*Prose*, p. 852). By retirement in later life he hoped to enter a timeless realm in which childhood feelings of intimacy with nature might be recaptured. But this paradisaical dream yielded like all of his others to the monitors, the trees, to which he fled. In the year he began *Yardley Oak* he wrote to a friend:

A yellow shower of leaves is falling continually from all the trees in the country. A few moments only seem to have passed since they were buds, and in a few moments more they will have disappeared. . . . It is impossible for a man conversant with such scenes as surround me not to advert daily to the shortness of his existence here, admonished of it as he must be by ten thousand objects. There was a time when I could contemplate my present state and consider myself as a thing of a day with pleasure, and I remembered seasons as they passed in swift rotation as a schoolboy remembers the days that interpose between the next vacation when he shall see his parents and enjoy his home again. But to make so just an estimate of life as this is no longer in my power. I would live and live always, and am become such another wretch as Maecenas, who wished for long life, he cared not at what expense of sufferings.[17]

Cowper could keep the past immune from destruction in his memory, but, as Young warned, all the rest of his life showed in relief as a blasted ruin. As the early part of his life increasingly took on the aspect of perfection it came within a finger's reach, as close as the moment following death. In his backward looks Cowper was by turns disinterested and morbid. The very closeness of his childhood terrified him, as the above quotation suggests, because the distance of years he traversed to arrive at Berkhamstead was more than double the years he could expect to live henceforth. Here is a variation of Blair's syndrome: "Of joys departed / Not to return, how painful the remembrance." The ambiguous nature of his nostalgia posed unique questions for his poetic descendants. It is worth noting that when *Yardley Oak* first appeared in print Wordsworth copied it into his daybook.

    Throughout his poems and letters Cowper discovers in English life a degeneration as painful, as vicious, and as melancholy as his own. "He that has seen both sides of 50," he wrote in 1782, "has lived to little purpose, if he has not other views of the world than he had when he was much younger. He finds, if he reflects at all, that it will be to the end what it has been from the beginning, a shifting, uncertain, fluctuating scene; that nations as well as individuals have their seasons of infancy, youth, and age, and if he be an Englishman, he will observe that ours in particular is affected with every symptom of decay, and is already sunk into a state of decrepitude" (*Prose*, p. 652). Occasionally he argues on the other side of the issue, but in general England takes on the appearance of Yardley Oak, its best energies having catabolized it, century after century, into a state of dissolution.

Historical events of Cowper's time did not offer him opportunities for cheer. The American Revolution, especially, exacerbated his doubts about English destiny. He accepted the fact of British colonial expansion. As a patriot, he believed that the growth of commerce would benefit all nations and that Christianity would follow in the wake of English trade. But he perceived also the negative effects of an aggressive imperialism. He wrote often against the slave trade and recognized the harrowing danger to the English body politic of foreign conquest, in America and elsewhere. If England "is already sunk into a state of decrepitude" then the spreading abroad of its infirmity was not an activity which a Christian could conscientiously approve. As to the hopeful propaganda about England's entry into a renewed Golden Age, Dyer's dream in *The Fleece*, Cowper scornfully answered that such a dream was impossible in his own time "when virtue is so scarce, / That to suppose a scene where she presides, / Is tramontane, and stumbles all belief" (*Task*, IV.531–33).

Cowper's uncertainty about colonial policy is most elaborately articulated in a letter to Joseph Hill (1781) concerning the American war. He begins by imagining a conversation between Hill and himself on the war, much as Spenser framed his own doubts about Ireland by casting them into a dialogue. "Well, Cowper—what do you think of this American war?" he has Hill begin, and then answers, "To say the truth I am not very fond of thinking about it; when I do, I think of it unpleasantly enough. I think it bids fair to be the ruin of this country" (*Prose*, p. 646). He drops the dialogue form soon after to discourse on the paralyzing effect of the dilemma: that England will continue to sink year after year into calamity if it pursues the war but that the success of these revolutionaries would be a model for all of England's colonies and of course for England's own dissenters as well. "I consider the loss of America as the ruin of England," he concludes, a loss that he added shortly afterward to his already lengthy burden of mortalities.

Because Cowper considered imperial ambition analogous to individual pride he expected the Providence that punished Adam to overturn the vain hopes of England as well. He imagined himself as the emblem of his country's ruin because he harbored the same worldly desire for self-preservation and fame as kings. "*I have, what perhaps you little suspect me of, in my nature an infinite share of ambition,*" he writes emphatically in a letter, though he adds immediately, "But with it, I have at the same time... an equal share of diffidence" (*Prose*, p. 800). Cowper hardly seems the type of an ambitious author, but despite his repeated deprecations of his talent he aspired in the most obvious way to the role of preacher and prophet to his age. *The Task* is a compendium of opinions on the most diverse subjects imaginable, from the growing of cucumbers to the character of the Messiah. Beyond that masterwork are verse sermons like *Truth, Hope, Charity*, and *Retirement*. Cowper believed that in the body he could accomplish much good for his small community at Olney and for the larger community of England. His ambition committed him to the preservation of a body which his reason warned him was destined for oblivion. In his letters we find him writing as if he could carry his flesh into paradise. When he meets John Milton in a dream, he halts his conversation to recall that Milton is "about 200 years old, I said that I might fatigue him by much talking and took my leave" (*Prose*, p. 991). The subconscious desire that aging and by extension worldly personality might persist in heaven reflects his inability to accept entirely the doctrine of transfiguration. He judged that very incapacity a proof of his damnation. Of England he wrote, "Certain vices have infected it which more than anything else threaten its dissolution, and which therefore I wish to see eradicated" (*Prose*, p. 983). To eradicate them he had to tighten his grasp on life, live longer and longer, all the time knowing that Providence would not overlook his extravagant ambition.

Cowper perceived no way out; the contradictions in his mind, of which this was only one, found no resolution but madness. In one dream a doctor tells him that death is the only cure for his condition, a prescription whose horror deepened his insanity throughout the 1790s until his death in 1800. His last original poem, *The Cast-Away*, powerfully depicts his alienation from grace ("No voice divine the storm allay'd"), and his gradual descent into the deepest gulfs of madness. Poets of the next generation looked on Cowper himself as a monitor of the ruin he described in his work, an example of the "infinite despair" which graveyard writing, despite its good intentions, memorialized for the new century.[18]

7 The Deserted Village:
The Politics of Nostalgia

"THE ONLY TRUE PARADISE is the Paradise we have lost." This apothegm of Marcel Proust echoes ancient and modern expressions of longing for a Golden Age. It presumes that immediate experience does not and cannot satisfy a person's imaginative needs and that the culture in which he has adult being will inevitably appear in a degenerate form. Some of Proust's contemporaries located their lost paradise in history; they praised the Dionysian joy, the piety, the austere wisdom of a particular epoch. Proust himself disdained a utopian model; he wished to reoccupy the territory he had already possessed in the body. His capacious memory secured from the storms of mutability a perfect place both ideal and actual. In *Le Temps Retrouvé* Marcel confronts the ruin of Gilberte Swann and insists that she is not the real presence which haunts his imagination. He restores her (and himself) to the lost paradise of their childhood in the landscape of Combray. Until he takes pen in hand Marcel is a walking shadow, an exile, a victim of time; so armed, however, he is able to preserve a homeland intact and organically whole.

Homesickness is a theme dignified by the most serious and enduring literature. The lamentations of Israel during its captivity and the voyage of Ulysses to Ithaca are ancient examples; the modern literature exemplified by Proust belongs to the same tradition. Such writings have long been interpreted as dramatizations of the soul's desire for completion and perfection. Home is the dwelling place of the primordial self (or soul, or local spirit) which accumulates feeling in retrospect as the living man travels farther toward the horizon, growing in intellectual power but vitiated in his purer feelings. To the extent he is conscious of living amid evil he yearns backward to a model of integrity and innocent pleasures. For this reason a modern commentator can say that "homesickness . . . is an involuntary conscience, a moral conscience, positive rather than prohibitory. It re-

95

minds a person, by way of giving him the experience, of the good he
has known and lost."[1]

Proust's biographer, Samuel Beckett, dramatizes in *Krapp's Last
Tape* nostalgia of a more superficial kind. The aged Krapp, alone in a
cave with his tape recorder, relives sensations and events described
by the voice of his former self. Here is not the yearning for unity of
being but a pathetic numbering of life's "straw-like trifles." From the
same impulse William Cowper looks at a portrait from former days
and exclaims, "Oh, if I could be as I was then." Aaron Hill, in his
poem, *Alone in an Inn at Southampton* (1737), writes

> Twenty lost years have stolen their hours away,
> Since in this inn, e'en in this room, I lay:
> How chang'd! what then was rapture, fire, and air
> Seems now sad silence all, and blank despair![2]

The lament for youthful spirits must be distinguished from the more
powerful and complex emotion of homesickness. Lament-for-youth
is whimsical; it looks backward a year as easily as fifty, it respects no
particular landscape but touches accidental and superficial qualities:
an illusion, an ambition, a bodily grace, an adventure or perfect moment. An artist needs these qualities for the texture of his autobiographical work, but he knows that the more he insists on them the
closer he approaches to sentimentality and bathos. A work essentially
composed of such memories, like *Krapp's Last Tape*, must be satiric, a
comedy that explodes nostalgia as Molière does avarice or hypocrisy.

Eighteenth-century writers of Oliver Goldsmith's generation
were divided, often against themselves, on the matter of nostalgia.
Because humanists like Samuel Johnson based their faith in moral
progress on the study of the past, they judged the faculty of remembrance as the chief influence for good on the human soul. In individuals no less than in nations, Johnson wrote in *The Rambler* (no. 41),
the recollection of virtue restores the sense of purpose which worldly
distractions may have impaired. But recollection is not nostalgia.
Johnson always censured the yearning to draw an earlier state of
being into the present, for his whole moral philosophy assumes that
"Providence has fixed the limits of human enjoyment by immovable
boundaries, and has set different gratifications at such a distance from
each other, that no art or power can bring them together. This great
law it is the business of every rational being to understand, that life
may not pass away in an attempt to make contradictions consistent,
to combine opposite qualities, and to unite things which the nature of
their being must always keep asunder."[3]

Nostalgia, at best, brings powerful emotion to the service of reason and rational conduct. But, as Johnson realized, it degenerates easily into self-pity and despair if the longed-for home or source of good is in fact inaccessible. The pleasures of memory then become pains, and the emotional charge of recalled images is turned upon time itself and the conditions of growing up. To flail against such an enemy is to destroy forever all chance of happiness in oneself. Johnson is therefore as much concerned in his writings with the faculty of forgetting as of remembrance. "It would add much to human happiness," he writes in *The Idler* (no. 72), "if an art could be taught of forgetting all of which the remembrance is at once useless and afflictive, if that pain which never can end in pleasure could be driven totally away, that the mind might perform its functions without incumbrance, and the past might no longer encroach upon the present." In an earlier paper of *The Idler* (no. 44), he lamented that "the shades of the dead" which memory summons to haunt the mind inevitably bring with them unwelcome stories of death and disappointed hopes. For this reason he deprecates homesickness throughout his work; revisitation of the past in thought or act is mocked and surrounded with irony.

Goldsmith, by contrast, continually seeks the shades of the dead. The resonance in such a phrase is not accidental. The *Odyssey* and the *Aeneid* describe the meeting of dead and living in the underworld as a heroic enterprise. The plea of Aeneas, particularly, for some charm from the Sibyl that he may "go to my beloved father, to see him face to face," seems precisely the kind of self-afflictive act that Johnson disapproved in everyday life. Goldsmith's finest narratives, however, derive their form and their emotion from imaginative revisitation of a patriarchal home. Born in Ireland but a resident of England from the age of twenty-four, he recurs habitually to home in letters and literary productions. "My very country comes in for a share of my affections," he recounts in one of his first letters from abroad, "Unaccountable fondness for country, this maladie du Pays, as the french call it. Unaccountable that he should still have an affection for a place, who never received when in it above civil contempt."[4] Goldsmith, by all objective accounts, did not have a joyful childhood in the village of Lissoy. We find no scenes of rapture like Wordsworth's at Hawkshead, but rather the settled confidence, the benevolence, and bond of community Goldsmith describes in *The Deserted Village* and *The Vicar of Wakefield*. Having no new city to found, but only Grub Street to labor in year after year, he increasingly sought inspiration from his lost pastoral paradise. It is the task of the modern, he discovered, to linger at the Sibyl's cave.

Homesickness is generated by homelessness, either of exile or travel. Goldsmith is the type of a displaced artist whose life at the inns of the world turns his imagination toward the archetype of return. In his dedication of *The Traveller* to his brother, Henry, he remarks ruefully that Henry chose the wiser destiny of the two by remaining at home, while Oliver set off ambitiously to increase his knowledge of the world by European travel and academic study. Henry pursued their father's profession in the ministry and inherited his living. Henry grew into the continuous selfhood that Oliver, the prodigal, abjured and left behind in quest of fame. Goldsmith was aware that his flight to the city perfectly symbolized the disintegrating effect of urban civilization on the rural virtues. His letters home are a string of apologies for his defection, which they justify by reminders of Oliver's genius. He will someday guide the English flock, he promises, as Henry does the Lissoy faithful; he will be an arbiter of taste and a purveyor of truth. In a letter written at age twenty-eight, he imagines a Chinese philosopher of the future lecturing about him: "Oliver Goldsmith flourished in the eighteenth and nineteenth centuries. He lived to be an hundred and three years old, and in that age may justly be styled the sun of literature and the Confucius of Europe."[5] Goldsmith understandably prefers to look with foreign eyes upon England. When he later creates Lien Chi Altangi, his "Citizen of the World," he is careful to note that the displaced cosmopolitan has been forbidden by his emperor to return home.

Goldsmith spent his years of exile in the republic of letters, as he often called it, a foreign country caged by a nation even more forbidding (for an Irishman), England. In the eighteenth century the ambition which led to Grub Street cohabited uneasily with the simple piety and virtue that characterized the world Henry inherited. Nobody of his time knew better than Goldsmith the profanity of spirit that was Grub Street. His first published volume, *An Enquiry into the Present State of Polite Learning in Europe*, was written with the intention "to mark out . . . the corruptions that have found way into the republick of letters, to attempt the rescuing of genius from the shackles of pedantry and criticism, to distinguish the decay, naturally consequent on an age like ours grown old in literature, from every erroneous innovation which admits a remedy."[6] The "shackles of pedantry and criticism," we quickly learn in the *Enquiry*, are forged in the political mills, for "the great and avaricious" have most to fear from genius and most to gain by suppressing it. While substantial payments flowed from Westminster to the hacks whom Johnson called the lowest of all human beings, scribblers for party, the best writers of the age often labored in poverty and obscurity. Goldsmith, as a self-proclaimed genius, had no choice but to enter the jailhouse, a pen for hire like the rest. Shackled in this vile republic, like Samson at the mill with slaves, Goldsmith haunted himself with familial shades. His father, especially, makes frequent appearances in his work: as the Vicar of Wakefield, the Man in Black's father in *Citizen of the World,* and the village preacher in *The Deserted Village.* The meeting of father and son is beautifully dramatized in chapter 28 of *The Vicar of Wakefield* when Dr. Primrose discovers his wandering son George, on whom all the family fortunes depend, in prison, "all bloody, wounded, and fettered with the heaviest irons."

The pathos of Goldsmith's plight arises from the irrevocable effects of his decision to isolate himself from the nurturing home. This decision Goldsmith recognized as a natural consequence of the Fall, a gesture of kinship with Adam. The world Adam inherits by his pride is larger, more dangerous, and in an obvious way more stimulating in its freedom than the garden.[7] When Johnson writes that "Providence has fixed the limits of human enjoyment by immovable boundaries," he implies, at least, that the recreations of the exile are legitimate and, in their own being, compelling. A letter of Cowper's describes the mixed nature of the Adamic presence, free and enslaved at once. The italics are mine.

Thus am I both free and a prisoner at the same time. The world is before me; I am not shut up in the Bastille though often as miserable as if I were, there are no moats about my castle, nor locks upon my gates but of which I have the key—but an invisible, uncontrollable agency, a local attachment, an inclination more forcible than I ever felt, *even to the place of my birth,* serves me for prison-walls, and for bounds which I cannot pass. (*Prose,* p. 687).

Goldsmith never did revisit Lissoy even though he reiterated his desire to do so and on at least one occasion, following the success of *The Deserted Village* in 1770, had the funds, time, and health to make the journey. He traveled instead to Paris, in search, he wrote Joshua Reynolds, of distracting adventures.

Goldsmith's sense of captivity in London was increased by his Irishness. At first he met the most direct prejudice when employers refused him because of his nationality. When his ability overcame that obstacle he confronted a further and inescapable dilemma. In order to rise in his adopted republic of letters he had to assume English attitudes, and to some extent—depending on the periodical—he had to praise imperial policies whose effect on Ireland was devastating. Nothing had improved in Anglo-Irish relations since Spenser's day. If anything, the draconian Penal Laws passed against Catholics in Ireland during the eighteenth century sustained the conquest recommended by Spenser in his *Vewe*. They insured the transfer of all Catholic property to non-Catholics and excluded Catholics from the bar, the bench, the university, the navy, and all public bodies. Goldsmith's friend and countryman, Edmund Burke, called the penal code "a machine of as wise and elaborate contrivance for the impoverishment and degradation of the people, and the debasement in them of human nature itself, as ever proceeded from the perverted ingenuity of man."[8] Not only the Catholics suffered. High tariffs against Irish goods, coupled with prohibitions forbidding the Irish to trade elsewhere than with England, ruined Irish commerce. At the same time, as much as one third of the whole rental of Irish land was annually drained away to England for the support of absentee landlords. The emigration of Irish families became a familiar sight in the latter part of the eighteenth century, causing Irish leaders like Grattan and Flood to argue with greater urgency for home rule.

The enmity of these two islands created in Goldsmith a painful division of loyalties. He had to praise English laws, policies, and freedom (which he genuinely admired) in order to eat, but throughout most of his career he dared not modify his praise by charges of English cruelty toward his homeland. The young Goldsmith deliberately painted a prospect of Ireland to suit the prejudices of his readership. "They live in a fruitful country," he writes in *The Royal Magazine* (1760), "sequestered from the rest of mankind, protected by a powerful nation from foreign insult.... They have no important national concerns to make them anxious, or cloud their tempers with the solemnity of pride. In such circumstances they are contented with indolence and pleasure, take every happiness as it presents, are easily excited to resent, and as easily induced to submission" (*CW*, III, 84). The tone is that of a smug landlord who patronizes *The Royal Magazine* in order to remain self-deceived. Forced to write such dishonest drivel Goldsmith could not help but imagine his adopted republic as Babylon, a city of oppression.

He develops this analogy in the first of his long poetic works, *The Captivity*, an oratorio written for Robert Dodsley in 1764, but never performed. It is a play for conflicting voices: lamentations by Israelites in Babylon versus the arrogance and exultation of their captors. It concludes with news of Cyrus's war on Babylon which brings promise of liberation for the Jews. This obvious vehicle for expressions of homesickness contains images and phrases Goldsmith used in his

later writings to communicate the same yearnings and the same despair. The play opens with sighs of maladie du pays by a Jewish
Prophet:

> That strain once more; it bids remembrance rise,
> And calls my long-lost country to mine eyes.
> Ye fields of Sharon, dressed in flowery pride,
> Ye plains where Jordan rolls its glassy tide,
> Ye hills of Lebanon with cedars crowned,
> Ye Gilead groves that fling perfumes around,
> These hills how sweet! those plains how wondrous fair,
> But sweeter still, when Heaven was with us there!

> *Air*
> O memory, thou fond deceiver,
> Still importunate and vain;
> To former joys recurring ever,
> And turning all the past to pain.   (15–26)

Goldsmith repeats this last line in *The Deserted Village* when he meditates on his own homeland: "Remembrance wakes with all her busy
train, / Swells at my breast, and turns the past to pain." The Hebrews
are imagined by Goldsmith as great singers of devotional verse and
prophetic utterance, an apotheosis of the republic of letters. The
Babylonian Priest is given the clichés of Whig rhetoric, the gospel of
wealth and power. The Priest states confidently that "our fixed empire shall for ever last" (194), and he brags of the Monarch's foreign
conquests. The Jewish Prophet, however, knows that Babylon does
not command the loyalties of its conquered peoples.

As a hostage in the oppressor's camp, Goldsmith could speak
through the victimized prophets, and like them pronounce doom on
his captors. No formula comes to his pen more easily than the ruin
sentiment. The most famous example is the "city night-piece" from
The Citizen of the World:

What cities, as great as this, have once triumph'd in existence, had their
victories as great, joy as just, and as unbounded, and with short-sighted
presumption, promised themselves immortality. Posterity can hardly trace
the situation of some. The sorrowful traveller wanders over the awful ruins of
others, and as he beholds, he learns wisdom, and feels the transience of every
sublunary possession.   (CW, II, 452–53)

In *The Deserted Village* the "poor houseless shivering female" must
carry her weight of adjectives because her misery foretells the ruin of

the state. Once "ambitious of the town," her virtue has been betrayed by the indifferent seducer, her "wheel and robes of country brown," an image significantly withheld until the end of the verse paragraph, abandoned in the pursuit of an unproductive luxury. Goldsmith points the moral shortly afterward:

> O luxury! Thou cursed by Heaven's decree,
> How ill exchanged are things like these for thee!
> How do thy potions with insidious joy,
> Diffuse their pleasures only to destroy!
> Kingdoms, by thee to sickly greatness grown,
> Boast of a florid vigour not their own.
> At every draught more large and large they grow,
> A bloated mass of rank unwieldy woe;
> Till sapped their strength and every part unsound,
> Down, down they sink and spread a ruin round.   (385–94)

Goldsmith's severity owes much to his own victimization by the idea of luxury. Luxury had lured him from Ireland because, as he insisted in *The Bee*, luxury was only another name for elegance and taste (*CW*, I, 435). The English public flattered mediocrity but it also sustained genius by indiscriminately supporting good and bad alike in its playgoing, its purchase of fiction and verse and some fifty-five London periodicals. Money for these artistic efforts flowed from the profits of commerce·and the indulgence of vanity. Though Goldsmith's praise of luxury has often been held up by critics as an example of his confused thinking on the subject, he knew very well the internal contradictions of his position. Consider his formulation in *The Citizen of the World*: "The more various our artificial necessities, the wider is our circle of pleasure; for all pleasure consists in obviating necessities as they rise; luxury, therefore, as it encreases our wants, encreases our capacity for happiness" (*CW*, II, 51).[9] Goldsmith must have smiled as he contrived the deceptive logic of that sentence. The oxymoron "artificial necessities" would make any sensitive reader of his time pause with suspicion, as would the dubious morality implied when he attributes *all* pleasure to the relief of such redefined necessities. He is again flattering the beliefs of his wealthier readers by lumping gaudy consumption with what in *The Traveller* he calls "the luxury of doing good" (22). Not self-deception but self-pity underlies this rhetoric, for Goldsmith has in mind his own transformation into an article of commerce in Grub Street. Like Roxana he must plead necessity in a hostile world of luxury, and submit to the "insidious joy" of London prosperity.

His long poem, *The Traveller*, is an impressive analysis of the commercial spirit, as he observed it in his European travels and as he embodied it in his own exile. His starting point, as usual, is an axiom of Whig philosophy. This time it is the assumption well expressed by Dyer in *The Fleece* that "they / The clearest sense of Deity receive / Who view the widest prospect of his works, / Ranging the globe with trade through various climes" (II.628–31). In Goldsmith's revision of this claim such expansion is an illusion; merchant and traveler alike drag a lengthening chain. Their clearest view of Deity comes when they return in thought or act to the primordial paradise which God patterned for man's terrestrial home. In his formulation avarice and pride, the bases of commercial success, are degenerate forms of the love that grew from day to day in the home from which all persons are exiles. At home the "hoard of human bliss" actively circulates in an affectionate bond with the community that shares it. By leaving this "spot to real happiness consign'd" the exile falls into a world whose competitive spirit is a demonic parody of the bond. Master and slave are exchanged for father and son, the patron usurps the parson, the critic stands in for the brother. And commerce itself, which from the perspective of home, from the center, seemed to be the mighty brotherhood Dyer said it was, alters its character when observed from inside its own vortex. As in Holland, so in England; where "convenience, plenty, elegance, and arts" are pursued, the result may be "a land of tyrants, and a den of slaves." As the poem draws to a conclusion, Goldsmith knits the personal and public themes together:

> Yes, brother, curse with me that baleful hour,
> When first ambition struck at regal power;
> And thus polluting honour in its source,
> Gave wealth to sway the mind with double force.   (393–96)

The address to Henry recalls Goldsmith's distinction in the dedication between Henry's pastoral retirement and his own ambition. His own desires are here recalled in the "first ambition" which suggests the Fall while tracing the ethics of competition back to dimmest antiquity. And finally, the passage serves as an effective transition to Goldsmith's first attack on rural depopulation caused by enclosure, a subject he could use as a vehicle for self-pity and prophecy alike.

Goldsmith's dependence on a rural home for his model of excellence made him uniquely attuned to the evils of enclosure which befell the English and Irish countryside during this period. Dispossessed himself, his social criticism became most acute when he discovered whole villages displaced by the vanity of London. In his essay, "The Revolution in Low Life" (1762), he recounts how he visited a little village about fifty miles from London, "inhabited by a race of men who followed the primeval profession of agriculture." But these people, "the strength and ornament of their country," were compelled to relocate themselves because a wealthy merchant decided to establish a seat of pleasure for himself. Here was not only an affront to humanitarian principles but an ominous threat to national destiny. Goldsmith makes an extended comparison to latter-day Rome at the conclusion of his account. When he surveyed Italy in his travels he found peasants practicing pastoral economy amid the ruins of Rome, and he took this as a positive sign of Italy's regeneration. Rome, when an imperial power, drove peasants from the land, as we observe in Virgil's first Eclogue. Now in England the empire-builders, refusing to look backward and be saved by historical example, had initiated a new cycle of dispossession (CW, III, 195–98).

Many writers on *The Deserted Village* have added examples to Goldsmith's in "The Revolution in Low Life," and two of these might be cited as further instances of the devastation wrought by Timons of Goldsmith's generation. John Scott narrates a story, repeated by Marx in *Das Kapital*, of the Earl of Leicester, who, being complimented on the completion of his great design at Holham, replied, "It is a melancholy thing to stand alone in one's country. I look round; not a house is to be seen but mine. I am the giant of giant-castle, and have eat up all my neighbors."[10] Few of the gentry had such reservations. F. L. Lucas tells of Joseph Damer, the future Earl of Dorchester, who in 1786 "objected to the village of Milton ... being in sight of his mansion. He removed the whole place—a hundred houses, a brewery, a grammar-school that had bred Nelson's Hardy, almshouses, inns, even the very tombstones. Even so, it is recorded that Mr. Damer was much annoyed because the bones of past Miltonians kept turning up as he laid out his gardens."[11]

Where did the dispossessed go? According to *The Deserted Village* a few moved on to fields unpleasant enough to keep landlords away, and more gravitated to the cities. But Goldsmith, eager to demonstrate that "trade's proud empire hastes to swift decay" (427), follows with particular attention those rural folk who of necessity volunteered for settlement or service in new colonies. Behind these exiles he locates a tyrant's hand (37, 76) which as a symbol unites landlord and warlord. The unkind portrait of America in the poem is not meant to be realistic any more than the America of Blake's prophecies. The "poisonous fields with rank luxuriance crowned" (351) shoot out from the "bloated mass of rank unwieldly woe" which Goldsmith in *The Traveller* described as luxury's ruinous impact on the kingdom.

The infections are as universal as the empire; they reach into America as they do into Auburn and Grub Street.

Goldsmith took the most unsympathetic view possible of the acquisition of foreign territories and commercial intercourse with them. New colonies entered British hegemony at such an accelerated rate that by 1763, after the Peace of Paris, the British Empire had tripled in size over its 1754 boundaries. British armies had to guarantee security along the eastern seaboard of North America from Nova Scotia down to Florida, not to mention its burdensome responsibilities in India, Africa, and elsewhere. This aggrandizement Goldsmith considered the utmost folly. To him Canada was a frozen wasteland, the southern part of the continent a pestilential bog, and the frontier a savage desert. The settlement of such areas, necessitating wars with native and European competitors, did not secure worthwhile advantages for England. His description of the war with France over Canadian trading routes illustrates his opinion. The land actually belongs to the natives—"they have all the pretentions which long possession can confer"—but because a small portion of the English and French public covet fur, for coats and muffs, not only must the natives be violently subjugated but the lives of young men of both countries must be squandered in warfare (*CW*, II, 73).[12]

If this is true of Canada, how much truer of the Falkland Islands. What did England acquire by its contest with Spain over these islands, asked Samuel Johnson—"What, but a bleak and gloomy solitude, an island thrown aside from human use, stormy in winter, and barren in summer; an island which not the southern savages have dignified with habitation; where a garrison must be kept in a state that contemplates with envy the exiles of Siberia."[13] Colonial enterprises that did benefit the English treasury, like the East India Company, dishonored England in other ways, as Edmund Burke was soon to demonstrate in the trial of Warren Hastings. In the *Weekly Magazine* a concerned Goldsmith wrote:

There is another maxim, which experience has ever testified the truth of; I mean, that an empire, by too great a foreign power may lessen its natural strength, and that dominion often becomes more feeble as it grows more extensive. The ancient Roman empire is a strong instance of the truth of the assertion. . . . To be as explicit as possible, I see no reason why we should aggrandize our colonies at our own expence; an acquisition of new colonies is useless, unless they are peopled; but to people those deserts that lie behind our present colonies, would require multitudes from the mother-country; and I do not find we are too populous at home.   (*CW*, III, 32–33)[14]

Goldsmith was compiling a history of the Roman Empire at the time he wrote *The Deserted Village*, and the extremity of language in some parts of the poem clearly reflects his unhappy recognition that England could not be prevented from its imitation of the imperial model. Pitt had openly boasted that his intention in conducting the war for empire was simply to conquer and keep what he could. Modern historians have tended to take him at his word. "This 18th Century Empire... was a straightforward institution of plunder," A. J. P. Taylor writes. "It was a 'good thing' for those who profited from it and for no one else."[15]

When Goldsmith was a boy, a general named Napier dispossessed cottagers in Lissoy of their land in order to enlarge his estate. When the original of Auburn became a tourist attraction after Goldsmith's death, Napier's mansion, Littleton, was pointed out as an emblem of the desolating spirit lamented by the poet. In his lifetime as well, Littleton and Lissoy were contraries by which Goldsmith interpreted the meaning of his experience, a provincialism that served him well in Grub Street. The nostalgia common to city dwellers was for Goldsmith an article of commerce that he could craft more skillfully than others because he had reasons to understand it more fully. The longer he remained an exile, in a landscape elsewhere than his home, the more beautifully he could sing of his loss. Remembrance turned the past to pain and pain turned the past to art. A long-standing criticism of *The Deserted Village*, expressed most forcefully by Thomas Macaulay, has been that depopulation was an Irish and not an English phenomenon. Examples like those of Scott and Lucas suggest otherwise, but the criticism does bear upon Goldsmith's motives in composing the poem. Clearly it *is* Ireland and not England that stirs in his consciousness, though the poem is set in England. The poet discovers in a historical problem the exact form of his own alienation, and by regarding his case as typical of all humanity he establishes spiritual dispossession as a permanent fact of modern life.

The first eighty-two lines of the poem are a catalogue of changes in the "seats of my youth." They document how a remembered landscape has been usurped by "trade's unfeeling train." The elegiac tone commands authority by the use of universal, one might almost say stock, images of ruin, and by comparisons of past and present. The dislocation in time is rendered by physical contrasts: the gamboling children versus the hollow-sounding bittern; the cultivated farm versus the "shapeless ruin" of sunken bowers and long grass; the glassy brook now choked with sedge and weeds. Goldsmith prepares us for

THE

DESERTED VILLAGE,

A

P O E M.

By Dr. GOLDSMITH

The sad historian of the pensive plain.

LONDON:

Printed for W. GRIFFIN, at Garrick's Head, in Catharine-ſtreet, Strand.

MDCCLXX.

The ruins of Auburn, title page of *The Deserted Village*, 1770.

his personal response by moving the images of contrast closer to his own condition. Finally, the speaker includes himself: "Remembrance wakes with all her busy train, / Swells at my breast, and turns the past to pain." Goldsmith has adapted from graveyard poetry the art of rendering the immediate perception unpleasant by adding to it the consciousness of decay. Memory is Adam's fatality, for it brings to every garden the inward spectacle of the Fall.

Goldsmith provides a model of this conversion in his essay, "The History of a Poet's Garden," written shortly after *The Deserted Village*. He wanders through William Shenstone's estate, Leasowes, which a succession of owners had "improved" with new ideas:

As I was turning my back upon a beautiful piece of water enlivened with cascades and rock-work, and entering a dark walk by which ran a prattling brook, the Genius of the place appeared before me, but more resembling the God of Time, than him more peculiarly appointed to the care of gardens. Instead of sheers he bore a scythe.... Having remembered this place in its pristine beauty, I could not help condoling with him on the many alterations which had been made, and all for the worse: of the many shades which had been taken away, of the bowers that were destroyed by neglect, and the hedge-rows that were spoiled by clipping.   (*CW*, III, 206–07)

Leasowes is not Goldsmith's home, so his tone is less impassioned and personal, but his vision of this ruined garden resembles that of the opening lament in *The Deserted Village*. As in Pope's *Epistle to Burlington* it is the owner's bad taste that Goldsmith disapproves and on which he is revenged by his commentary. In Pope's imagination bad taste has a way of expanding to apocalyptic dimensions, as in the concluding lines of *The Dunciad* where the "dream Empire, CHAOS! is restor'd" when the uncreative triumphs. In Goldsmith as well, the effect of neglect and active desolation puts the spirit of place in thrall to "the tyrant's power," a power which fuses the monstrous overgrowth of luxury and empire with their spiritual daimon, the scythe-bearing God of Time. Goldsmith's strategy in *The Deserted Village* is to draw these overwhelming forces into the poem by phrases and figures and set them in opposition to his enfeebled though creative word.

Goldsmith dramatizes his erstwhile hopes by means of a conventional *topos*, the desire of revisitation. Here he draws on his own obsession, never more comfortable than in the *persona* of an Englishman rejoicing in his return to native haunts. An essay in the *Royal Magazine* characteristically insists on the preservation of the home landscape in its every feature:

To grow old in the same fields where we once were young; to be capable of every moment beholding objects that recal our early pleasures; to measure our own years by the trees that our hands have planted, are more truly pleasing than may at first be imagined. We entertain for every mountain, stream, or cottage, that we have been accustomed to see, an habitual fondness; and each is capable of improving our sensations. "Methinks, says the sensible Menage, I would not wish to see even an old post removed with which I had been long acquainted."

After a life of the most dissipated variety, after having strayed through so many countries without being regarded, or known, with what enthusiasm do I again revisit the happy island where I drew my first breath, and received the early pleasures and institutions of life? . . . here let me spend the small remainder of my days in tranquillity and content.   (CW, III, 67)[16]

The essay, which might be contrasted with Johnson's sardonic paper in *The Rambler* (no. 165) on the same theme, has its parallel in the following passage from *The Deserted Village:*

> In all my wanderings round this world of care,
> In all my griefs—and GOD has given my share—
> I still had hopes my latest hours to crown,
> Amidst these humble bowers to lay me down;
> To husband out life's taper at the close,
> And keep the flame from wasting by repose.
> I still had hopes, for pride attends us still,
> Amidst the swains to show my book-learned skill,
> Around my fire an evening group to draw,
> And tell of all I felt and all I saw;
> And, as a hare whom hounds and horns pursue,
> Pants to the place from whence at first she flew,
> I still had hopes, my long vexations past,
> Here to return—and die at home at last.   (83–96)

When these two passages are considered together, we observe the complexity of the revisitation theme. A returned prodigal both gives and receives. He receives, most significant, an improvement in sensual enjoyment from objects endeared to the self by childhood affections. So long as these objects are permanent they can preserve that archaic part of his self which might otherwise atrophy, leaving the adult man at the mercy of memory. To a citizen of the world the haunting by ephemeral shades, though desirable as a token of the lost paradise, is also a condition of imprisonment in the enemy camp. "We lose more than we gain by remembrance," Lien Chi Altangi concludes (CW, II, 187). Only the actual repossession of native landscape can heal the breach between the two lives—of childhood and old age.

In recompense, the prodigal gives to the community he revisits the benefits of his wayward experience. Since he has ("as a hare") been chased back to his home by the hunters of men, the descendants of Nimrod, his wisdom will almost certainly consist of warnings against the imperial tyrants with whom the figure of Nimrod was associated. As he knows, the community leaders he praises in *The Deserted Village*—the preacher and the schoolmaster—had anticipated him not only in the inculcation of the virtuous life but in the embodiment of it. They freely chose the life of continuity, maintaining the integrity of self by spanning generations in a single place and by communicating the spiritual truths that made their experience in time meaningful. Finding that the hunters have reached Auburn before the hare, the poet still carries out his tutelary obligation. He directs his warnings to readers of the poem rather than to the village swains. He fills the bulk of the poem with a detailed delineation of his loss: the games, work, rites of courtship, characters, and favored spots of the rural village. The irony of his unintended discourse, telling the oppressors about the victims rather than vice versa, underlies the sentimental tone (perhaps accounts for it), and emerges in the conclusion when honest poetic discourse itself is playfully dismissed as another victim of the tyrant's hand.

The disfigurement of a beloved object "capable of improving our sensations" leads to an elaborate simile:

> As some fair female unadorned and plain,
> Secure to please while youth confirms her reign,
> Slights every borrowed charm that dress supplies,
> Nor shares with art the triumph of her eyes;
> But when those charms are passed, for charms are frail,
> When time advances and when lovers fail,
> She then shines forth, solicitous to bless,
> In all the glaring impotence of dress:
> Thus fares the land, by luxury betrayed,
> In nature's simplest charms at first arrayed;
> But verging to decline, its splendours rise,
> Its vistas strike, its palaces surprise;
> While scourged by famine from the smiling land,
> The mournful peasant leads his humble band;
> And while he sinks, without one arm to save,
> The country blooms—a garden and a grave.   (287–302)

In this passage the city usurps the country, the place of change extends itself by means of wealth and vanity to the place of continuity.

The country had as its life-giving virtues typical customs and local scenes so regularly present that no remembered event could die out; past and present were simultaneous in the sense of general experience Goldsmith describes in the opening lines of the poem. But the physical alteration of a human community to a lifeless estate reminds the poet how change in landscape is linked to the ruin of a human community. Images of reversal operate in this passage for similar effects: splendor is decline, beauty is decay, the garden is a grave. Throughout *The Deserted Village* Goldsmith describes nature and the village by images of fragility—especially the blooming of fruits and flowers—and we see how this reversal of conventional associations of rural life (robust, invigorating) serves the theme of degeneration on both personal and historical levels.

In the passage above, for example, the land is compared to an aging woman. Comparisons of earth and woman are of course a poetic commonplace, and generally center on fertility and reproductive qualities as a basis for analogy. Goldsmith inverts this convention, insisting on the contrary implications of the metaphor: that woman's life is linear, historical, ended by death. In this new context, the land is "betrayed" by the seducer, luxury; for the land, unproductive luxury is equivalent to death. The earth is dislocated into human history, it dies into time. For this reason, the appropriate emblem of Auburn, signified visually in the frontispiece to the poem, is an old woman, a "widowed, solitary thing" who scavenges for food and fuel in a landscape as bereft of support as she. And when Goldsmith affixes to her the epithet that clearly belongs to himself, "the sad historian of the pensive plain" (36), we realize again that the historian of necessity participates in the ruin he or she traverses as a figure of mourning.

In *The Deserted Village* Auburn becomes recognizable as a lost Arcady. In 1769, while Goldsmith was composing his poem, Joshua Reynolds showed Samuel Johnson his newly completed portrait of Mrs. Bouverie and Mrs. Crewe seated before a tombstone whose inscription reads *Et in Arcadia Ego.* Johnson did not understand the graveyard sentiment, but if Goldsmith saw the picture he must have recognized the iconographic structure of his own poem, which insists on the conversion of a living community into a death's-head voicing despair from the internal spaces of the speaker's imagination. "Vain, very vain, my weary search to find / That bliss which only centres in the mind," Goldsmith wrote in *The Traveller* (423–24). The inward descent led him to the most familiar of eighteenth-century tableaux, a place covered by a tomb. In this sense, Goldsmith's confronting of the ruin of his worldly self is analogous to Johnson's denouement in *Rasselas.* In the penultimate chapter of that novel the travelers de-

scend into the Egyptian catacombs to gaze upon the mummified remains of a people who yearned for the everlasting above all things.
As the most terrifying stop on their journey it summons the most
fundamental questions about the meaning of life. Johnson guides
their conversation into an affirmation—not so hearty as we might
expect—of the immortality of the soul. Goldsmith's poem, after its
bereaved vision of the ruin of kingdoms in the penultimate verse
paragraph, seems to be proceeding also toward a religious affirmation.

But instead it ends with a witty address to Poetry which laments
that verse is "unfit, in these degenerate times of shame, / To catch the
heart or strike for honest fame." Goldsmith knows that he leaves
unanswered the crucial question, what is honest fame? "Honest
fame" like "inclement clime" was a cliché phrase of the period. As in
The Deserted Village it was often contrasted to monuments erected by
the tyrant's hand. An anonymous poem which appeared with Dyer's
Grongar Hill in a 1726 miscellany made a clear moral distinction:

> The lofty Pyramid that threats the Skies!
> For what august Possessor does it rise?
> You've there a little formless Mummy shown;
> A Human Carcase harden'd into Stone.
> Ascends for this the huge stupendous Tomb?
> For this includes whole Acres in its Womb?
> For this were drain'd the Tributes of the Nile?
> Was so much Treasure spent, and Time, and Toil?
>   Be pure my Heart, and upright be my Deed,
> Give me of Honest Fame a Pyramid;
> This grant me, Heav'n! and for my Monument
> My length of humble Earth; and I'm content.[17]

The "stupendous Tomb" is the same pyramid which Imlac deplores
in *Rasselas* as a monument to the insufficiency of human enjoyments.
Himself a poet, Imlac describes in chapter 10 of that novel the immense labors which a true poet must undertake in order to build a
reputation—honest fame—as enduring as the ancients'. "He must
divest himself of the prejudices of his age or country," Imlac maintains, "he must disregard present laws and opinions, and rise to
general and transcendental truths, which will always be the same."
Goldsmith's nostalgic poem accomplished these aims as a kind of
vengeance. Like the Jewish Prophet in *The Captivity* he assaulted
Babylon and laid to its sinister charge dispossession and exile. He
showed how in him and through him London had achieved more

than Babylon by extinguishing the terrestrial symbol of his redemption.

Because it can propose no solution, "sweet Poetry," including the bittersweet poem he has just composed, must in England become monumental, like the tombstone in Reynolds's painting. Poetry has none of the powers that Romantic poets will claim for it; it offers no religious comfort, no rebirth, no marriage of man's desire to external nature. Rather it is the verbal expression of the wound other poets must heal. Nothing is more characteristic of Goldsmith than the irony of this farewell. It is an attack on the commercial spirit which, by announcing the withdrawal of opposition, secures the power of Grub Street over the author. Those who followed, however, had at least *The Deserted Village* as a model for their increasingly serious accounts of journeys to a childhood place.

8 · Wordsworth at Grasmere

Ne'er can the way be irksome or forlorn
That winds into itself for sweet return.
                    —Departure from the Vale of Grasmere

Remembrance and Repetition

The Deserted Village, and poems like it, were ounces of white melancholy digested periodically by the English public to strengthen its constitution against an anticipated loss of awesome dimensions. Pessimism about the course of empire continued to provoke speculations of an apocalyptic cast in the latter part of the eighteenth century. Books of the four last things retained their large readership, joined in this age by historical scholarship that suggested lessons for England's future in ancestral models of imperial glory. The last chapter of Gibbon's *Decline and Fall of the Roman Empire* is both the type and culmination of Augustan monitions. Gibbon begins that chapter with the description by Poggius in 1430 of the ruins of Rome. Like Dyer some three centuries later, Poggius emphasizes the sublime horror of "shapeless and enormous fragments," the great edifices "prostrate, naked, and broken, like the limbs of a mighty giant and the ruin is the more visible, from the stupendous relics that have survived the injuries of time and fortune." Gibbon remarks ruefully that a single edifice like the Pyramids may survive indefinitely but "a complex figure of various and minute parts is more accessible to injury and decay." Though he is speaking of architecture, we know that he refers to civilization also, a complex of traditions and rites which even as he composed this chapter (in 1787) clearly was approaching a transformation. A belief in progress, he had suggested in his "General Observations on the Fall of the Roman Empire in the West," might

114

involve the art of being well-deceived, for the lesson of Rome is that human progress "has been irregular and various, infinitely slow in the beginning, and increasing by degrees with redoubled velocity; ages of laborious ascent have been followed by a moment of rapid downfall."[1] For those who imagined themselves the agents and caretakers of a progressive civilization these downfalls were a mockery of effort and faith. As the histories of Rome multiplied— Goldsmith wrote one while composing *The Deserted Village*—despair of national destiny deepened.

To the public at large the lessons of history tended to legitimize its withdrawal into smaller, more controllable spheres of concern. Retirement to a country seat offered one possibility, but a competing pleasure was the cultivation of "ideal property" as it came to be called. Real property possessed the same hazards as the empire, for historical change could desolate it, as Goldsmith had demonstrated. A landscape held in the mind was impervious to decay and benefited from the improvements of fancy. It was an accessible Good, a vision of the paradise to come as well as a remembrance of the paradise lost. For those who dealt regularly in the strife of commerce the landscape of reverie endowed absolute security. We find in periodical literature of the time a continuing celebration of painless nostalgia which soothes because it makes no claim for compensation on its sum-moner. Remembrance, we see in this commentary from *The Lounger* (1787), causes pleasure by revitalizing natural objects and beings:

Time mellows ideas as it mellows wine.—Things in themselves indifferent acquire a certain tenderness in recollection; and the scenes of our youth, though remarkable neither for elegance nor feeling, rise up to our memory dignified at the same time and endeared. As countrymen in a distant land acknowledge one another as friends, so objects, to which when present we gave but little attention, are nourished in distant remembrance with a cordial regard. If in their own nature of a tender kind, the ties which they had on the heart are drawn still closer, and we recal them with an enthusiasm of feeling which the same objects of the immediate time are unable to excite.... The hum of a little tune to which in our infancy we have often listened; the course of a brook which, in our childhood, we have frequently traced; the ruins of an ancient building which we remember almost entire; these remembrances sweep over the mind with an enchanting power of tenderness and melan-choly, at whose bidding the pleasures, the business, the ambition of the present moment fade and disappear.

Our finer feelings are generally not more grateful to the fancy than moral to the mind. Of this tender power which remembrance has over us, several uses might be made; this divinity of memory, did we worship it aright, might lend its aid to our happiness as well as to our virtue.[2]

Memory, condemned a century previous as the disjointed ruins of experience in the mind, a danger to sanity unless tamed by reason, has by Wordsworth's time become the preeminent contributor to human virtue and wisdom. When a literary critic like John Ogilvie makes this claim in his *Observations* (1774) there are few to dispute him: "It is therefore obvious that as Memory is by no means naturally subversive either of judgement or imagination, so these on the other hand are so far from being incompatible with it, that this last acquires its extent by an effort of the one, and becomes tenacious of particular objects in consequence of being accompanied by the other."[3]

In chapter three I discussed a scene in John Dyer's poem, *The Country Walk*, in which the appearance of a deer chases away the poet's ambitious thoughts. In the Lounger's remarks the "divinity of memory" provides the same kind of salvation by making "the ambition of the present moment fade and disappear." This transfer of grace to an act of the mind has ominous implications. Memory may, by its very power to influence imagination and judgment, vitiate sensual delight. A perceived tree competes for attention with a remembered tree, and if the latter has the advantage of tender emotion under it the outcome is predetermined. To avoid being overwhelmed by nostalgia, therefore, the landlord of ideal property must constantly seek living symbols of continuity which bind past and present in such a way as to secure the future as well. One favored symbol is people who sustain their peace of mind unchanged by fortune.

The Lounger is most Wordsworthian in the way he subsumes such persons into his description of "things in themselves indifferent." He is attracted in the present to figures who having no obvious reason for virtuous good spirits are nevertheless content. He searches for fellow stoics not among the wealthy or powerful, the empire-builders, but among the rejected and destitute. In a passage following that on memory he encounters an old soldier in the environs of London "leaning on a crutch, and rather accepting than soliciting the aid of the charitable." The soldier tells of suffering in foreign campaigns and of the ingratitude of his superiors. "But I forget and forgive, as the saying is; and, thanks to such as your Honour, I can make shift to live. It is true, I have seen others get halberts, ay, and commissions too, that were not better men than myself; but that don't signify. *It will be all the same an hundred years hence*" (italics in text). The "happy Stoicism" of the soldier delights the Lounger, for he testifies to man's ability to endure the decline of his kingdom without bitterness or despair. The old soldier, in other words, is not a *memento mori*. Neither his past misfortunes nor his present decay depress him. Like the memories the Lounger had just celebrated, the old soldier chases away ambition, and remains, through his forgiveness and gratitude, free.

The Lounger's interest in the soldier must be distinguished from, say, Defoe's portraits of social outcasts. Defoe is fascinated by the way people thrown back on hardship, like Roxana or Moll, better their condition by a relentless, often ruthless, will to climb above their oppressors. The absence of this ambition draws the interest of later writers; it corresponds to their own desire for relief both from the inward compulsion to improve and extend the self by professional effort, and from the demands levied upon them by England's eminence in global affairs. Wordsworth begins the major phase of his career by seizing upon unfortunate or decrepit figures and celebrating them—not simply as Stoics but as genii of place. He sees local history in them, the kind of history that provides a binding and solacing continuity of past and present. "Let us not rashly quit our hold upon the past," Hazlitt cried, "when perhaps there may be little else left to bind us to existence."[4] For Hazlitt and Wordsworth the significant past is composed of those particular, local, domestic figures who have impressed, in the Lockean sense, their presences upon the memory. Wordsworth bound himself to figures who, like the Waggoner in the poem of that name, were "living almanacks" of their locality and whose chartered rounds constituted a territorial boundary creative of human form.

The Old Cumberland Beggar is an especially significant figure. He points up the distance between the Lounger's needs and Wordsworth's, for the beggar does not, as even the Discharged Soldier in Book IV of *The Prelude* and the Leech-Gatherer do, offer obvious stoic assurances. To the eye of almost any writer before Wordsworth the beggar would teach a despairing lesson about the vanity of human aspirations and the frailty of flesh. Wordsworth, however, sees at least two important things about the beggar. He understands that the beggar represents all natural forms in a crucial way by not being of obvious use in social intercourse or social improvement. He produces nothing, he only consumes, and therefore his value, like that of the lilies of the field, must be measured by nonutilitarian means. If he is put to use by society then what is to prevent all of nature being put to use or sacrificed for end products as trivial as those the beggar would turn out in a "House—misnamed of Industry"? The beggar comes to symbolize, at the very least, unconscious animal being which even if incognizant of the beauty around it still participates in that beauty by its presence. Life, not consciousness, is his contribution. Where sensual deprivation is not so extreme, as in the old man of *Animal Tranquillity and Decay*, the example is enhanced in value. The character in that poem is "by nature led / To peace so perfect that the young behold / With envy what the Old Man hardly feels." The question of who the young should envy is of central importance in all of Wordsworth's writing, and this early expression anticipates the new kind of heroic argument that Romantic writers will introduce into English poetry.

Another effect of the Old Cumberland Beggar's presence is that

> While from door to door,
> This old Man creeps, the villagers in him
> Behold a record which together binds
> Past deeds and offices of charity
> Else unremembered, and so keeps alive
> The kindly mood in hearts which lapse of years,
> And that half-wisdom half-experience gives,
> Make slow to feel, and by sure steps resign
> To selfishness and cold oblivious cares.   (87–95)

The beggar is an outward symbol of the moderating power of memory, as the Lounger defined it. He is not only antiquity himself but he binds the past of each member of the community by the sympathy he enforces on them. The beggar preserves the kindly mood which, lacking objects of charity, would lose ground to the pressing claims of self-esteem and self-aggrandizement. Children especially must be instructed to give sympathy not for obvious material rewards but freely, for the pleasure of preserving animal life. The beggar, in this sense, is part of the ministry of love that Wordsworth describes in The Prelude, which "impregnates" the mind, to borrow his own suggestive metaphor, with feelings that will not have observable, measurable being until later in life.

It is not just local attachment, then, that underlies Wordsworth's poetic interest in a figure like the Old Cumberland Beggar. If he can demonstrate that the decrepit beggar more persuasively symbolizes life than death he can banish one more phantom from the reader's imagination. The beggar, after all, continues to live in the hearts of all who give him charity, and in the acts of kindness these people bestow on others. Just as other natural forms have a kind of immortal life— "woods decaying, never to be decayed"—(Prelude, VI.625), so the beggar overcomes time by remaining alive to those he bound in sympathy and love. In this sense he is like the Dalesmen that Leonard comments on in Wordsworth's poem The Brothers, composed a couple of years after The Old Cumberland Beggar. Leonard returns to his old village after a life at sea, and coming upon a priest in the local

churchyard, he inquires about the absence of monuments. The priest
replies:

> We have no need of names and epitaphs;
> We talk about the dead by our fire-sides.
> And then, for our immortal part! *we* want
> No symbols, Sir, to tell us that plain tale:
> The thought of death sits easy on the man
> Who has been born and dies among the mountains.
>
> (178–83)

Leonard replies, "Your Dalesmen, then, do in each other's thoughts /
Possess a kind of second life." Wordsworth added a note in 1800
which explains, "There is not anything more worthy of remark in
the manners of the inhabitants of these mountains, than the tranquillity, I might say indifference, with which they think and talk
upon the subject of death" (*PW*, II, 467–68). The divinity of memory
operates more effectively in a community whose visible history is
local and whose inhabitants gladly entrust their fame to oral tradition.

A graveyard scene in Book V of *The Prelude* clarifies the interaction of past and present, and Wordsworth's own part in the ongoing
process. It follows the Boy of Winander section (364–97), in which
Wordsworth has described how the Boy hooted to the owls and,
awaiting their response, received "unawares into his mind" the
whole and solemn imagery of the visible scene before him. The Boy
died in childhood, and as a youth the poet visited his grave. Now an
adult, he recollects in his "mind's clear eye" the burial place. Instead
of charnel horrors and darkness Wordsworth sets the scene in day-
light on a green hill where the Boy "slumbers" and, above him, the
local church, a "throned Lady," listens to the "gladsome sounds"
that ascend from a contiguous schoolyard. "May she long / Behold a
race of young Ones like to those / With whom I herded," Wordsworth prays. As readers we are not asked to grieve or fear, but
are comforted by the calm and naturalness that marked the graveyard
scene in *The Brothers*. Death does not radically sever one state from
another; the cycle of life passes on without agony. If we think of the
Boy of Winander as Wordsworth himself, which was his original
intention, we see a curious instance of self-perpetuation occurring in
the process of composition. The Boy is father to this man. The Boy is
resurrected first in his own body and made to repeat the actions
Wordsworth remembers having performed. In the next passage the
playmates by their feverish energy, "mad at their sports," sustain the
Boy's mimic hootings after his death; the "Lady" connects them in

space and time. Wordsworth wrote in his preface to the Poems of
Imagination: "Guided by one of my own primary consciousnesses, I
have represented [in *There Was a Boy*] a commutation and transfer of
internal feelings, co-operating with external accidents to plant, for
immortality, images of sound and sight, in the celestial soil of the
Imagination."[5] Though "immortality" here means something akin to
"infinite extension," the term profits by its ambiguity. Drawing on
sublime experiences like these, Wordsworth can resurrect the Boy not
only in himself but in those successors who, like the poets he foresees
in the opening of *Michael*, will be a "second self when I am gone."

The perpetuation of life by oral and written records remains an
obsessive concern of Wordsworth's mature work. The principal life
he wishes to preserve is of course his own, either directly or through
the use of dramatic *personae* like the Boy of Winander. Wordsworth is
a perpetual analyst of such memories, not as a technician who murders to dissect but as a map maker who apprehends the minute particulars of a landscape traversed only once. To sustain this mental
concentration Wordsworth required an extraordinary bodily constitution, one that struck De Quincey by its "animal sensibility superior to
that of most men, diffused through *all* the animal passions (or appetites)."[6] As it happened, the first scientific experiments aimed at dis-
covering the effect of experience on the brain were performed in the
1780s. The conclusions, then as now, were that enriched experience
in early life, especially increased opportunities for play, increase both
the weight of the cortex and the number of synaptic junctions in it. In
a highly sensitive child like Wordsworth, removed from an unhappy
family situation at age nine to the release of an ecstatic schooltime in
Hawkshead, the physiological effect of his newly enriched experience
must have been profound, altering the chemistry of his being in ways
he attempted to describe all his life. Wordsworth's concern with the
"impressive discipline" (*Prelude*, I.603) of nature's ministry makes use
of the metaphors empirical psychologists employed for the impressions of experience, the wax and *tabula rasa* on which the lineaments of
external nature are reproduced and retained. Wordsworth's revalua-
tion of the body originated in the superb confidence he had in his own
sensitivity to sights and sounds planted "for immortality." Chris-
topher Salvesen makes the point that "memory was, for Wordsworth,
a sensuous mode of experience—first made apparent to him through
the sense of sight, becoming more calm and diffused through a general sense of being."[7]

Memory itself owes its sensuous power to repetition. In
Wordsworth's universe something acquires value by being repeated
in thought or act, as often as possible. When Wordsworth praises the

paradise of his childhood we note the unique insistence he gives to repetition. The italics are mine.

> —And if the vulgar joy by its own weight
> Wearied itself out of the memory,
> The scenes which were a witness of that joy
> Remained in their substantial lineaments
> Depicted on the brain, and to the eye
> Were visible, *a daily sight;* and thus
> By the impressive discipline of fear,
> By pleasure and *repeated* happiness,
> *So frequently repeated,* and by force
> Of obscure feelings representative
> Of things forgotten, these *same scenes* so bright,
> So beautiful, so majestic in themselves,
> Though yet the day was distant, did become
> *Habitually* dear, and all their forms
> And changeful colours by invisible links
> Were fastened to the affections.   (I.597–612)

This insistence reversed the dominant attitude of two centuries. William Drummond of Hawthornden spoke for his time (1623) when he asserted that "one year is sufficient to behold all the magnificence of nature, nay even one day and night, for more is but the same brought again."[8] Intensity of experience, it was assumed, depended on variety and quantity of images, not increased familiarity. The satire on rural society in these centuries owed much of its point to the narrow range of experience encountered by all the Tony Lumpkins who dwelt away from the city. Because the mind's vitality depends on novelty, rural residence would depress wit and increase melancholy. The graveyard writers, who usually did live in the country, seemed to be obliging examples of the prejudice. They tended to view repetition as a sordid boon which by exhausting man's attachment to sensual objects turns his loyalty away from sensual pleasures. Edward Young puts the case in *Night Thoughts:*

> Ere man has measured half his weary stage,
> His luxuries have left him no reserve,
> No maiden relishes, unbroach'd delights;
> On cold-served repetitions he subsists,
> And in the tasteless present chews the past;
> Disgusted chews, and scarce can swallow down.   (III.316–21)

In a nostalgic writer like Cowper we see a movement away from such attitudes, but with residual allegiance to them. In Book I of *The*

Task he conducts Mary Unwin to a familiar prospect, described in rural imagery (groves, rivers, hedgerows) identical to Wordsworth's Wye Valley scene in *Tintern Abbey*. The vista is preceded by a catalogue of youthful attributes whose degeneration in time Cowper laments. He then takes care to point out that he is "still unsated" by nature. His admiration is increased, in fact, because

> Scenes must be beautiful, which, daily view'd,
> Please daily, and whose novelty survives
> Long knowledge and the scrutiny of years.   (177–79)

The assumption is that long knowledge does bring satiety but that in this instance Cowper has escaped it. The singularity of the scene is emphasized further when he remarks in the same book:

> It is the constant revolution, stale
> And tasteless, of the same repeated joys,
> That palls and satiates, and makes languid life
> A pedlar's pack, that bows the bearer down.
> Health suffers, and the spirits ebb; the heart
> Recoils from its own choice—at the full feast
> Is famish'd.   (462–68)

Though Cowper refers here to the languid life of society, he applies the sentiment, in the passage immediately following, to prospects and views of the "shelter'd vale" as well.

The situation of *Tintern Abbey* differs from that of Cowper's daily prospect; Wordsworth has not seen the Wye Valley for five years. But we know from his other work that even daily repetition does not weary his sight; on the contrary, he considers a continuity of sensations essential for well-being. *Tintern Abbey*, like Cowper's passage, admits to certain bodily changes and confesses also a "sad perplexity" caused by the vagueness of his memory. But the very dimness of his recollection leads him to express a renewed delight in the scene before him. The stamping-in of this second impression will give him "life and food for future years," a metaphor perhaps chosen as a rebuttal to Cowper's "tasteless" joys and Young's "cold-served repetitions." At the conclusion of the poem, Wordsworth turns to his younger sister, Dorothy, and expresses gratitude for her presence: "in thy voice I catch / The language of my former heart, and read / My former pleasures in the shooting lights / Of thy wild eyes." She gives a second life to the poet's extinguished past. She recapitulates or repeats his being, as the schoolboys do the Boy of Winander's, and the poet's second self does in *Michael*. [9]

The distinction of Wordsworth from Cowper is significant because Wordsworth's appreciation of the need for repetition at first
conflicted with a craving for novelty akin to Cowper's. His earliest
poetry imitates the "country walk" tradition of *The Task* in which
discrete impressions of picturesque nature are bundled together. On
a hurried trip through Europe in 1790, Wordsworth realized that the
rapid shifts of scene, rather than nourishing the imagination, made
few or no enduring pathways in his brain. "Ten thousand times in the
course of this tour," he wrote Dorothy, "have I regretted the inability
of memory to retain a more strong impression of the beautiful forms
around me." "Every new picture was purchased by the loss of
another," he complains in the same letter. In desperation he would
return to the most remarkable views and concentrate on them, hop-
ing, as he said, to impress them deep enough "that perhaps scarce a
day of my life will pass [in] which I shall not derive some happiness
from these images" (*Letters*, I, 35–36). Wordsworth identifies the condition in which the eye is master of the soul as the particular plague of
adolescence, a state of being that creates a thirst for novelty leaving
the youth parched and melancholy. He can neither concentrate on
nor retain any object or purpose. And without "unfading recollections" (*Prelude*, I.491) the youth will all his life possess only a mechanical ability to value people, places, and things.

When Wordsworth describes this "thraldom" in *The Prelude*
(XII.127–51), he relies deliberately on political metaphors. The bodily
eye is "the most despotic of our senses," it exercises "tyranny" and
holds the profounder powers of the mind "in absolute dominion." At
this dangerous time of life

> I roamed from hill to hill, from rock to rock,
> Still craving combinations of new forms,
> New pleasure, wider empire for the sight.

This psycho-political disease is the state of mind which he as a prophetic poet seeks to reform. It is the remnant in him of the eighteenth
century itself. Novelty imagined as a multiplication of spatial objects
is the will-o-the-wisp, the "fleeting good" Goldsmith pursued in *The
Traveller*, and compared to the retreating horizon, "That, like the circle, bounding earth and skies, / Allures from far, yet, as I follow, flies"
(27–28). Wordsworth's emphasis on the habitual repetition, in
thought and act, of local perceptions underlaid with affections, carries
with it a critique of imperial politics. People seek quantity as a good
because they lack the satisfaction which discrimination of thing from
thing, action from action, makes possible. If repeated access to the

124 RUINS AND EMPIRE

affections is not permitted, then people, places, and things are only a desert of phenomena dancing dreamlike before the senses. Their novelty of form and feature invites acquisition, but like Blake's maiden in *The Crystal Cabinet*, they retreat before the grasp when their "inmost form" becomes an object of sensual desire. The tyrannical will seeking "wider empire for the sight," like Mozart's Don Giovanni, accumulates new conquests "pel piacer di porle in lista," to add them to the list. Memory, through its guiding power of homesickness, enlightens the will and turns it back to the primordial landscape in which the creative spirit abides.

Grasmere and Stonehenge

Ultraviolet photography has revealed that the cave paintings of Lascaux, Pech Merle, and other Paleolithic sites were retraced again and again by successive generations of primitive artists. Wordsworth is like these artists, retracing in his memory and by his senses the outward (then inward) forms that awakened and amplified his consciousness. It is apparent, then, that revisitation of his childhood paradise would come to be an obsessive desire of his adult life. This desire for renewed contact with the fostering spirit of place necessarily coincides with the inception of Wordsworth's most ambitious poetic work. As Geoffrey Hartman notes, "the existence of a Genius loci . . . is intrinsically related to vision and prophecy: to determining the destiny of an individual or a nation."[10] Even before the publication of the *Lyrical Ballads* in 1798 Wordsworth felt a "paramount impulse not to be withstood" (*Prelude*, I.240) to compose a long poem. As he confesses in the opening paragraphs of *The Prelude* he had no idea of what subject his great project (tentatively called *The Recluse*) was to consist. *The Recluse*, in fact, was Coleridge's conception and, it was understood by both poets, would be largely dependent on Coleridge's notes. These notes were not then, or ever, forthcoming. In the first few hundred lines of *The Prelude*, which are commonly dated 1798–99, Wordsworth laments his inability to write a long poem on either a historical or philosophical subject, having no "perfect confidence" (I.162) in either area.

Following the composition of the introductory passages, William and Dorothy established residence at Grasmere, a small vale in the Lake District. Grasmere was a scene of Wordsworth's childhood raptures, beginning in his ninth year, while attending school in nearby Hawkshead. With Goldsmith's unhappy experience in mind, Wordsworth confessed some anxiety about the return. The "Vale" he addresses in this sonnet is a composite of several childhood shelters:

> "Beloved Vale!" I said, "when I shall con
> Those many records of my childish years,
> Remembrance of myself and of my peers
> Will press me down: to think of what is gone
> Will be an awful thought, if life have one."

In fact, the return had the effect of validating the high value
Wordsworth had given to remembrance and revisitation in poems
like *Tintern Abbey*. The sonnet concludes:

> But, when into the Vale I came, no fears
> Distressed me; from mine eyes escaped no tears;
> Deep thought, or dread remembrance, had I none.
> By doubts and thousand petty fancies crost
> I stood, of simple shame the blushing Thrall;
> So narrow seemed the brooks, the fields so small!
> A Juggler's balls old Time about him tossed;
> I looked, I stared, I smiled, I laughed; and all
> The weight of sadness was in wonder lost.   (PW, III, 2)[11]

They discovered not Father Time with his scythe, but the genius of
the place, here imagined as a kind of merry Prospero holding the
forces of time in check. The "Vale" was secure from the ravages of
change, still nursing the natural forms Wordsworth had known and
loved in childhood, those he had endued with his own vitality and
thereby bound to him as emblems of his self.

Wordsworth had never actually lived in Grasmere before but the
opening of his long poem, *Home at Grasmere*, states that his enthusiasm for the secluded vale began when he came upon it as a
roving schoolboy. In 1794, at age twenty-four, he adapted a Horatian
ode in praise of retirement as a vehicle for his own fondness for
Grasmere. *Septimi Gades* is addressed to Mary Hutchinson, whom he
later married, and recalls for her "that delicious spot obscure" which
will one day be their home (PW, I, 296).[12] Wordsworth's removal to
Grasmere, then, fulfills the need for a country seat illuminated by his
past history. The vale is in this sense

> A termination, and a last retreat,
> A Centre, come from wheresoe'er you will,
> A Whole without dependence or defect,
> Made for itself; and happy in itself,
> Perfect Contentment, Unity entire. (*Home at Grasmere*, 147–51)

To celebrate his return, Wordsworth composed in the spring of
1800 the blank verse encomium, *Home at Grasmere*. It was further

identified by him, in manuscript, as "The Recluse. Part First. Book First." As Ernest de Selincourt suggests, "It is clear that in its initial stages Wordsworth regarded his spiritual autobiography [The Prelude] as an integral part of The Recluse, and not as a separate poem preparatory to it. . . . It seems likely that until the early months of 1800 . . . the history of his early life was not viewed as an independent work."[13] Apparently it was revisitation of his childhood locale that shocked him into a full recognition of the one theme upon which he could write with perfect confidence: the circular odyssey of the poetic soul back to the natural sources of its creativity. Wordsworth substantiates by homesickness his vision of "Unity entire." That specter of abstract philosophy, The Recluse, is put aside, postponed until the personal epic of the poet's spiritual journey could be completed.

Also put aside is the possibility of "some old / Romantic tale by Milton left unsung" (I.168–69). There had been no decrease in the fondness for historical poems and fictions by the English public, but by Wordsworth's time a certain satiety had set in. Perhaps the prose histories, like Gibbon's and Hume's, had stamped in the pessimistic view of man's progress too deeply. When John Ogilvie wrote the advertisement to his antiquarian poem, The Fane of the Druids, in 1787 he felt it necessary to distinguish his positive treatment of Druid civilization from the usual history:

It is not without reason that we complain of the general histories of nations, as giving us so much reason to detest the species, by offering to our view successive scenes of wars, massacres, and devastations, from which the feeling heart recoils with horror: while man, simple and independent in his original state, establishing gradually, from rational motives, government and subordination; deviating, by a process almost imperceptible in its movement, from the boldness of innocence into the chicanery of artifice; and from the simplicity of nature into the refinements of policy; remains wholly unknown to us.[14]

Wordsworth knew that his great project, whatever its subject, would have as its aim the truth of human nature. We can assume that he had the ability to write a historical narrative. Even after his creative powers began to wane he wrote a thoroughly competent historical poem, The White Doe of Rylstone (1815). But he lacked an essential interest in antiquarian themes. During the first years of the French Revolution, Wordsworth and Michel Beaupuy had discussed the application of Roman models to the new French republic, but the defeat of the Girondists by the Catilines of Paris, the Jacobins, and the renewal of Caesarism marked by Napoleon's ascendancy had made a mockery of Wordsworth's humanism. He would not indulge in serious study of the Roman histories again until the period of his pamphlet on the Convention of Cintra (1809). At the turn of the century Wordsworth devoted his exclusive attention to the history that inhered in local places, the traditions and legends gathering at a particular spot or about some natural object. The ruin at Hart-Leap Well and the decayed sheep-fold of *Michael* aroused his story-telling faculties, not the columns of Trajan. To write expertly and truthfully in that historical vein he had to return to the Lake District.

The circular pattern which returns the protagonist of a long poem or fiction to his homeland is an enduring structural device of all narrative art. Coleridge believed that "the common end of all *narrative,* nay, of *all* Poems, is to convert a *series* into a *Whole:* to make those events, which in real or imagined History move on in a *strait* line, assume to our Understandings a *circular* motion—the snake with its tail in its mouth."[15] Wordsworth elevates the importance of his return by granting it the status of myth: he conceives himself as Adam reentering paradise. Eighteenth-century writers employed the conceit of "Paradise" for a pleasure garden so casually that the term by itself carries little significance. Wordsworth develops the conceit, however, he exploits the mythic potential Milton gave to the comparison when he located his Garden of Eden in an earthly place. That Grasmere is paradise we are told repeatedly in *Home at Grasmere,* and Wordsworth retained the term in later years. He invited William Sotheby (in 1804) to visit "the hidden wonders and little boudoirs of our Paradise, such as flying travellers [like Wordsworth in 1790] know nothing about" (*Letters,* I, 456). "What a beautiful spot this is! the greenest in all the earth," Dorothy enthuses in another letter (*Letters,* I, 393).[16] The vale is not only Edenic, Wordsworth remarks in *Home at Grasmere,* it is better than Eden, because Adam and Eve could not rediscover their paradise; they had never longed for it, as William and Dorothy had done. The presence of Dorothy at Grasmere was an essential aspect of Wordsworth's successful revisitation, because she participated in his natural education as a child and was also responsible for his restoration to Nature following his self-destructive lapse into the flux of historical events in France. Wordsworth can therefore pay tribute to Dorothy as a perfect female counterpart to his male, a completion of the whole life represented by the vale. Far from the ruin Goldsmith confronted, Wordsworth has discovered the beloved landscape of his most profound yearning:

> —What Being, therefore, since the birth of Man
> Had ever more abundant cause to speak
> Thanks, and if favours of the heavenly Muse

> Make him more thankful, then to call on verse
> To aid him, and in Song resound his joy.
> The boon is absolute; surpassing grace
> To me hath been vouchsafed; among the bowers
> Of blissful Eden, this was neither given,
> Nor could be given, possession of the good
> Which had been sighed for, ancient thought fulfilled
> And dear Imagination realized
> Up to their highest measure, yea and more.   (98–109)

The structure of *Home at Grasmere* is a series of images which suggest how the vale becomes an emblem of one creative mind, its physical properties extensions of the poetic intelligence that perceives them. The self-enclosed and self-sufficient vale embodies the "one interior life" that Wordsworth describes in a manuscript fragment of this period:

> —In which all beings live with god, themselves
> Are god, existing in one mighty whole,
> As indistinguishable as the cloudless East
> At noon is from the cloudless west, when all
> The hemisphere is one cerulean blue.[17]

The images of activity and rest in *Home at Grasmere* are associated with recurring or unchanging phenomena; there is no significant object in the poem which Wordsworth would not have met with in his childhood. By evoking these perennial images of continuity, as Goldsmith could not, Wordsworth preserves a unified, even godlike, self experienced as landscape. The purposive manner in which he compares the vale to heaven, to the sky and stars, underscores his insistence that this "symbol of Eternity and Heaven"[18] embodies the cosmic unity that is the poet's dream. Images of reflection (in Grasmere Lake) which link heaven and earth into one being, generalized descriptions of "warm woods, and sunny hills, and fresh green fields" (127) which contrast to the closely observed forest scenes in the 1805 *Prelude,* the dream imagery that clouds over distinctions—all these suggest a world removed from time and change, a fairyland in which the poet seems to be Prospero and Adam in the same flesh.

Wordsworth composed another poem with mythic aspirations during his first year in Grasmere. *Song for the Wandering Jew* contrasts the satisfactions of home with the anxiety that we know Wordsworth experienced before his revisitation. Six quatrains (one of them added in 1827) show us in turn, torrents, clouds, a Chamois, a Sea-horse, a

Raven, and an Ostrich, all by their very nature finding the home comforts they seek. The last stanza turns to the human species:

> Day and night my toils redouble,
> Never nearer to the goal;
> Night and day, I feel the trouble
> Of the Wanderer in my soul.

Only the title, very likely an afterthought, associates the Wandering Jew with the poem. Why did Wordsworth bring in this figure at all? According to legend (not the Gospels), the Wandering Jew mocked Jesus on the road to Calvary and was told by the angry Christ that he must abide on earth until the Last Judgment. The legend is thus another ectype of the Fall, in which a prideful man is driven into exile because of an impious action. Shelley conceives the Wandering Jew in *Queen Mab* as the victim of a jealous God who stamps his oppressive pattern on all social institutions. Coleridge and Wordsworth, less overtly polemical, used the legend to dramatize human depravity, outside the social context in *The Rime of the Ancient Mariner*, and on its fringes in Wordsworth's drama, *The Borderers*.

Wordsworth identified the spiritual despair of the Wandering Jew, the "trouble" of the above stanza, with his own miserable wanderings after the triumph of the Jacobins in France and England's declaration of war against the republic had together dispossessed him of a place where he could settle his affections. His most compelling symbolic landscape of that trouble is the Salisbury Plain, which he traversed on foot in 1793 and where he set his long poem of 1793–94, *Salisbury Plain*.[19] That poem describes a character called the "traveller," with whom the poet feels such a close affinity that his authorial voice opens the poem with the first person plural:

> The thoughts which bow the kindly spirits down
> And break the springs of joy, their deadly weight
> Derive from memory of pleasures flown
> Which haunts us in some sad reverse of fate,
> Or from reflection on the state
> Of those who on the couch of Affluence rest
> By laughing Fortune's sparkling cup elate,
> While we of comfort reft, by pain depressed,
> No other pillow know than Penury's iron breast.   (19–27)

This formulation follows Goldsmith's lead: remembrance turns the past to pain, a process conjoined to a national ambience where wealth accumulates and men decay. As Auburn is Goldsmith's culminating symbol of desolation so the Salisbury Plain, "more wild and more forlorn" (61), becomes the inevitable path of Wordsworth's nameless victim.

On the plain he encounters a "female wanderer" who completes the terms of Goldsmith's prophecy by recounting how she and her father, once the rural tenants of a "hereditary nook" were dispossessed: "His all was seized; and weeping side by side / Turned out on the cold winds, alone we wandered wide" (260–61). The daughter marries and starts a family; the happy father dies; but more hard times force the young couple and their children to Goldsmith's "horrid shore," America. There she loses her whole family to disease and famine, and returns to England broken in body and spirit. Wordsworth repeats this dramatic situation in his poem of 1795–96, *The Ruined Cottage*, where a wanderer is told the story of Margaret, a miserable woman abandoned by her husband who joins the foreign service. By the end of the poem the "tranquil Ruin" the wanderer beholds incorporates Margaret's fate, and, to the extent she represents her class, the fate of the rural poor as well.

Wordsworth's figure of the wanderer, then, is a witness to the depravity of thought and act which sacrifices human beings to imperial policy. By his own exposed situation the wanderer in *Salisbury Plain* becomes a sacrificial victim in turn. When Wordsworth revised the poem in 1795 to the version entitled *Adventures on Salisbury Plain* he made the desperately poor wanderer rob and kill a man; at the end of the poem he dies on the gallows. Wordsworth had used the theme of human sacrifice in a long juvenile lyric, *The Vale of Esthwaite*, in which he confronts some putative Druid remains in the Lake District. The posturing in that poem owes much to the Gothic revival and especially to the example of William Collins's *Ode to Fear*. In *Salisbury Plain*, however, an older and poorer Wordsworth turns to eighteenth-century models with a better understanding of the political themes underlying the ruin sentiment. When the wanderer makes his way to Stonehenge, a disembodied voice warns him of that ruin's horror in lines which deliberately recall John Dyer's passage from *The Ruins of Rome* beginning "The pilgrim oft / At dead of night, 'mid his oraison hears / Aghast the voice of time." Wordsworth's passage is this:

> "For oft at dead of night, when dreadful fire
> Reveals that powerful circle's reddening stones,
> 'Mid priests and spectres grim and idols dire,

> Far heard the great flame utters human moans,
> Then all is hushed: again the desert groans,
> A dismal light its farthest bounds illumes,
> While warrior spectres of gigantic bones,
> Forth-issuing from a thousand rifted tombs,
> Wheel on their fiery steeds amid the infernal glooms."   (91–99)

As a rule Wordsworth is not, like Dyer, taken aback by huge and mighty forms, nor distressed by the sublime prospect of vacant time they arouse in the observer's mind; even Wordsworth's juvenile poems show an enthusiasm for such vistas. But the vision at Stonehenge, recalled again in Book XIII of *The Prelude*, links past and present under the aspect of tyrannical oppression. The "powerful circle" of Stonehenge recalls Dyer's concentric images of the Colosseum, a place of human sacrifice surrounding its victims on every side. Wordsworth's use of the Spenserian stanza calls attention to the deadly echoes: reddening stones, human moans, desert groans, gigantic bones. Stonehenge is the emblem of England's mad Leviathan. As he wrote in the Advertisement to the poem, when it finally emerged in its final draft as *Guilt and Sorrow* (1842):

The monuments and traces of antiquity, scattered in abundance over that region, led me unavoidably to compare what we know or guess of those remote times with certain aspects of modern society, and with calamities, principally those consequent upon war, to which, more than other classes of men, the poor are subject.

As the most remote man-made forms that Britain possessed, these megaliths make civilization and violence coeval historical entities. Stonehenge becomes a native memento of the Fall.

If this is so, then the male and female wanderers of Salisbury Plain are a version of Adam and Eve as victims, like the Wandering Jew in search of some resting place. Wordsworth probably has in mind the situation of himself and Dorothy in 1793, dispossessed and yearning for some permanent home removed from the monuments of despotism. In a letter of that year, Dorothy uses Goldsmith's poem of exile, *The Traveller*, to describe the feelings of attraction between her and William:

We have been endeared to each other by early misfortune. We in the same moment lost a father, a mother, a home, we have been equally deprived of our patrimony by the cruel Hand of lordly Tyranny. These afflictions have all contributed to unite us closer by the Bonds of affection notwithstanding we

Stonehenge, by John Constable. Crown Copyright. Victoria and Albert Museum.

have been compelled to spend our youth far asunder. "We drag at each
remove a lengthening Chain" this Idea often strikes me very forcibly.

(Letters, I, 88)

The Wordsworths were unwilling to remain within this evil. By returning to Grasmere, Wordsworth hoped to escape the whole ruins of
tyrannic history, of which Stonehenge remained in his imagination
the persistent emblem. But Salisbury Plain and its shades, its "warrior spectres," continued to haunt Wordsworth in many forms, even
in his regained refuge. In *Home at Grasmere* and *The Prelude* terms like
"waste" and "wilderness" join city and Plain, and because "the living
and dead wilderness / Of the thronged world" (*Home*, 613–14) values
quantity above all things, no obscure nook can be wholly safe from
violation. It takes only the most superficial sense of historical inevitability to recognize the dangers in the grandiose claims made for "A
Whole without dependence or defect." Grasmere, no less than Auburn, did not live without dependence, and it is only a dreamer's
paradise that does. In 1807 Wordsworth had "Great Pan himself"
speak comforting words in a sonnet: "Be thankful, thou; for, if unholy
deeds / Ravage the world, tranquillity is here!" (*PW*, III, 127). But by
that time his first enthusiasm had been shaken, as the "abyss" that
yawns in the opening of the sonnet suggests. It is not just Napoleonic
threats of invasion that disturb his peace. We shall see in chapter ten
other shades creep across the protective home of the poet's soul.

Whatever his second thoughts, however, Wordsworth never re-
pudiated the salvation which this return represented. In his essay,
"Letter to Mathetes" (1809–10), Wordsworth took up the question of
human progress, which writers like Gibbon had construed pessimis-
tically. Wordsworth claims that progress in the species is not direct
like a Roman road but "may be more justly compared to that of a
River, which both in its smaller reaches and larger turnings, is frequently forced back towards its fountains, by objects which cannot
otherwise be eluded or overcome." What seems to be a downfall or
regression may actually be a gathering of energy from an original
source which "contributes as effectually to further [the river] in its
course, as when it moves forward uninterrupted in a line" (*Prose*, II,
11). He might have cited as a personal example his revisitation of
Grasmere. He had regained in body the ideal property preserved and
strengthened by memory. But after the proper exultation what progress, what flow of purpose could result? The poet watches the
aquatic fowl fly in circles above the lake, an emblem of that activity
characteristic of a vigorous mind. In their "tracing and retracing that
large round" (211) they show Wordsworth the concentric force of his

own active memories, welling restlessly in him since his revisitation of the Lakes, and even before then. In what way can he give creative vent to these "spots of time," as he will call them in *The Prelude*? If *Home at Grasmere* is a prelude to *The Prelude*, we see in this question the beginning of the project that ends in Grasmere itself.

The aquatic birds are "inmates... Of Winter's household" but undaunted "they keep festival" (194–95) and express their joy in all seasons. Their exuberance contrasts to the dreariness of Stonehenge in *Adventures on Salisbury Plain*, described as the "inmate of lonesome Nature's endless year" (157). Stonehenge is an inmate in the institutional sense, condemned to a life sentence by the tyrants who performed human sacrifice there. The Grasmere birds wheel in a motion "whose way / Is a perpetual harmony, and dance / Magnificent," but Stonehenge is the site of a whirlwind, the demonic version of concentric grace. "Winds met in conflict," Wordsworth wrote in a revision, "each by turns supreme." The warrior specters that "wheel on their fiery steeds amid the infernal glooms" return to beat upon the victimized wanderers. Can those specters pursue them even into paradise? In *Home at Grasmere* he describes at some length a human voice from the mountains that summons the sheep home but which Wordsworth perversely converts by "superstitious fancy" into a demonic cry, the voice of man's trouble. Like Dyer in *The Fleece*, Wordsworth must reassure the reader that his pastoralism attends to the real expressions of human nature:

> I look [in Grasmere] for Man,
> The common Creature of the brotherhood
> Differing but little from the Man elsewhere,
> For selfishness, and envy, and revenge,
> Ill neighbourhood—pity that this should be—
> Flattery and double-dealing, strife and wrong.   (352–57)

The "Demoniac" voice speaks for the wilderness within and without, but the warning is both needful and bracing. Against this voice Wordsworth decides to raise his own prophetic song and through poetry overcome in others the errors he overcame in himself.

Dame Nature, for not unselfish reasons, endorses his preservative instinct. At the end of *Home at Grasmere* she advises the poet:

> "Be mild and cleave to gentle things,
> Thy glory and thy happiness be there.
> Nor fear, though thou confide in me, a want
> Of aspirations that *have* been, of foes
> To wrestle with, and victory to complete,

> Bounds to be leapt, darkness to be explored,
> All that inflamed thy infant heart, the love,
> The longing, the contempt, the undaunted quest,
> All shall survive—though changed their office, all
> Shall live—it is not in their power to die."   (735–44)

At the end of his troubled wanderings, still haunted by a lost civilization's ruins, Wordsworth turns back to a kindred spirit, Edmund
Spenser, and borrows from his *Mutabilitie Cantos* both the figure and
the argument he needs for solace. The last two lines of the above
passage reflect Dame Nature's summary in Spenser's philosophic
poem:

> I well consider all that ye [Mutabilitie] have sayd,
> And find that all things stedfastnes doe hate
> And changed be: yet being rightly wayd
> They are not changed from their first estate;
> But by their change their being doe dilate:
> And turning to themselves at lengthe againe,
> Doe worke their owne perfection so by fate:
> Then over them Change doth not rule and raigne;
> But they raigne over change, and doe their states maintaine. (VII.58)

Spenser considered himself, as an artist, an agent of the fate by which
all things are preserved from the oblivion which change and loss
threaten in every age. Wordsworth, having like all the other things
of nature turned to his true self again, borrows this hope from
Spenser as well. The medium of verse will be the element he must
wrestle with, and that struggle itself will represent the onward flow of
creative life which, he told Mathetes, would inevitably follow a return
to sources of spiritual power. His poetry will be continuous with his
home landscape and from that center he will preach of preservation
and continuity.

9 The Arab Rider

The City of Man

WORDSWORTH DIRECTS a simple prayer to his vale in *Home at Grasmere:*

> Embrace me then, ye Hills, and close me in,
> Now in the clear and open day I feel
> Your guardianship; I take it to my heart;
> 'Tis like the solemn shelter of the night.   (110–13)

The simile recalls the grammar of graveyard literature, in which the sheltering night forces thought inward and allows the writer to commune with his immortal soul. By insisting on "the clear and open day" as one term of the comparison, however, Wordsworth attempts to join together the most positive aspect of graveyard literature—its endorsement of man's insatiable quest for enduring life—with his own location of that life in the everyday garden of Grasmere. Grasmere is a "symbol of Eternity and Heaven" because it offers within its small topographical compass an infinitude of hills, trees, flowers, animals, and people—all catalogued in the poem as potential objects of his ever-expanding imagination. "Objects gross and the unseen soul are one," Whitman wrote in his *Song for Occupations,* and Wordsworth, like the American poet, sees his task in life as a binding of the one with the other as "inmates" of his terrestrial paradise.

Grasmere, then, is not an imprisoning place but a liberating one. According to Wordsworth, man is most fettered when he is homeless, wandering, at the mercy of political forces which add more weight to the lengthening chain. Wordsworth resorts to prison imagery whenever he describes an overwhelming of the creative will by some landscape associated with historical change. Notebook entries for *Salisbury Plain* imagine Stonehenge as a kind of Bastile for unwary travelers. "That stupendous monument / Has closed them in its black immensity" is one of several variations.[1] In the poem Wordsworth traces the horror back to its origin, the seat of empire, and watches its malign effects radiate outward:

> From the pale line to either frozen main
> The nations, though at home in bonds they drink
> The dregs of wretchedness, for empire strain,
> And crushed by their own fetters helpless sink,
> Move their galled limbs in fear and eye each silent link.   (446–50)

As in Wordsworth's epistemology, so in his politics. Quantity confines and limits; the landscape which is apparently confined (like Grasmere) is capable of inifinite spiritual expansion.

The philosophy of quantity, Goldsmith's "fleeting good," assumes that man can will his own and his nation's freedom, and find in the enjoyment of that freedom the satisfaction of his fundamental desires. Hannah Arendt, in a discussion of this belief, cites Thomas Paine's remark, "To be free it is sufficient [for man] that he wills it." Lafayette applied the principle to the nation-state: "Pour qu'une nation soit libre, il suffit qu'elle veuille l'etre." Arendt then describes the malign effects when this belief is translated into action:

It is . . . as though the moment men *willed* freedom, they lost their capacity to *be* free. In the deadly conflict with worldly desires and intentions from which will-power was supposed to liberate the self, the most willing seemed able to achieve was oppression. Because of the will's impotence, its incapacity to generate genuine power, its constant defeat in the struggle with the self, in which the power of the I-can exhausted itself, the will-to-power turned at once into a will-to-oppression. . . . The fact that an I-will has become so power-thirsty, that will and will-to-power have become practically identical, is perhaps due to its having been first experienced in its impotence. Tyranny at any rate, the only form of government which arises directly out of the I-will, owes its greedy cruelty to an egotism utterly absent from the utopian tyrannies of reason with which the philosophers [like Plato in *The Republic*] wished to coerce men and which they conceived on the model of the I-think.[2]

The I-think represents the channeling of the will into speculative reverie and discourse, the states of dream and poetry that Wordsworth affirms for himself in *Home at Grasmere*. His seclusion in Grasmere resembles in one sense the logic of Plato's allegory of the cave, in which the truth seeker must dwell in sunlit exile from his fettered and deluded fellows, but Wordsworth differs from Plato in his adherence to material objects as sources of spiritual nourishment. In so doing, he commits himself to the defense of such objects, by means of his art, from the pure expressions of the I-will.

In *Home at Grasmere*, then, Wordsworth necessarily concludes his praise of enduring objects with an attack on the forces which threaten their endurance:

> Say boldly then that solitude is not
> Where these things are: he truly is alone,
> He of the multitude whose eyes are doomed
> To hold a vacant commerce day by day
> With objects wanting life, repelling love;
> He by the vast Metropolis immured,
> Where pity shrinks from unremitting calls,
> Where numbers overwhelm humanity,
> And neighbourhood serves rather to divide
> Than to unite.   (592–601)

He had described the presences of Grasmere in celestial imagery throughout; they are "blessed" and "angelic." But from his prospect he looks out at the numbers who "overwhelm humanity," whose impotence has been intensified and made desperate by captivity in the city until they seem to threaten war in heaven itself. *The Prelude*, concerned with the distinction of spiritual weakness and power, attempts to separate in Wordsworth's own life the complex attractions of the I-will and the I-think. By 1800 he had already composed many of the famous "spots of·time" that give the poem its great lyrical beauty. After his revisitation of Grasmere, he decided to draw these episodes into a larger discursive structure and make of the whole a prophetic work, one that combined vision and monition. There are two principal forces, according to the poem, that oppress and disintegrate the "true self" (XI.342) he had rediscovered in Grasmere. One is the city, and the other, political action. They are connected by the power they possess to overwhelm the I-think in humanity.

The city requires less discussion because Wordsworth's approach to it is more conventional. He grants to London a physical beauty that belies its internal mechanism. The domes and bridges he praises in a poem like *Composed on Westminster Bridge* reflect, as they nourish, the creative spirit. The visitor to London receives "a sense / Of what in the Great City had been done" (VIII.625–26), a majesty and power which in certain moments exalts him as effectively as does nature's ministry. This, it must be said, is an advance over Cowper's withering comparisons of London with Babylon and Sodom in poems like *Expostulation* and *The Task*. But on the whole the two poets see the metropolis alike, as more degrading than uplifting. In Cowper's memorable analogy, the city is like a cheese teeming with mites, its activity a measure of its corruption (*Prose*, p. 575). When Luke travels to the city, in *Michael*, Wordsworth's readers need only a few lines to encapsulate his fall, so conventional and inevitable is that event in an eighteenth-century pastoral.

The opening lines of *The Prelude* are characteristic of Wordsworth's attitudes. The poet has been a "captive" in the city, which is "a prison where he hath been long immured" (1805 version). His carefully nurtured natural self has been repressed and perverted in the city but now " 'tis shaken off, / That burthen of my own unnatural self." The poet characteristically asks first where he can retire, what "harbour" or refuge, to allow the paramount impulses of his newly released imagination a congenial outlet. The city is compared (in 1805) to "the tiresome sea" which the poet has quitted to dwell on shore; he yearns for those palpable and permanent objects of affection that make up the catalogues in *Home at Grasmere*. Recent scholarship has now established that the refuge he refers to in this preamble of November 1799 is almost certainly Grasmere.[3]

Wordsworth's aversion to the city derives partly from his former desire for it. The young poet who wrote "I begin to wish much to be in town; cataracts and mountains are good occasional society, but they will not do for constant companions" (*Letters*, I, 136), sought from the city what sociologists, adapting Schiller's definition, call "disenchantment." Disenchantment is part of the breakdown of primitive consciousness. Primitivism depends on a magical view of natural phenomena, which perceives the world as an inclusive cosmological system in which everything has life, in which objects have indwelling spirits who exercise influence over the thoughts and actions of human beings and are in turn influenced by them. Disenchantment seeks to exorcise the divinity of natural objects and thereby liberate the mind from magical terrors and restrictions. Wordsworth felt the power of cataracts and mountains from an early age, but according to his record in *The Prelude* these presences could not be recognized in their true form until they were submitted to the competing forces of novelty. He describes in Book VII the fascination London had for a country boy, "living cheerfully abroad / With unchecked fancy ever on the stir, / And all my young affections out of doors" (74–76). His mobility is purely pedestrian; he walks through the streets collecting impressions as he had walked through the Lake District. He assumes, without worrying about it, that his London rambles extend the seedtime and by quantity enhance the natural forms already implanted in his Imagination.

Wordsworth's first reaction to London is that it disappoints his expectations. He had thought of it as some "Fairy-land" and allowed his fancy to work upon images imbibed from books and conversation, until the real London could only de-dramatize them. The disenchantment, then, worked opposite to his intentions. Nothing is surprising in this turn of events, but we ought to notice that his poetic response is necessarily a satire on the giant urban forms. He defensively criticizes the very features which tantalized his fancy, but which in reality threatened to overwhelm his provincial habits of mind. We can measure the limited scope of his chronicle by comparing it briefly to Balzac's account of young Eugène de Rastignac in *Père Goriot*. Rastignac engages the city on its own terms in order to discover its unique magic. Moving beyond the sordid surroundings of the Maison Vauquer, he locates the life-enhancing spirit of Paris, Society, in her extravagantly beautiful native landscape. As Wordsworth would distinguish the "Nature" of Salisbury Plain from the "Nature" of the Lakes, so Balzac distinguishes Parisian wilderness from Parisian paradise. The women Eugène pursues in the Faubourg Saint-Germain "personified for him the sort of beauty he had before seen only in dreams." To attain these creatures he must, like them, become enchanted by a Satanic ambition. The rewards are intense and ecstatic pleasures, the cost a perpetual yearning for aggrandizement: "The demon of luxury gnawed at his heart, a fever for gain seized him, a thirst for money dried his throat." Beauty and anxiety heighten each other's potency; in order to rise above the temperate life of his fellows Eugène must descend into moral sloughs. Like Roxana, Eugène confirms his damnation by worldly success. "I am in hell," he tells a friend at the novel's conclusion, "and I have to stay there. Whatever evil you are told about society, you can be sure it's true. It would take more than a Juvenal to describe the horror under the gold and the jewels."[4]

Balzac may or may not be more than a Juvenal but Wordsworth is certainly less. Perceiving no essential vitality in London he participates in no magical attraction. He "filled / An idler's place; an idler well content / To have a house (what matter for a home) / That owned him" (VII.71–74). And yet his limited experience of London illuminates a significant condition of urban life that the enchanted Balzac overlooks. By never engaging the city on its own terms, by remaining a tourist, he could intensely feel and exhaustively record the disorganized mechanism of its daily activity:

> How often in the overflowing Streets,
> Have I gone forward with the Crowd, and said
> Unto myself, the face of every one
> That passes by me is a mystery.
> Thus have I look'd, nor ceas'd to look, oppress'd

> By thoughts of what, and whither, when and how,
> Until the shapes before my eyes became
> A second-sight procession, such as glides
> Over still mountains, or appears in dreams;
> And all the ballast of familiar life,
> The present, and the past; hope, fear; all stays,
> All laws of acting, thinking, speaking man
> Went from me, neither knowing me, nor known.
> (1805 version, VII.594–606)

In this pastoral epic the country boy's visit to London corresponds to the conventional descent into hell. Not Balzac's hell of ever-increasing thresholds of pleasure but the hell of anonymity and confusion. The self, overwhelmed by the external apparitions of passing faces and forms, grows as phantomlike as they. More than a century before *The Waste Land*, Wordsworth documented the alienation of deracinated man ("all stays, / All laws . . . / Went from me") from the oppression of the city. When he describes the city the catalogue of appearances is not constructed in his characteristic rhetoric, one that emphasizes the process by which external and internal modes of being intertwine; rather, the city forces on the individual consciousness a condition in which the bodily eye, "the most despotic of our senses," gains such strength by the advantage of novelty that it holds the mind in absolute dominion. The rhetoric of Book VII of *The Prelude* ("Residence in London") resembles the frantic itemization of new sights that Wordsworth sent back to Dorothy during his first trip to Europe. His verse is a deliberate parody of that mode, a mode he associates with his own early travelogues, *An Evening Walk* and *Descriptive Sketches*:

> Now homeward through the thickening hubbub, where
> See, among less distinguishable Shapes,
> The Italian, with his frame of Images
> Upon his head; with Basket at his waist
> The Jew; the stately and slow-moving Turk
> With freight of slippers piled beneath his arm.
> Briefly, we find, if tired of random sights
> And haply to that search our thoughts should turn,
> Among the crowd, conspicuous less or more,
> As we proceed, all specimens of Man.   (1805 version, 227–36)

> Here there and everywhere a weary Throng
> The Comers and the Goers face to face,
> Face after face; the string of dazzling Wares,
> Shop after shop, with Symbols, blazon'd Names,

> And all the Tradesman's honours overhead;
> Here, fronts of houses
>
> . . . .
>
> There, allegoric shapes, female or male.
>
> (1805 version, 171–79)

A heap of broken images, "all jumbled up together" as he says of the Parliament of Monsters he finds at Bartholomew Fair. The parody works two ways, like the mock romance of Cervantes. The structure of random images, a "train of ideas" Locke called them, is satirized by being identified with a mental state of utter confusion—"Oh, blank confusion! a type not false / Of what the mighty City is itself" (1805 version, 695–96)—and the city is satirized by being described in a style reflective of an overwhelmed intelligence.

Batholomew Fair is the scene of Wordsworth's most extravagant caricature, and the most disjointed verse he ever wrote. The fair emblematizes the urban horror he described in *Home at Grasmere*: "vacant commerce day by day / With objects wanting life, repelling love." Bartholomew Fair shows us trade, the exchange of multitudinous objects, by means of its own fragmenting empirical form. A direct influence on Wordsworth, perhaps, is a passage in Dyer's *The Fleece*, where the poet, against the best interests of his argument, surrenders his prosodic control. "Augusta" here is London:

> To these thy naval streams,
> Thy frequent towns superb of busy trade,
> And ports magnific add, and stately ships
> Innumerous. But whither strays my Muse?
> Pleased, like a traveller upon the strand
> Arrived of bright Augusta: wild he roves
> From deck to deck, through groves immense of masts;
> 'Mong crowds, bales, cars, the wealth of either Ind;
> Through wharfs, and squares, and palaces, and domes,
> In sweet surprise; unable yet to fix
> His raptured mind, or scan in ordered course
> Each object singly; with discoveries new
> His native country studious to enrich.   (I.172–84)

Nothing could be more apt than Dyer's comparison of his muse to a foreign traveler who seeks to aggrandize his native treasury. Dyer's muse is cosmopolitan, deracinated. Wordsworth's, by contrast, is always Mnemosyne, or Memory, the mother of all the other muses in classical myth. His muse remains at home and thereby blends in his imagination with Dame Nature, who provides his soul and his art with more than the wealth of either Ind; he was "bred up 'mid Nature's luxuries . . . in daily intercourse / With those crystalline rivers, solemn heights, / And mountains" (III.354–56). Just as his mind was composed by harmony, so his verse proceeds from a unified sensibility, internal memories and external nature experienced as one. Only for satirical effect does he borrow the balances from Spenser's egalitarian Giant and like the city itself create a secondary world of lifeless shapes and images.

Perhaps Wordsworth is not so far from Juvenal after all. Coleridge recalled in 1832 that when Wordsworth conceived the idea of a long poem it was his intention to describe "the pastoral and other states of society, assuming something of the Juvenalian spirit as he approached the high civilization of cities and towns, and opening a melancholy picture of the present state of degeneracy and vice."[5] But it is useful to remind ourselves that Wordsworth's total view of London appears in retrospect one of the most judicious and even-handed of his contemporaries'. Blake is more savage in his lyric *London* and in his description of Los's walk through London in *Jerusalem* (31:2–43), where he sees "every Minute Particular of Albion degraded & murder'd." De Quincey is more savage in his address to Oxford Street in the *Confessions:* "stony-hearted stepmother, thou that listenest to the sighs of orphans and drinkest the tears of children."[6] Wordsworth withheld images of human sacrifice because London, in his scheme of *The Prelude* as in his life, preceded a more harrowing vision of oppression.

Ruins and Revolution

The metaphors of tyranny by which Wordsworth communicates his experience of London derive from his entire vision of the human condition; not only because the philosophy of quantity has imperial implications, but because the city as a human fabrication is by its nature a model of oppression. Hannah Arendt comments:

An element of violence is inevitably inherent in all activities of making, fabricating, and producing, that is, in all activities by which men confront nature directly, as distinguished from such activities as action and speech, which are primarily directed toward human beings. The building of the human artifice always involves some violence done to nature—we must kill a tree in order to have lumber, and we must violate this material in order to build a table. In the few instances where Plato shows a dangerous preference for the tyrannical form of government, he is carried to this extreme by his own analogies. This, obviously, is most tempting when he speaks about the right way to found new communities, because this foundation can be easily seen in the light of another "making" process. If the republic is to be made by somebody who is the political equivalent of a craftsman or artist, in accordance with... the rules and measurements valid in this particular "art," the tyrant is indeed in the best position to achieve the purpose.[7]

It was obvious to the young Wordsworth that the accumulation of men in cities, as later in factories, violated the laws of nature. Communities must be limited in size, and the artifacts made within them must be organically related to the whole life of the area. The sheepfold and spindle in *Michael* are perfect Wordsworthian symbols of such artifacts; they provide for the necessities of survival and therefore signify the primordial democracy of the vale.

Wordsworth's enthusiasm for the French Revolution, according to *The Prelude*, emerged from his philosophical discussions with Beaupuy, and their agreement that the laws of external nature and human nature were constant and informative one to the other. This was, in fact, the fundamental tenet of moral philosophy during the Enlightenment. In his influential book, *The Ruins* (1791), C. F. Volney had a divinely appointed legislator announce that "there existed in the regular order of the universe, and in the physical constitution of man, eternal and immutable laws, which only required his observance, in order to render him abundantly happy."[8] The new spirit of progress, radiating outward from Paris to the whole of mankind, would create an immortal state by illuminating the system of values implanted by God for man's enduring benefit. These values—of which equality is paramount—would preserve and perfect man and society. None would wish to abrogate or challenge them. This new myth of the immortal state differed from earlier versions by substituting knowledge for power as an instrument of preservation. The I-think underlies its imperial hopes, not the I-will.

Volney patterns some of his ideas on Plato's *Republic*, particularly his attack on luxury, which parallels that of Socrates in every way. The fate of nations that do indulge in luxury, and thereby violate the immutable laws within their breasts, is surveyed in the haunted ruins which give the book its title. Writing after the fall of the Bastille, Volney relates the ruins he visits to French, as Dyer and Spenser did to English, fortunes. Volney takes heart from speeches by the Genius of Liberty affirming that natural law would urge the populace to active construction of a new pyramid—not an artifact of vanity but a "pyramid of the legislators." This would consist of an eternally stable society of governors, responsive to the people forming its supportive base. This iconographic conception is typical of the Enlightenment, or at least of the French *philosophes* who, looking backward into history, perceived little more than the ruined artifacts of past tyrannies, and therefore looked forward instead.

The Revolution had as its goal the figurative trampling of these ruins into dust. "Empire is no more," Blake cried, and imagined the liberation in dances of "females naked & glowing with the lusts of youth" (*America*, 15:22). The French painter, Hubert Robert, used the same image in his canvas *Young Girls Dancing around an Obelisk* (1798), in which a train of maidens is set against a background of three pyramids, an obelisk, and a sphinx. The art of this time is full of a joyful destruction of monuments. To the revolutionary spirit all of history, preserved in architecture, amounted to a monument of tyrannical cruelty. Robert Southey, in *Joan of Arc*, has his hero speak for the mood of vengeance in Southey's own time:

> "Perish these mighty ones,"
> Cried Conrade, "these who let destruction loose,
> Who walk elated o'er their fields of fame,
> And count the thousands that lie slaughtered there,
> And, with the bodies of the innocent, rear
> Their pyramid of glory! Perish these,
> The epitome of all the pestilent plagues
> That Egypt knew, who send their locust swarms
> O'er ravaged realms, and bid the brooks run blood!
> Fear and destruction go before their path,
> And Famine dogs their footsteps. God of justice!
> Let not the innocent blood cry out in vain!"[9]

Southey's hero wants to match ravage with ravage, crime with crime, though the agent of destruction will be God. Southey appeals constantly in his work of this period to the example of the Puritan revolution. The model in the above passage is Milton's sonnet, *Avenge O Lord thy slaughter'd Saints* and beyond it the whole Samson-like force of Milton's revolutionary imagination. Milton's star rose to unparalleled heights during the republican enthusiasm because he was part of the prophetic experience that Southey, like Wordsworth and Blake, required for the dismantling of the Satanic temple:

> For by experience taught shall man at length
> Dash down his Moloch-idols, Samson-like,
> And burst his fetters.[10]

The destruction of the Bastille had been the first such overthrow, and opponents of the Revolution, like Edmund Burke, foresaw that the logic of the Puritan example would lead to regicide and the emergence of a military leader as powerful as Cromwell.

Defenders of the Revolution could not themselves decide how to value the event in relation to previous history. They wanted to convince the doubtful that the Revolution did in fact originate in historical examples (like the Puritan) and evolutionary principles. That is the argument of Mary Wollstonecraft's *An Historical and Moral View of the Origin and Progress of the French Revolution* (1794). With one eye on Burke's objections, she argues that Versailles and all it symbolizes was a ruin even before the revolutionaries occupied it, and though she grants that the French Assembly had "suffered themselves to be hurried forward by a multitude on whom political light had too suddenly flashed," she traces that light back to the very constitutional principles that Burke himself had defended in the debate over the American colonies.[11] Even before the Bastille fell, Richard Price had assured his audience at the Old Jewry that forces were at work that would reshape human destiny, and that their effects would be limitless (italics in text):

The observations now made may be of use in assisting you to form just ideas of the progressive course of human improvement. Such has it hitherto been; and such the natures of things assure us it must continue to be. Like a river into which, as it flows, new currents are continually discharging themselves, it must increase till it becomes a wide-spreading stream, fertilizing and enriching all countries, and *covering the earth as the waters cover the sea.*[12]

The Revolution confirmed Price's belief in the progressive growth of enlightenment, and he celebrated its inception in another speech at the Old Jewry, a discourse known to us now principally through Burke's attacks on it in his *Reflections on the Revolution in France.*

Though writers like Wollstonecraft and Price attempted a melioristic view, there were others, principally the poets, who preferred the apocalyptic account. The Revolution, in this view, is a providential occurence that will establish eternally a new heaven and new earth, as prophets like Isaiah, Peter, and John had promised. Christ would rule on earth and man return to the pastoral simplicity he had lost when the Fall sent him into the wilderness of history. Blake's *Songs of Innocence* is certainly the purest expression of this dream, a green world nourished and watched over by the Sun of the Divine Vision. This Sun, like Wollstonecraft's, flashes "political light" on the multitude; it is not the sun by which fallen man measures his decay but a timeless Sun. Blake distinguishes the material sun (Apollo or Satan) from the spiritual Sun (Jesus), and affirms in his work that only the former shines in the cycles of history. The new earth has a new sun. Wordsworth added a passage to his first published poem in 1794 with a similar sentiment. He addresses the spirit of the sun:

> Spirit who guid'st that orb and view'st from high
> Thrones, towers, and fanes in blended ruin lie,
> Roll to Peruvian vales thy gorgeous way
> See thine own temples mouldering in decay,
> Roll on till hurled from thy bright car sublime
> Thyself confess the mighty arm of Time
> Thy star must perish, but triumphant Truth
> Shall tend a brightening flame in endless youth.   (PW, I, 20)

The sun belongs to the creation myths of past civilizations; human sacrifices were made to it by the Druids of all continents. It is the icon of ruined empires, the sign of tyranny. And so time must destroy it, for time has brought a new source of illumination, truth. Southey has a similar sentiment in *Wat Tyler* (1793), in which the hero, John Ball, prophesies that "The destined hour must come / When it [truth] shall blaze with sun-surpassing splendor."[13]

Wordsworth, when he traveled through France in the summer of 1790, and when he returned in November of 1791, would have located the center of this new political light in Paris. Paris remained a holy city in Wordsworth's imagination all his life, the promise of its first blazing hopes a prefiguration of the New Jerusalem he later transferred to a place beyond the grave. The apocalyptic views cited above derived directly from the most powerful of the prophetic writings in the Western world, the Revelation of St. John the Divine. In chapter 21 John imagines a transfigured city:

And the city had no need of the sun, neither of the moon, to shine in it: for the glory of God did lighten it, and the Lamb is the light thereof.

And the nations of them which are saved shall walk in the light of it: and the kings of the earth do bring their glory and honour into it.

And the gates of it shall not be shut at all by day: for there shall be no night there.   (21:23–25)

Those poets who had the vision of truth paid homage to it in their later work, even after disillusionment with the events in France. Wordsworth's Solitary, who experienced the bliss of revolutionary enthusiasm, is given in *The Excursion* the vision of a "mighty city" patterned after John's. And Blake became the forger of Golgonooza, the City of Art, which rightly seen "is the spiritual fourfold London in the loins of Albion" (*Milton*, 20:40).

It is the apocalyptic belief that a new heaven and a new earth lay within man's grasp that accounts for Wordsworth's movement of mind from the speculative to the prescriptive, from the I-think to the I-will. He was convinced that the Revolution was "nothing out of nature's certain course" (*Prelude*, IX.247), that far from being one more turn in the cycle of empires it portended an immortal state in which truth not tyranny would reign. He joined his sympathies with a political force so that the London he visited in 1790 and resided in during 1791 would not be in its oppressive form the city of the future. In *Descriptive Sketches*, his long poem of 1793, Wordsworth concluded with hopes that the Revolution would spread throughout the world. His images for the Revolution are the conventional ones of the "master pamphlets of the day" (IX.97), light and deluge.

> —Tho' Liberty shall soon, indignant, raise
> Red on his hills his beacon's comet blaze;
> Bid from on high his lonely cannon sound,
> And on ten thousand hearths his shout rebound;
> His larum-bell from village-tow'r to tow'r
> Swing on th' astounded ear it's dull undying roar:
> Yet, yet rejoice, tho' Pride's perverted ire
> Rouze Hell's own aid, and wrap thy hills in fire.
> Lo! from th' innocuous flames, a lovely birth!
> With it's own Virtues springs another earth
>
> . . . .
>
> Oh give, great God, to Freedom's waves to ride
> Sublime o'er Conquest, Avarice, and Pride
>
> . . . .
>
> And grant that every sceptred child of clay,
> Who cries, presumptuous, "here their tides shall stay,"
> Swept in their anger from th' affrighted shore,
> With all his creatures sink—to rise no more.   (*PW*, I, 88–90)

In his poem, *Destruction of the Bastille* (1789), Coleridge addressed freedom with the same hopes:

> And wider yet thy influence spread,
> Nor e'er recline thy weary head,
> Till every land from pole to pole
> Shall boast one independent soul!   (35–38)

Wordsworth and his contemporaries had decided to participate in the founding of a new and universal republic, and, as Hannah Arendt points out, the readiest model for such foundations is the tyrannic one. In these early poems the rhetoric of imperialism comes easily to their pens. The tone is not speculative but vindictive; it threatens annihilation to all defenders of the old civilization.

One example will be sufficient. Richard Watson, bishop of Llandaff and a countryman of Wordsworth's, issued a pamphlet in 1794 which contained a critique of the Revolution. Watson had formerly supported the aims of the republic but the execution of the king alarmed him and caused a reversal of position. "Other nations may deluge their land with blood in struggling for liberty and equality," he warned his readers, "but let it never be forgotten by ourselves, and let us impress the observation upon the hearts of our children, that we are in possession of both." Wordsworth answered Watson's charges in an essay not published during his lifetime, *A Letter to the Bishop of Llandaff on the Extraordinary Avowal of his Political Principles ... by a Republican*. Wordsworth begins the letter by consigning the bishop to the same fate as the "sceptred child of clay" in *Descriptive Sketches:* "It is feared you have at last fallen through one of the numerous trap-doors, into the tide of contempt, to be swept down to the ocean of oblivion." The bishop, he goes on, has withdrawn himself from the real world of suffering and oppression, and lost sight of "the eternal nature of man." The Revolution expresses that nature and will eventually bring it to perfection. Wordsworth defends the violence of the Terror as the "overflow of spirits" to be expected from any animal newly released from its stall.[14] Like Wollstonecraft, he excuses such excess as an overabundance of political light. As he later described it in *The Prelude:*

> And above all—for this was more than all—
> Not caring if the wind did now and then
> Blow keen upon an eminence that gave
> Prospect so large into futurity;
> In brief, a child of Nature, as at first,
> Diffusing only those affections wider
> That from the cradle had grown up with me,
> And losing, in no other way than light
> Is lost in light, the weak in the more strong.   (XI.164–72)

The bishop represented a decayed civilization, a dark ruin, that radical change would enlighten by altering manners, art, and institutions. The light would grow "more strong" by making use of the most destructive passions. Though less radical, Mary Wollstonecraft affirmed the same principle:

Every nation, deprived by the progress of its civilization of strength of character, in changing its government from absolute despotism to enlightened freedom, will, most probably, be plunged into anarchy, and have to struggle with various species of tyranny before it is able to consolidate it's liberty; and that, perhaps, cannot be done, until the manners and amusements of the people are completely changed.[15]

"Civilization," we notice, is debased as a concept in this remark by the concluding reference to "manners and amusements," as if the two were synonymous. Wordsworth uses the same strategy in his *Letter* when he dismisses the aristocratic milieu of the bishop as an emasculated mockery of the "eternal nature" which the Revolution promises to resurrect.

The first years of the Revolution, then, even its bloodshed, satisfied Wordsworth's imperial desires. He understood the Terror as

> a terrific reservoir of guilt
> And ignorance filled up from age to age,
> That could no longer hold its loathsome charge,
> But burst and spread in deluge through the land.   (X.477–80)

He left France in December of 1792 for a number of reasons. One is that his family made it clear that he could not depend on them for more money unless he returned to England. Another is that the poet's remoteness from actual power, a power he craved to exercise, dissipated some of his revolutionary enthusiasm. The declaration of war by England against the republic shortly afterward, and then the foreign campaigns, when "now, become oppressors in their turn, / Frenchmen had changed a war of self-defence / For one of conquest" (XI.206–08), plunged him into despair of all worldly action. The images of hunting, human sacrifice, catastrophe, and uprooting which dominate the French Revolution sections of *The Prelude* express his disenchantment in retrospect.

In Book IX of *The Prelude* Wordsworth provides the character of a royalist officer to illustrate the ruinous effect of wholehearted dedication to political life. The portrait is worth quoting in full, along with its disillusioning effect on Wordsworth, who some fifty lines previous described himself as "unconcerned, / Tranquil almost, and careless as a flower / Glassed in a green-house" (IX.86–88):

                          One, reckoning by years,
Was in the prime of manhood, and erewhile
He had sate lord in many tender hearts;
Though heedless of such honours now, and changed:
His temper was quite mastered by the times,
And they had blighted him, had eaten away
The beauty of his person, doing wrong
Alike to body and to mind: his port,
Which once had been erect and open, now
Was stooping and contracted, and a face,
Endowed by Nature with her fairest gifts
Of symmetry and light and bloom, expressed,
As much as any that was ever seen,
A ravage out of season

                          .   .   .   .

                          'Twas in truth an hour
Of universal ferment; mildest men
Were agitated; and commotions, strife
Of passion and opinion, filled the walls
Of peaceful houses with unquiet sounds.
The soil of common life, was, at that time,
Too hot to tread upon. Oft said I then,
And not then only, 'What a mockery this
Of history, the past and that to come!
Now do I feel how all men are deceived,
Reading of nations and their works, in faith,
Faith given to vanity and emptiness;
Oh! laughter for the page that would reflect
To future times the face of what now is!'
The land all swarmed with passions, like a plain
Devoured by locusts,—Carra, Gorsas,—add
A hundred other names, forgotten now,
Not to be heard of more; yet, they were powers,
Like earthquakes, shocks repeated day by day,
And felt through every nook of town and field.   (139–80)

The royalist officer is one of those figures, like Bishop Watson, who stood against the tide of Revolution, but the difference in Wordsworth's treatment is absolute. Wordsworth wrote this section in 1804, in Grasmere, after more than a year of invasion threats had spurred him to a sequence of defensive poems against the imperial power of France. When he looks back on the royalist he sees him as a vulnerable landscape, "admirably fair" in the early draft and revised to "endowed by Nature with her fairest gifts" as Wordsworth himself grew into the overmastered figure of the royalist himself. History is no longer "nothing out of nature's certain course," but is a ravaging of natural beauty, "doing wrong / Alike to body and to mind." The royalist belongs to the same figurative nexus as the Convent of Char-treuse, which nature's voice tries to protect from "riotous men" in Book VI. In that book Wordsworth imagines the Revolution as a "State-whirlwind" which, like the locusts in the passage quoted above, devastates the land. This is the France of Burke's *Reflections*, "the fresh ruins of France" dispossessed of its great civilization by the mad passions of the Jacobins: "Laws overturned; tribunals subverted; industry without vigour; commerce expiring; the revenue unpaid, yet the people impoverished; a church pillaged, and a state not relieved; civil and military anarchy."[16] The presiding "powers" in Words-worth's passage are not those spirits which bind man and nature in unity, as in *Home at Grasmere*, but Girondist and Jacobin lead-ers who kill and are killed by those who themselves are sacrificed at the guillotine. The warrior spirits that Wordsworth had seen at Stonehenge in 1793, and accused as demonic specters of English im-perialism, now were the only bulwark against powers of annihilation swarming across the English Channel. The extraordinary patriotism of his *Poems Dedicated to National Independence and Liberty* derives from his fears of invasion, but their extreme militance can only be ex-plained by his refusal to have himself and his vale, the "Centre" of his soul and art, ravaged by the same overpowering force he had once cheered into being. He still looked to Providence for deliverance, but now it was from the deluge itself he wished to be delivered.

The fall of the Bastille, radiating outward in effect, inaugurated what came to be known as the *révolution en permanence*, the unend-ing social disequilibrium that constitutes modern politics. The idea of everlasting revolution became, in an ironic way, the "inheritance" passed from generation to generation that Burke called the prime requisite of a civilization. The French experience of liberation did not lead, as Wordsworth hopefully predicted in his *Letter to the Bishop of Llandaff*, to a secondary construction of freedom, consisting of univer-sal suffrage and decreasing autonomy of the chief executive. The Revolution never discovered its boundaries, as the American Revolu-tion did in composing the Constitution and the Bill of Rights. The Revolution instead embodied the principle of infinite expansion and ended by adopting the imperial model it had formerly deposed. Given its commitment to a new heaven and a new earth it could not do otherwise. It became, as Wordsworth wrote of the city, a uniform mass having "no law, no meaning, and no end" except spatial exten-sion, a desire to overwhelm all of time and space. The end result, he realized in Grasmere, might be a universal wilderness in which, all consumed, the age would fall back to old idolatry.

The Dream of the Deluge

Book V of *The Prelude* opens with an enigmatic dream-vision which all critics of Wordsworth agree is central to his narrative of the growth of the mind, but which possesses an anagogical complexity of reference that defies definitive interpretation. The most common reading relates the dream to Wordsworth's discussion of the function and operations of the creative imagination in Book V.[17] His biographer, Mary Moorman, believes that the dramatic structure and symbolism of the dream belong to the period of nightmares and "ghastly visions" (X.402) he underwent during 1794. "It is clearly a 'Revolution dream,'" she writes.[18] My own opinion should not be in doubt by this time. I would place the dream, if it actually occurred, sometime during Wordsworth's residence in Grasmere, when his fears of being overwhelmed seemed to reach panic proportions. The threat of invasion can be termed the final cause of the dream, but Napoleon and his armies would not have terrified Wordsworth so much if the first consul (then emperor) did not appear to be an embodiment of "perpetual emptiness, unceasing change" threatening from all sides (*PW*, III, 116). It *is* a Revolution dream but its anxiety belongs to the later period of the Revolution, the one Wordsworth recalled in his *Ode* of 1816 as he contemplated the Spirit of France:

> My soul, a sorrowful interpreter,
> In many a midnight vision bowed
> Before the ominous aspect of her spear
>
> . . . .
>
> So did she daunt the Earth, and God defy!
> And, wheresoe'er she spread her sovereignty,
> Pollution tainted all that was most pure.   (*PW*, III, 123–24)

It is Napoleon's master, the imperial will in all men, the I-will itself, that Wordsworth dramatizes in his dream.

The dream is prefaced by an expression of sorrow that man, who "hast wrought, / For commerce of [his] nature with itself, / Things worthy of unconquerable life" should have to live with the knowledge that these things must perish.[19] The sentiment is a conventional one; it appears throughout Spenser's *The Ruines of Time* and before that in poems like Petrarch's *The Triumph of Time*. Wordsworth, however, is not talking about the oblivion that passing time inflicts; he has in mind an apocalyptic catastrophe:

> A thought is with me sometimes, and I say,
> Should earth by inward throes be wrench'd throughout,
> Or fire be sent from far to wither all
> Her pleasant habitations, and dry up
> Old Ocean in his bed left sing'd and bare,
>
> . . . .
>
> The consecrated works of Bard and Sage,
> Sensuous or intellectual, wrought by men,
> Twin labourers and heirs of the same hopes,
> Where would they be?

The fire "sent from far" recalls the biblical narratives of the flood and the destruction of cities like Sodom for wickedness. The book of Revelation and millennial thinking in general inform the dream and suggest a divinely imposed punishment for current evils. The language and above all the tone resemble the apocalyptic claims in anti-Jacobin writing of the decade preceding the composition of Book V. Burke's imagination of disaster had been no less prophetic in its warnings than *Descriptive Sketches* or Coleridge's *The Destiny of Nations* in their advocacy. The conservative view was that an unparalleled catastrophe had fallen upon France. "The very elements of civilization have been destroyed in a moment, and society itself disbanded," proclaimed one periodical.[20] And the same fate threatened England.

As the dream itself opens, the fire seems already to have taken place. The dreamer is in an "Arabian Waste, / A Desert" and a "wide wilderness." Again, the immediate connection is to the prophetic books:

For the LORD shall comfort Zion: he will comfort all her waste places; and he will make her wilderness like Eden, and her desert like the garden of the LORD.   (Isaiah, 51:3)

The waste land can be, paradoxically, Zion and Babylon, the city under the curse of God for its worship of false idols:

Your mother shall be sore confused; she that bare thee [idolators] shall be ashamed: behold, the hindermost of the nations shall be a wilderness, a dry land, and a desert.

Because of the wrath of the LORD it shall not be inhabited but it shall be

wholly desolate: every one that goeth by Babylon shall be astonished, and
hiss at all her plagues.   (Jeremiah, 50:12–13)

The desert is an iconographic equivalent of Wordsworth's city, a "picture" that can "weary out the eye" (VII.731). Wordsworth associated
the two in the 1805 *Prelude:* "And now it pleas'd me my abode to
fix / Single in the wide waste" (VII.75–76), though the epithet was
altered in revision. Wordsworth let stand his other significant use of
"wide waste" in the 1805 *Prelude,* during his recollected vision of the
sacrificial altar on Salisbury Plain (XIII.336). The two landscapes cohere in his prophetic imagination. London, as the seat of empire, had
degraded all of England and returned it to the barbaric code of the
Druids.
     Wordsworth suffered fresh perceptions of London's degeneracy
on every visit. This sonnet, *Written in London, September, 1802,* is addressed to Coleridge, though in one draft the first line is "O thou
proud City! which way shall I look." The italics are mine.

>O Friend! I know not which way I must look
>For comfort, being, as I am, opprest,
>To think that now our life is only drest
>For show; mean handy-work of craftsman, cook,
>Or groom!—We must run glittering like a brook
>In the open sunshine, or we are unblest:
>The wealthiest man among us is the best:
>No grandeur now in nature or in book
>Delights us. Rapine, avarice, expense,
>*This is idolatry; and these we adore:*
>Plain living and high thinking are no more:
>The homely beauty of the good old cause
>Is gone; our peace, our fearful innocence,
>And pure religion breathing household laws. (PW, III, 115–16)

     But London, and all of England, is also Zion, the beloved home-
land. In prophecy the waste land must be both destroyed and preserved, punished by ruin so that it may be rebuilt in glory. It is the
task of the prophet to pronounce this mixed fate upon nations. And
that is exactly what happens next in the dream.
     The dreamer meets with an Arab mounted on a dromedary who
carries a stone and a shell. He identifies the stone as "Euclid's Elements" and the shell as "something of more worth," or poetry. The
shell is, as a later passage puts it, a "Poor earthly casket of immortal
Verse! / Shakespeare, or Milton, Labourers divine!" When the dreamer

puts his ear to the shell, he learns that these achievements are threatened:

> And heard that instant in an unknown Tongue,
> Which yet I understood, articulate sounds,
> A loud prophetic blast of harmony,
> An Ode, in passion utter'd, which foretold
> Destruction to the Children of the Earth,
> By deluge now at hand.

The fears expressed by eighteenth-century moralists of "Ambition's overwhelming wave" (see chapter six) here become apocalyptic in a vision of civilization's total overthrow. The twentieth century, justly preoccupied with its own horrors, finds it difficult to imagine that an earlier time, when the perverted ingenuity of man seemed less in evidence, could or did undergo the fears of annihilation common to the era of Buchenwald and Hiroshima. But in Wordsworth's poetry we confront a sensibility steeped in the ultimate horror. Not only did he face the prospect that a tyrant he considered the agent of Satan might blot out the civilization of Shakespeare and Milton, but he saw that the protectors of those supreme poets were themselves idolators of power. One object of their worship, in fact, was Napoleon himself. In 1802, during a truce, it was estimated that close to ten thousand English tourists flocked to Paris to catch a glimpse of the romantic first consul and his court.[21] In 1803 Wordsworth indicted his country for its errors:

> England! all nations in this charge agree:
> But worse, more ignorant in love and hate,
> Far—far more abject, is thine Enemy:
> Therefore the wise pray for thee, though the freight
> Of thy offences be a heavy weight:
> Oh grief that Earth's best hopes rest all with Thee! (*PW*, III, 119)

Wordsworth is the more alarmed because he once participated in the idolatry of power. The prophetic blast he hears in the shell is a repetition of his own youthful enthusiasm as he consigned all the conservators of tradition to the deeps.

Wordsworth is of course aware of this irony, and a recollection of his republican fervor in *The Prelude* seems to echo in phrase and situation the passage from the dream quoted above. He seems even to have revised the recollection to accord with the particulars of the dream:

> To Nature, then,
> Power had reverted: habit, custom, law,
> Had left an interregnum's open space
> For *her* to move about in, uncontrolled.
> Hence could I see how Babel-like their task,
> Who, by the recent deluge stupified,
> With their whole souls went culling from the day
> Its petty promises, to build a tower
> For their own safety; laughed with my compeers
> At gravest heads, by enmity to France
> Distempered, till they found, in every blast
> Forced from the street-disturbing newsman's horn,
> For her great cause record or prophecy
> Of utter ruin.   (XI.31–44)

Wordsworth is here alluding to people like Watson and Burke, lackeys of the tyrannical empire, who persisted in furthering Nimrod's mad work, the Tower of Babel. Such people imagined that they were preserving the mind of Europe from the deluge; every "blast" of news about the deluge's closer approach seemed a prophetic warning about the destruction of England near at hand. Then Wordsworth laughed with his friends at this preservative instinct, but a decade later he was no longer laughing.

Because he has become the thing he once condemned, his retrospective attitude is necessarily ironic; it mocks his own hopes as it deflates theirs. The complexity of feeling is transferred successfully to the preserver of stone and shell:

> A wish was now ingender'd in my fear
> To cleave unto this Man, and I begg'd leave
> To share his errand with him. On he pass'd
> Not heeding me; I follow'd, and took note
> That he look'd often backward with wild look,
> Grasping his twofold treasure to his side.
> —Upon a Dromedary, Lance in rest,
> He rode, I keeping pace with him, and now
> I fancied that he was the very Knight
> Whose Tale Cervantes tells, yet not the Knight,
> But was an Arab of the Desart, too;
> Of these was neither, and was both at once.

The Quixote face of the Arab appears in the dreamwork because the dreamer has been reading Cervantes before falling asleep. Book V of *The Prelude* carries the heading "Books" and Wordsworth tries in each episode to make some connection between his childhood reading and the experience of death in the external world. His basic premise is that fantasy literature, by expanding the imagination beyond the customary confines of time and space, makes the mind "lord and master" (as he puts it in XII.222) and not the slave of circumstance and mutability. *Don Quixote* is especially pertinent because it tells of a man whose reading of romantic literature exalts his view of human nature, with ironic results when he confronts the real world.

Don Quixote remains the perfect example in our literature of the attempted translation of I-think into I-will. Conservatives like Burke had frequent recourse to Cervantes when faced with the kind of radical claims Wordsworth made in his *Letter to the Bishop of Llandaff* and *Descriptive Sketches*. Burke begins his *Reflections* by making such an analogy:

> Can I now congratulate the same nation [France] upon its freedom? Is it because liberty in the abstract may be classed amongst the blessings of mankind, that I am seriously to felicitate a madman, who has escaped from the protecting restraint and wholesome darkness of his cell, on his restoration to the enjoyment of light and liberty? Am I to congratulate a highwayman and murderer, who has broke prison, upon the recovery of his natural rights? This would be to act over again the scene of the criminals condemned to the galleys, and their heroic deliverer, the metaphysic knight of the sorrowful countenance. (P. 6)

But Quixote can also serve as a symbolic figure for the preservation of virtue and vision against the vulgar reality of rapine and avarice, the idolatry of the swinish multitude in England and France alike. One of Burke's favorite rhetorical postures is that of the romantic nourished on heroic dreams and affronted daily by the blasts of news reports. Nowhere is this more true than in the most famous passage of the *Reflections,* on Marie Antoinette:

> I thought ten thousand swords must have leaped from their scabbards to avenge even a look that threatened her with insult. But the age of chivalry is gone. That of sophisters, economists, and calculators, has succeeded; and the glory of Europe is extinguished for ever.... On this scheme of things, a king is but a man, a queen is but a woman; a woman is but an animal, and an animal not of the highest order. All homage paid to the sex in general as such, and without distinct views, is to be regarded as romance and folly. (Pp. 73–74)

Marie Antoinette is Burke's Dulcinea, and he defends her against all the leveling blasts of radical literature and radical action. He will preserve intact in his imagination the "romance and folly" that insists on a hierarchy of value.

The figure of Don Quixote, then, contains a fruitful paradox in the dreamwork. It functions as a proleptic emblem of the deluge which destroys and preserves, for the waters of the deep—in a crude reduction, the democratic wave of the future—retain their political light from the phoenix birth of 1789 in their desolating force:

> And, looking backwards when he look'd, I saw
> A glittering light, and ask'd him whence it came.
> "It is," said he, "the waters of the deep
> Gathering upon us," quickening then his pace
> He left me: I call'd after him aloud;
> He heeded not; but with his twofold charge
> Beneath his arm, before me full in view
> I saw him riding o'er the Desert Sands,
> With the fleet waters of the drowning world
> In chase of him, whereat I wak'd in terror,
> And saw the Sea before me; and the Book,
> In which I had been reading, at my side.

Dreams tend to dramatize psychic tensions rather than reveal their solution. The dreamer's perplexity here is typical. He asks where the light comes from and is told only what it is. The unanswered question in the dream is one that troubled Wordsworth throughout the rest of his career: who sends the deluge?

By the archetypal logic of the Bible, it should be God who delivers punishment on England as he engineered the catastrophe that befell the first generations of Adam. In *Paradise Lost*, Michael describes the deluge to Adam in a way that emphasizes the justice of the event:

> all dwellings else
> Flood overwhelm'd, and them with all thir pomp
> Deep under water roll'd; Sea cover'd Sea,
> Sea without shore; and in thir Palaces
> Where luxury late reign'd, Sea-monsters whelp'd
> And stabl'd.   (XI.747–52)

The reign of luxury is ended by mass annihilation, and Michael rebukes Adam's sorrow at the spectacle by reminding him of the one just man (Noah) who will preserve a community of the faithful. But did Wordsworth and his fellow conservatives at this time really believe that England was being punished by the agency of Napoleon? Their answer seems to have been, "Alas, yes." They had witnessed and exposed the apostasy of London ("the freight / Of thy offences"), and therefore could not disown the punishment that seemed to hurry close behind their maledictions.

If it had been only London which would feel a conqueror's wrath, perhaps Wordsworth would have affirmed the justice of being overwhelmed, though, like Adam in Milton's epic, with appropriate grief. But having decided that Grasmere was a "Centre" and "Unity entire" he could not countenance the annihilation of the one terrestrial place he considered perfection itself. Grasmere is a symbol of eternity and heaven, it represents the *potentiality* of being without which no secondary creative order can arise. Poetry would be an immediate victim of external force, for without the continuity of habitual perceptions characteristic of existence in Grasmere, an imagination like Wordsworth's could not function. Proverbial wisdom has it that, "When the cannon thunders, the muses are silent." Whether this is true in all cases, it would certainly have been the case if the cannon were located in Grasmere.

Burke wrote in his *Reflections* that France and England recovered from previous rebellions and civil wars because the leaders in those conflicts, whatever their other faults, had not slain the mind of their countrymen. But he saw the French Revolution as an engine of "total destruction," citing as the mood of French libertarianism the manifesto of one revolutionary leader.[22]

Tous les établissments en France couronnent le malheur du peuple: pour le rendre heureux il faut le rénouveler; changer ses idées; changer ses loix; changer ses moeurs; . . . changer les hommes; changer les choses; changer les mots . . . tout détruire; oui, tout détruire; puisque tout est à recréer. (P. 164)

Of the leaders, Burke wrote, "They conceive, very systematically, that all things which give perpetuity are mischievous" (p. 85).[23] The stone and shell are frail synecdoches for the mind, which, as Wordsworth states in the preamble to the dream, has no element in nature more permanent to stamp its image on. In a world where everything, including words, is to be changed, all such images of perpetuity will disappear. Wordsworth had already visited one monument of such an annihilation, Stonehenge. And in his poem set at Stonehenge, *Salisbury Plain*, he lamented another civilization entirely blotted out by a European conqueror, Pizarro:

> Oh that a slave who on his naked knees,
> Weeps tears of fear at Superstition's nod,

> Should rise a monster Tyrant and o'er seas
> And mountains stretch so far his cruel rod
> To bruise meek Nature in her lone abode.
> Is it for this the planet of the pole
> Hangs out his stedfast lamp: Merciful God
> Who viewest us ride with Misery to her goal
> Disclose thy light of Truth to guide man's erring soul.[24]

God had guided Wordsworth to Grasmere, and that revisitation had overcome his doubts about the wisdom of Providence. But once again the prospect of usurpation creates the same doubts. If Pizarro could cross an entire ocean, cross mountains, and penetrate jungles "To bruise meek Nature in her lone abode," how much easier for Napoleon to cross the English channel and destroy Grasmere as Pizarro had annihilated the Inca civilization. The idea drove Wordsworth into despair:

> When, looking on the present face of things,
> I see one man, of men the meanest too!
> Raised up to sway the world, to do, undo
> With mighty Nations for his underlings,
> The great events with which old story rings
> Seem vain and hollow; I find nothing great:
> Nothing is left which I can venerate;
> So that a doubt almost within me springs
> Of Providence, such emptiness at length
> Seems at the heart of all things.   (PW, III, 119–20)

As in the portrait of the royalist soldier, history loses all of its glory when its desolating effects are seen close up. And if God is not truly absent but immanent within history then he too must suffer the annihilation he inflicts.

The Arab Dream, then, shows Wordsworth practicing the mode of graveyard literature which achieves its ultimate triumph in visions of universal destruction. "Will not an injured God be avenged on such a nation as this," James Hervey asked, quoting Isaiah, "Will he not be provoked to sweep it with the besom of destruction?"[25] The flood of revolution that a republican Wordsworth wished upon the world in order to remake it according to the Divine Will, that flood seemed a decade later to the contented resident of Grasmere a terrifying retribution for his and his nation's old idolatry. Infinite power, he discovered, had the polymorphous potential of overwhelming his best hopes. Imaged as the sea, it drowned his brother John in 1805 and by doing so infected Wordsworth's imagination with despair, just as the biblical flood was once conceived to have "curroded and putrified the seede" of the earth.[26] He must henceforth live with the harrowing knowledge that his paradise of Grasmere may only be a country of romance and its protector a Quixote riding before a future as inimical to human tradition as the sea. To preserve what the imperial forces of history seek to sunder becomes, in Wordsworth's imagination, the highest prophetic task. No wonder he "felt / A reverence for a Being thus employ'd" while gazing at the Arab rider.

The Auburn Syndrome:
Change and Loss in Grasmere

IN THE FIRST YEAR of William and Dorothy's revisitation of the Lakes (1800), the poet composed some inscriptions for various locations he wished to memorialize. One is titled with unusual particularity, *Written with a Slate Pencil upon a Stone, the largest of a Heap lying near a deserted Quarry, upon one of the Islands at Rydal*. Wordsworth begins by informing the stranger who has stopped to read that this is no ancient ruin he perceives but the aborted "embryo" of a pleasure-house designed by Sir William Fleming of Rydal Hall in the previous century. Like other Timons of the eighteenth century Sir William was careless of the outrage which an ostentatious building, in this case glaring white, would perpetrate in a mountainous district. The project was abandoned when Sir William realized the lake was shallow enough to allow pedestrian access to the island. Wordsworth forgives Sir William, and warns the reader to "think again" if he designs a similar change for any local spot:

> leave
> Thy fragments to the bramble and the rose;
> There let the vernal slow-worm sun himself,
> And let the redbreast hop from stone to stone. (*PW*, IV, 200)

Wordsworth enjoys Sir William's folly because it represents such a clear victory for the local forces of nature over human vanity. The Lake District had few ancestral estates, but as cities like Manchester and Birmingham evolved into manufacturing centers, the nearby Lakes became more popular as places of retirement and recreation. Deforestation, new erections, radical "improvements"—these began to suddenly (or so it seemed to Wordsworth) dismantle the inner sanctum. The pleasure-house symbolizes a destructive force of unlimited potential. Sir William cannot be satisfied by the spirit of place; he must extend his self-distinction into a space where it can be observed

163

and envied. "Something they must destroy, or they seem to themselves to exist for no purpose," Burke had written of the Jacobins.[1] From the perspective of Grasmere, not only revolutionaries but the propertied and civilized, like Sir William, seemed to make an annihilating menace of liberty. The longer Wordsworth resides in Grasmere, and later in Rydal, the more he perceives the onrush of desolation; not only as a threatened invasion over water, but as a wearing away of his spiritual center by the Sir Williams of his own time.

Wordsworth had always kept an eye on the movement of private homes and monuments into the Lake District. He writes to Dorothy in 1799, for example, that he and Coleridge "were much disgusted with the New Erections and objects about Windermere" (*Letters*, I, 271). But it is not until the year 1805 that Grasmere itself begins to undergo a marked physical change. Writing in that year, Wordsworth describes one example:

Woe to poor Grasmere for ever and ever! A wretched Creature, wretched in name and Nature, of the name of *Crump*, goaded on by his still more wretched Wife... this same Wretch has at last begun to put his long impending threats in execution; and when you next enter the sweet paradise of Grasmere you will see staring you in the face upon that beautiful ridge that elbows out into the vale... a temple of abomination, in which are to be enshrined Mr. and Mrs. Crump. Seriously this is a great vexation to us, as this House will stare you in the face from every part of the Vale, and entirely destroy its character of simplicity and seclusion.   (*Letters*, I, 534)[2]

In November of the same year Dorothy Wordsworth raised "lamentations for the fate of Grasmere" in a letter:

Alas poor Grasmere! The first object which now presents itself after you have clomb the hill from Rydale is Mr. Crump's newly-erected large mansion, staring over the church Steeple. Then a farm-house opposite to ours, on the other side of the Lake, has been taken by a dashing man from Manchester who, no doubt, will make a *fine place* of it, and as he has taken the Island too, will probably erect a pavilion upon it, or, it may be, an Obelisk. This is not all. A very beautiful little Estate has been purchased in the more retired part of the Vale, and the first thing the Gentleman has done preparatory to building his house, has been to make a *sunk Fence* which you overlook on every side from the rocks, thickets, and green sloping hills! Add to all that Sir Michael Fleming has been getting his woods appraised, and after Christmas the Ax is to be lifted against them, and not one tree left, so the whole eastern side of the Lake will be entirely naked, even to the very edge of the water!—but what could we expect better from Sir Michael? who has been building a long high wall under the grand woods behind his house which cuts the hill in two by a straight line; and to make his doings visible to all men, he has whitewashed it, as white as snow. One who could do all this wants a sense which others have. To him there is no *"Spirit in the Wood."*   (*Letters*, I, 638)[3]

These alterations would continue throughout Wordsworth's lifetime. His letters are full of venom directed at the nouveau riche and families like the Flemings who ought to know better than to despoil the locality with tasteless improvements. The problem, it must be emphasized, is one of taste, not change *per se.* He did not desire an untrammeled wilderness, protected as a beauty spot from the ongoing activities of mankind. His love of the Lakes derived partly from their human associations, the lore and legendry, the often violent dramas enacted by visitors as well as residents. He appreciated the man-made structures throughout the region, provided they were of local materials for local purposes. He did abhor the imposition of "foreign" influences into the organic life of the Lakes. He illustrated this feeling, and extended its significance, in a letter of 1806:

I like splendid mansions in their proper places, and have no objection to large or even obtrusive houses in themselves. My dislike is to that system of gardening which, because a house happens to be large or splendid and stands at the head of a large domain, establishes it therefore as a principle that the house ought to *dye* all the surrounding country with a strength of colouring, and to an extent proportionate to its own importance. This system I think is founded in false taste, false feeling, and its effects disgusting in the highest degree.   (*Letters*, II, 8)

It is "false taste" that imperils the countryside by threatening to "dye" its visible being into conformity with the mastering source. Poetics, politics, and gardening, always closely linked in the Augustan period, are here rejoined as a critique of Augustanism. It is the moral universe of Pope's *Windsor Forest* that Wordsworth came to see as his specific enemy.

The imperial imposition of a false taste on a native one Wordsworth increasingly laid to the charge of Alexander Pope. Though Pope had satirized the excesses of Timon, the grotesque ambitions of a person eager for self-distinction, the poet himself had done much to establish a modified English style. Pope's home at Twickenham had a surfeit of ornaments—a shell temple, obelisk, statues, and urns. Pope's taste rested on the fundamental belief that nature must be methodized or improved upon to rid it of its inherent deformities, "a belief that Nature was not to be trusted," as Wordsworth charged in his *Essay, Supplementary to the Preface* (*PW*, II,

418). False taste originates in a failure of compassion, a lack of universal feeling, for it insists that the self, the craving ego, interpose its presence between person and person, person and place. Wordsworth's critique of Pope's epitaphs develops this point with a passion that speaks for some motive beyond a concern for style. "The Epitaphs of Pope cannot well be too severely condemned," he writes in his *Essay on Epitaphs*, "for not only are they almost wholly destitute of those universal feelings and simple movements of mind which we have called for as indispensible, but they are little better than a tissue of false thoughts, languid and vague expressions, unmeaning antithesis, and laborious attempts at discrimination" (*Prose*, II, 80). The style is the man, and if the style is the taste of the age it is mankind as well. When Wordsworth imagined the pastoral world he cherished in the Lakes, he dwelt on man-made structures rich in associations of love, hope, trust, patience, and suffering; the qualities invested, for example, in the house called the Evening Star and the unfinished sheep-fold in *Michael*. What he feared was the imposition of the Twickenham version of pastoral: statues of Venus and Mercury at every turn, an obelisk which Maynard Mack describes as "the point of visual and emotional climax for the observer in [Pope's] garden."[4]

As Mack points out, Pope's fondness for objects which look into several avenues of a garden corresponds with his fondness for pun and zeugma as verse techniques. The unnatural juxtaposition of objects to create perspectives underlies both the poetry of wit and the ornamental garden. The "picturesque" mode of landscape appreciation is sometimes considered a romantic reaction against such methodizing habits, but it derives in essence from the same impulse. It recommends, for example, replacement of the high fence by the sunk fence in order to provide a better view of distant scenery, but, as we see from Dorothy Wordsworth's letter above, a sunk fence is still objectionable: its rationale is still that of the removed spectator. James Thomson is the English poet most closely identified with the picturesque, and Wordsworth's critique of him in the *Essay, Supplementary to the Preface* emphasizes the artifice consequent upon detached views rather than intimate and repeated familiarity. "Notwithstanding his high powers," Wordsworth says, "he writes a vicious style; and his false ornaments are exactly of that kind which would be most likely to strike the undiscerning" (*PW*, II, 421).[5] Wordsworth's love of the natural figuration in landscape made him cautious about any change not essential to survival or approved by the most time-honored practice of the rural folk. The cult of the picturesque foreshadowed the changes he complained of in poems and letters of this period. One can imagine his feelings in reading a passage like the following from one landmark of the picturesque, William Gilpin's *Highland Tour* (italics in text):

A circuit round the lake [Derwentwater] naturally suggests the visionary idea of improving it. If the whole lake (I mean the whole district of land and water, contained within the circumference of the mountains) belonged to one person, a nobler scene for improvement could not well be conceived. This grand circumference, it is true, in all it's vastness and extent, sets at nought all human power; and resists every idea of human improvement: yet still in some parts an impression might be made. It might be rendered *more accessible*—it might be *cleared of deformities*—it might be *planted*—and it might be *decorated*. [6]

Wordsworth's fear of improvements by the wealthy and tasteless is part of a more general anxiety about the acceleration of the rate at which a small vale like Grasmere might be subject to change. Tourists, for example, were (and still are) a mixed blessing and curse to the integrity of the Lake communities. The flow of visitors was a phenomenon of Wordsworth's lifetime; by 1788, according to Wilberforce, "the banks of the Thames are scarcely more public than those of Windermere." [7] The invasion reached such proportions by 1805 that Wordsworth felt driven from his home into tours of his own during the busiest season. He appreciated the irony of this situation, that having secured the Good he would then be unsettled and even displaced by those competing for their share of its benefits, their glimpse of Zion. Unfortunately, tourists tended to bring with them the kind of debased values engendered by Pope, Thomson, and Gilpin. When the most enamored visitors settled in their newfound paradise they often brought with them, like Wordsworth, "a paramount impulse not to be withstood," but one that required an ax rather than a pen.

To counteract, and not to stimulate, the destructive extension of urban values into the Lakes, Wordsworth wrote, in 1810, *A Guide Through the District of the Lakes.* In that work he quotes approvingly Thomas Gray's description of eighteenth-century Grasmere: "Not a single red tile, no flaring gentleman's house or garden-wall, breaks in upon the repose of this little unsuspected paradise; but all is peace, rusticity, and happy poverty, in its neatest and most becoming attire." Commenting on this passage, he remarks:

What is here so justly said of Grasmere applied almost equally to all its sister Vales. It was well for the undisturbed pleasures of the Poet that he had no forebodings of the change which was soon to take place; and it might have been hoped that these words, indicating how much the charm of what *was*, depended upon what was *not*, would of themselves have preserved the an-

cient franchises of this and other kindred mountain retirements from trespass; or (shall I dare to say?) would have secured scenes so consecrated from
profanation.   (*Prose*, II, 208)

The *Guide* is a corrective application of Wordsworth's philosophy of
nature to particular localities. It tells the new landowner what to
build, with what materials, what trees to plant (evergreens, no
larches). It instructs the tourist how to look at natural scenes so as to
appreciate the manifold distinctions as well as the obvious similarities
in wilderness landscape. It praises places, like Grasmere, where these
distinctions are blended and not severely demarcated. In short, the
Guide pleads with new residents to learn from nature's genius at
composition. But the *Guide* does not contain much hope that favorite
scenes can be preserved from trespass or profanation; in fact, the very
existence of the *Guide* speaks to its futility. By 1810 Wordsworth had
become more reconciled to the prospect that his sacred wood might
have to yield to the "temple of abomination" erected by the Crumps
of the world, or, even worse, some picturesque monstrosity like the
glaring white Pantheon so much admired by landscape architects at
Stourhead in Wiltshire.

By retiring to the refuge of Grasmere, Wordsworth had removed
into what Blake calls the Circle of Destiny. He had chosen to depend
on physical objects as analogies to spiritual states, and so, in Blake's
mythology, was destined to lapse backward in the Circle from the
Beulah of Grasmere to the Ulro or hell of spiritual dispossession. This
movement has been chronicled by Wordsworth in a poem, *The Tuft of
Primroses*. The poem is some six hundred lines long and was completed in 1808. It describes feelings about events which date from
1805, though its specific occasion is probably to be found in the loss of
neighbors (by death) and the loss of evergreen groves that William
and Dorothy discovered when they returned in July of 1807 after a
disappointing reunion with Coleridge in Coleorton. The illness of
Wordsworth's sister-in-law, Sara Hutchinson, also prompted composition. Though it is not linked to *The Recluse* by title, de Selincourt
suggests that it might have been Book II had the philosophical poem
ever been finished. It contains the passage on the Grand Chartreuse,
the largest single addition to *The Prelude* after 1805. It also contains
passages which were reworked and inserted into *The Excursion*. Related as it is to those longer poems, *The Tuft of Primroses* emerges as
the *locus classicus* of Wordsworth's decline; it articulates as no other
single work does the collapse of those special conditions he needed to
compose great poetry.

The first verse paragraph of the poem is quintessential

Wordsworth, and reminds us immediately of the opening of *The Pre-lude*. The primrose is hailed and praised in its solitude and majesty. The fragility of the primrose, reminiscent of Goldsmith's frail flowers in *The Deserted Village*, becomes an emblem of the entire vale and, by extension, of Wordsworth's poetic soul. From this point the poem turns from celebration of preservation to lamentation over loss, as *The Prelude* descends into doubt and misgiving after its uplifting first paragraph. In this poem, however, there is no convincing cyclical return. "Farewell," the poet suddenly bids the flower, and we feel the poem diverted to a sequence of thoughts possibly unanticipated by Wordsworth when he began it. The poem becomes a catalogue of "the changes of this peaceful Vale" (131) from its pristine innocence of 1800. Remembering the popular choice of trees as *memento mori* in the eighteenth century, we have a shock of recognition at passages like the following:

> Alas how much,
> Since I beheld and loved thee first, how much
> Is gone, though thou be left. I would not speak
> Of best Friends dead, or other deep heart-loss
> Bewail'd with weeping, but by River sides
> And in broad fields how many gentle loves,
> How many mute memorials pass'd away.
> Stately herself, though of a lowly kind
> That little Flower remains and has survived
> The lofty band of Firs that overtopp'd
> Their antient neighbour the old Steeple Tower
> . . . .
> Ah what a welcome! when from absence long
> Returning, on the centre of the Vale
> I look'd a first glad look, and saw them not!
> Was it a dream? th' aerial grove, no more
> Right in the centre of the lovely Vale
> Suspended like a stationary cloud,
> Had vanish'd like a cloud—yet say not so
> For here and there a straggling Tree was left
> To mourn in blanc and monumental grief,
> To pine and wither for its fellows gone.   (71–81, 95–104)

This return journey contrasts painfully to the joyful revisitation recorded in the poems of 1800. Wordsworth is no longer an Adam regaining Eden and finding there a merry juggler as the presiding spirit of place; he is more like the "straggling Tree" which survives to report on its near escape from annihilation. The integrity of the vale

has been destroyed, and for Wordsworth, who identified the centrality
of his true self with Grasmere, the despoiling of its "Centre" is a
spiritual one.

One simile in the text is especially enlightening. Wordsworth
reflects on the death of an entire family, asserting that death has no
terrors for him, but that he does repine

> That after them so many of their works
> Which round that Dwelling covertly preserved
> The History of their unambitious lives
> Have perish'd, and so soon!   (188–91)

Trees and flowers are "ravaged," a protected bower is

> creeping into shapelessness, self lost
> In the wild wood, like a neglected image
> Or Fancy which hath ceased to be recalled.   (203–05)

That is, if we consider the natural figuration that man creates as an
extension of his own self, then the decay of that order is the complete
obliteration of the self. The simile comparing this waste to a forgotten
memory seems to diminish its significance until we remember that
the speaker is Wordsworth, to whom the remembrance of images is
an important salvation from spiritual decay. Following the passage on
the destruction of trees, then, we see that his lament for the desolated
bower is by psychic displacement a lament for the absence of those
objects which are the symbols of Wordsworth's inner life. The process
of change, in what might be called the Auburn syndrome, fragments
the continuous self by removing the outward embodiments of past
time. These are the implications of a philosophy of landscape.
Wordsworth's cry for protection of his peace of mind is certainly one
of the darkest passages in his work:

> O grant some wardenship of spirits pure
> As duteous in their office to maintain
> Inviolate for nobler purposes,
> These individual precincts, to protect
> Here, if here only, from despoil and wrong
> All growth of nature and all frame of Art
> By, and in which the blissful pleasures live.
> Have not th' incumbent Mountains looks of awe
> In which their mandate may be read, the streams
> A Voice that pleads, beseeches, and implores?
> In vain: the deafness of the world is here

> Even here, and all too many of the haunts
> Which Fancy most delights in, and the best
> And dearest resting-places of the heart
> Vanish beneath an unrelenting doom.   (249–63)

The vale is a secluded microcosm of "all growth of nature and all frame of Art," but if neither nature nor art can plead successfully for preservation then the prophetic power is undone. External agency will accomplish what time could not, the radical dismantling of the timeless and "dearest resting-places of the heart." Wordsworth is condemned from this point to see oncoming vacancy when he gazes at trees, to anticipate the doom which he admits in *The Tuft of Primroses* is unrelenting.

It is this situation, perhaps, which impelled Wordsworth, in 1809, to reply to a letter signed "Mathetes" which appeared in Coleridge's periodical *The Friend*. Mathetes (John Wilson) made certain complaints about the "accidents of Life" constantly at work to effect the mind's degradation. A youth, he wrote, carries high ideals and innocent enthusiasm into adult life, but may be betrayed by those very ideals into dishonorable causes and be misled by enthusiasm into embracing some will-o-the-wisp of progress which undermines the very strength which childhood energies insured. "The faith in the perpetual progression of human nature towards perfection, gives birth to such lofty dreams, as secure to it the devout assent of Imagination," Mathetes writes. Where, then, can the young man find a standard of moral excellence to set against the ideal of progress, so that if a youth has erred he will not undergo the ultimate horror, "to live and perish with the age to which he has surrendered himself" (*Prose*, II, 29, 31).

Such a letter must have seemed to Wordsworth the voice of his own disappointed hopes. He would have read in the analysis offered by Mathetes the story of his enthusiasm for the French Revolution and his later recognition that worldly progress, in essence impulsive, irrational, governed by the I-will rather than the I-think, was reckless of the frail spirits caught in its maelstrom. But what answer to give Mathetes? Wordsworth begins his "Reply" by recommending his own experience of revisitation, though we notice how he alters his formulation from the ecstatic affirmation of *Home at Grasmere*:

[A Youth] cannot recal past time; he cannot begin his journey afresh; he cannot untwist the links by which, in no undelightful harmony, images and sentiments are wedded in his mind. Granted that the sacred light of Childhood is and must be for him no more than a remembrance. He may, notwithstanding, be remanded to Nature; and with trust-worthy hopes; founded less upon his sentient than upon his intellectual Being—to Nature, not as leading on insensibly to the society of Reason; but to Reason and Will, as leading back to the wisdom of Nature. A re-union, in this order accomplished, will bring reformation and timely support; and the two powers of Reason and Nature, thus reciprocally teacher and taught, may advance together in a track to which there is no limit.   (*Prose*, II, 16)

To be "remanded" to nature is still Wordsworth's ideal, in spite of the problems he confronted in Grasmere. But those losses weigh upon his "Reply." The emphatic and uncharacteristic assertion that past time cannot be recalled, or relived, belongs to the despair of *The Tuft of Primroses*. In that poem he catalogues the familiar garden plants that have been "sullied and disgrac'd" or have disappeared: "a gulf / Hath swallowed them which renders nothing back." They have gone into a cave "which cannot be unlock'd" (214–17). These metaphors insist on an absolute demarcation between past and present, death and life. The same negative tone prevails when he interposes reason and will between youthful hopes and the wisdom of nature, a reason whose principal advantage, as we shall see, is its heightened consciousness of death.

   Wordsworth enters a Stoical phase of his career. In order to forestall disappointment in the erratic progression of human nature toward perfection, he diminishes his worldly hopes. His cure for the vexations of the spirit Mathetes had described is the abiding consciousness of death he associates with reason. Following the practice of graveyard literature he selects a monitor of mortality, and recommends it as a perpetual companion of adult meditation:

There never perhaps existed a School-boy who, having when he retired to rest carelessly blown out his candle, and having chanced to notice as he lay upon his bed in the ensuing darkness the sullen light which had survived the extinguished flame, did not, at some time or other, watch that light as if his mind were bound to it by a spell. It fades and revives—gathers to a point— seems as if it would go out in a moment—again recovers its strength, nay becomes brighter than before: it continues to shine with an endurance which in its apparent weakness is a mystery—it protracts its existence so long, clinging to the power which supports it, that the Observer, who had lain down in his bed so easy-minded, becomes sad and melancholy: his sympathies are touched—it is to him an intimation and an image of departing human life.   (*Prose*, II, 17)

The variation Wordsworth plays on the conventional "brief candle" of human life is a poignant one. The struggle of the taper to maintain its light after being snuffed, the endurance it shows in spite of an essential weakness, reminds us not only of the "departing human life" that Wordsworth mourned in recent years but of Grasmere itself. When he goes on to say that the struggle of the taper to keep alight is "a type of all death, Nature teaching seriously and sweetly through the affections," we see how Grasmere has been converted in his imagination to a place whose value lies precisely in its mutability. He has resigned himself to the unrelenting doom he now expects to overtake all his dearest resting-places, and the form of his resignation is the spellbound fascination with the dying taper. He continues:

Let us accompany this same Boy to that period between Youth and Manhood when a solicitude may be awakened for the moral life of himself.—Are there any powers by which, beginning with a sense of inward decay that affects not however the natural life, he could call up to mind the same image and hang over it with an equal interest as a visible type of his own perishing Spirit?— Oh! surely, if the being of the individual be under his own care—if it be his first care—if duty begin from the point of accountableness to our Conscience, and through that, to God and human Nature;—if without such primary sense of duty, all secondary care of Teacher, of Friend, or Parent, must be baseless and fruitless; if, lastly, the motions of the Soul transcend in worth those of the animal functions, nay give to them their sole value; then truly are there such powers: and the image of the dying taper may be recalled and contemplated, though with no sadness in the nerves, no disposition to tears, no unconquerable sighs, yet with a melancholy in the soul, a sinking inward into ourselves from thought to thought, a steady remonstrance, and a high resolve. —Let then the Youth go back, as occasion will permit, to Nature and to Solitude, thus admonished by Reason, and relying upon this newly-acquired support.   (*Prose*, II, 17–18)

The actual philosophy has not changed since *Tintern Abbey*, for the "high resolve" that comes from melancholy recollection of the dying taper descends from the "still, sad music of humanity" which Wordsworth identified in that earlier poem as a compensatory gift of maturity. And yet no one could miss in his "Reply to Mathetes" the shift of emphasis as he considers the progress of the soul through mortal life. In the earlier poem remembrance of the "beauteous forms" that he describes so particularly in the opening paragraph has provided balm when he fell victim to the melancholy of adult existence. Now it is melancholy thoughts themselves that are recommended as subjects of recollection. A youth might connect his expanding hopes, built as they are upon love of enduring forms, to a plot of ground like Grasmere, but he can save himself from this folly by remembering the dying taper, and recognizing that, as a later poem puts it, "no perfect cure grows on that bounded field" of natural landscape (*PW*, IV, 5). In his "Reply" Wordsworth is at pains to emphasize that the soul's yearnings transcend in worth those of the "animal functions." In a poem of 1798 he could advise his sister to put down her books and come out to feel the sun:

> Love, now a universal birth,
> From heart to heart is stealing,
> From earth to man, from man to earth:
> —It is the hour of feeling.
>
> One moment now may give us more
> Than years of toiling reason:
> Our minds shall drink at every pore
> The spirit of the season.   (*PW*, IV, 60)

Now, a decade later, Reason is interposed between the mind and its bodily pores and its function as an intermediary is to overlay sensation with recollections of death. "Feeling" will be educated by "toiling reason." Now books are recommended with a new urgency and contemplation preferred to action. Another tie to the earth has been broken, for contemplative Stoicism vitiates the influence of the Genius loci. The mind no longer expands to encompass the local forms beloved from childhood; rather it retreats, "sinking inward into ourselves" so that it may enhance the perfect "ideal property" promised to man in the Scriptures. As for the "accidents of life" of which Mathetes had complained, Wordsworth, knowing their power to depress, says only that one must hope for the best. The century that followed the rule of Henry IV, he writes, was "a hurling-back of the mind of the Country, a delapidation, an extinction," but this overthrow allowed new and better institutions, laws, customs, and habits to arise without resistance (*Prose*, II, 12). Wordsworth was not very optimistic about the future, but neither were the Tudor historians who lived in the period of revival, and he took some heart from that.

By 1809, then, Wordsworth realized that to avoid the repeated horror recorded in *The Tuft of Primroses* he would have to increase his consciousness of death, as Mithridates took small daily doses of poison to forestall the effects of a single potent draught. Wordsworth revisits the dying taper in his imagination as habitually as he had summoned a vista of the Wye Valley or Winander lake in earlier days. He had always been attracted to the trancelike "quiet of death," but in his earlier work this quietude arose from an intense experience of sensual pleasure, which in turn stimulated a joyful, and often mystical, amplitude of consciousness. In a journal entry of 1802 he writes:

> I have thoughts that are fed by the sun.
>   The things which I see
>   Are welcome to me,
>   Welcome every one:
> I do not wish to lie
>   Dead, dead,
> Dead without any company;
>   Here alone on my bed,
> With thoughts that are fed by the Sun,
> And hopes that are welcome every one,
>   Happy am I.
>
> O Life, there is about thee
> A deep delicious peace,
> I would not be without thee,
>   Stay, oh stay!
> Yet be thou ever as now,
> Sweetness and breath with the quiet of death,
> Be but thou ever as now,
>   Peace, peace, peace.   (*PW*, IV, 365–66)

Gradually, however, natural objects become, in the words of his "Reply," "a visible type of [man's] own perishing spirit." In adult life this type nourishes the mind as habitually as the timeless "things which I see" were impressed upon him in his youth. The poems collected in *Evening Voluntaries* (1832) exhibit the most extreme reversal of Wordsworth's attitude. They disdain all pagan thoughts fed by the sun. Now he prefers "thoughts that shun the glare of day." He wishes to enclose himself within the twilight of piety, and shut out the "petty pleasures of the garish day" (*PW*, IV, 15, 17). Grasmere under the aspect of darkness, a minor motif in *Home at Grasmere*, swells into a major theme as the landscape of memory is transformed into a graveyard.

As he filled his contemplative periods more and more with thoughts of mutability and death, Wordsworth began to change his mind about mementos of earthly survival. His *Essay on Epitaphs*, for example, a contribution in three parts to *The Friend* of 1810, represents a complete about-face from the sentiments expressed in *The Brothers*. In the earlier poem he had seemed to endorse the view of death which dispensed with the memorializing paraphernalia of urn burial, monuments, and epitaphs. In these essays Wordsworth not only declares his fondness for memorials but prescribes rules for their most effective forms. Unless biographical details are provided, Wordsworth reminds the reader, the past is in danger of becoming a gulf, a cave which cannot be unlocked. He maintains in the first essay that the sense of immortality precedes our rational understanding of mortal existence. Why then should we resist the psychic need to memorialize ourselves in this life? Where remembrance is denied to the community, virtue itself degenerates, lacking a full understanding of virtuous models. Wordsworth expounds on this idea at great length in *The Excursion*, where he seems to conceive the task of narrative itself as an extended process of memorialization. Though these words are directed at the Pastor in the local churchyard, they are directed in another sense to Wordsworth's own newly imagined role as a defender of the faith (italics in text):

> Or rather, as we stand on holy earth,
> And have the dead around us, take from them
> Your instances; for they are both best known,
> And by frail man most equitably judged.
> Epitomise the life; pronounce, you can,
> Authentic epitaphs on some of these
> Who, from their lowly mansions hither brought,
> Beneath this turf lie mouldering at our feet:
> So, by your records, may our doubts be solved;
> *To prize the breath we share with human kind;*
> *And look upon the dust of man with awe.*   (V.646–57)

Wordsworth's best and most typical work of his later years commemorates exemplary lives from the past, either the actual or the legendary past. *The Excursion* itself, *The White Doe of Rylstone, Artegal and Elidure, Dion, Laodamia* and many of the *Ecclesiastical Sonnets*—all these attempt to preserve and epitomise the exalted in spirit.

It was not long before Wordsworth had the unhappy opportunity to exercise his talent at writing actual epitaphs. His children Catherine and Thomas, aged four and six respectively, died in 1812, events so heartbreaking that the Wordsworths could not bear to live near the children's graves. In his fine sonnet *Surprised by Joy* Wordsworth wrote that Catherine's death "Was the worst pang that sorrow ever bore" (*PW*, III, 16). It required ten years before Wordsworth could write an epitaph of six lines for Thomas. The deaths of his children rekindled the horror of John's death in 1805, a horror that had overflowed to fill Grasmere itself. A landscape of memory that relies on habitual associations can be tainted throughout by the introduction of some element of despair. After John died, William and Dorothy felt him everywhere in Grasmere, in every scene they had visited and enjoyed with him. His drowned spirit became a Genius loci that deprived them of their former intense pleasure in familiar locations. Dorothy wrote that "I can turn to no object that does not remind me of our loss. . . . I know it will not always be so—the time will come when the light of the setting Sun upon these mountain tops will be as heretofore a pure joy—not the same *gladness*, that can never be—but yet a joy even more tender" (*Letters*, I, 559). Their thoughts will be fed after 1805 by the setting sun, a deliberate echo of *Tintern Abbey* where the declining light is listed as one dwelling of the presence that disturbs the poet with "the joy / Of elevated thoughts; a sense sublime / Of something far more deeply interfused." In those days Grasmere was the Eden toward which their troubled wanderings were directed. But after John's death Dorothy wrote, "this Vale is changed to us, it can never be what it *has been*" (*Letters*, I, 567).

The children's death consummated the estrangement from Grasmere which events had gradually precipitated. It brought back the horror with redoubled force and caused the Wordsworth family to flee a place now poisoned beyond redemption in their memory. Wordsworth wrote in a letter of 1813:

The House which I have for some time occupied is the Parsonage of Grasmere. It stands close by the Churchyard; and I have found it absolutely necessary that we should quit a Place, which, by recalling to our minds at every moment the losses we have sustained in the course of the last year, would grievously retard our progress towards that tranquillity of mind which it is our duty to aim at.   (*Letters*, III, 66)

With what feelings William and Dorothy must have removed from Grasmere to establish residence at Rydal Mount! They had become again the male and female wanderers of Wordsworth's early poem on Salisbury Plain. They had become exiles of the Eden which they had dared to claim in the body. For consolation they turned to the same writer who had in a very direct way sponsored their homesickness in the first place, Oliver Goldsmith. Even before the worst events dispossessed them from Grasmere, Wordsworth had written for *The Excursion* a prophecy of their leave-taking which echoes Goldsmith's *The Traveller* in several places:

> "Farewell, deep Valley, with thy one rude House,
> And its small lot of life-supporting fields,
> And guardian rocks!—Farewell, attractive seat!
> To the still influx of the morning light
> Open, and day's pure cheerfulness, but veiled
> From human observation, as if yet
> Primeval forests wrapped thee round with dark
> Impenetrable shade; once more farewell,

> Majestic circuit, beautiful abyss,
> By Nature destined from the birth of things
> For quietness profound!"
>   Upon the side
> Of that brown ridge, sole outlet of the vale
> Which foot of boldest stranger would attempt,
> Lingering behind my comrades, thus I breathed
> A parting tribute to a spot that seemed
> Like the fixed centre of a troubled world.
> Again I halted with reverted eyes;
> The chain that would not slacken, was at length
> Snapt,—and, pursuing leisurely my way,
> How vain, thought I, is it by change of place
> To seek that comfort which the mind denies.   (V.1–21)

Once out of the "fixed centre" trouble awaits the exile, the "trouble" Wordsworth applied to the Wandering Jew's condition but had now again become his own.

As Grasmere, in its own body and by association with other losses, undergoes the shocks of 1805–1812, Wordsworth begins to survey the countryside for consolatory images of permanence to replace the vale. His great poem, *Elegiac Stanzas Suggested by a Picture of Peele Castle*, written to commemorate John's death, points the direction of his quest. He becomes more and more fascinated by monumental "Piles" in country areas. Like epitaphs they are symbolic structures which bind together past and present, death and life. Wordsworth is especially interested in their tutorial function as ruins; he values the impression of death they make upon the living. In *Address from the Spirit of Cockermouth Castle* the Spirit tells Wordsworth that the two of them, "stricken as both are by years," have shared a bond since the poet's childhood when, upon entering the "soul-appalling darkness" of the castle, he had his innocent hopes made acquainted with the grave (*PW*, IV, 23). The castle performed the essential function of a memorial as Wordsworth had defined it in *The Excursion*, "to prize the breath we share with human kind." Man-made structures are the inheritances, in the Burkean sense, which insure the linkage of living and dead. They are historical tradition standing firm against those who would slay the mind by overrunning human limitations and by doing so leave the present scene a desert, a wide waste.

The Arab Dream in Book V of *The Prelude* had been a vision of such overthrow, and *The Tuft of Primroses* another. False taste and false feeling seemed to have infected the multitude. As the first decade of the nineteenth century ended, Wordsworth came to understand what the angel told the prophet John in Revelation 17:15. "The water which thou sawest, where the whore sitteth, are peoples, and multitudes, and nations, and tongues." In 1809 Wordsworth wrote in a letter that "this country is in fact fallen as low in point of moral philosophy (and of course political) as it is possible for any country to fall" (*Letters*, II, 296).[8] All classes wanted to dye the world around them by imposing their will, by overwhelming if necessary the sacred places of the creative spirit and placing them in captivity. Wordsworth's resistance takes the form of a conventional recourse to the guardian fortresses of English history. In the late verse we have poems addressed to or about ancient keeps, castles, fortresses, estates, and of course churches. If *Tintern Abbey* had been written after 1805, the abbey probably would have been the centerpiece of the poem. *Lowther* is a typical example:

> Lowther! in thy majestic Pile are seen
> Cathedral pomp and grace, in apt accord
> With the baronial castle's sterner mien;
> Union significant of God adored,
> And charters won and guarded by the sword
> Of ancient honour; whence that goodly state
> Of polity which wise men venerate,
> And will maintain, if God his help afford.
> Hourly the democratic torrent swells;
> For airy promises and hope suborned
> The strength of backward-looking thoughts is scorned.
> Fall if ye must, ye Towers and Pinnacles,
> With what ye symbolize; authentic Story
> Will say, Ye disappeared with England's Glory! (*PW*, IV, 48–49)[9]

Wordsworth wrote a multitude of poems with exactly these sentiments after 1810. "The democratic torrent" reminds us of the deluge in the Arab Dream, and here, as there, Wordsworth imagines an overthrow of all that lends glory to his time. The particular reference is almost certainly to the Reform Bill, which he strenuously opposed. "Perilous is sweeping change, all chance unsound," he wrote in another sonnet, for the Reform Bill seemed a sweeping aside of precisely those rights of property that protected English tradition from destructive whim (*PW*, IV, 129).[10] These whims of policy are often described hopefully in the imagery of airy elements, unsubstantial things opposed to the granite reality of earth, trees, stones, and piles. Once again, if we look back at *Home at Grasmere* we see that Wordsworth is exorcising the powers he hailed as Grasmere's local spirits. As a boy his imagination was composed "Of sunbeams, shadows, butterflies and birds, / Of fluttering Sylphs, and softly-gliding Fays, / Genii, and winged Angels that are Lords" (32–34). Now his disenchantment is complete. Lowther and piles like it are the legitimate lords of the vales, emblems of continuity and the local attachments Wordsworth associated with authentic patriotism. Lowther, like Burke's vision of the Keep of Windsor in *A Letter to a Noble Lord*, unites grace and sternness, a political structure adored by God and preserved by his adoration as an emblem of time, the time which can properly be called the mercy of eternity.

Wordsworth's admiring stance toward castles, churches, and lordly estates contrasts most dramatically with the final stanza of his youthful poem, *Salisbury Plain* (1793–94). Still in his revolutionary phase, he calls upon his fellow enthusiasts to demolish the archaic Bastilles of the spirit:

> Heroes of Truth pursue your match, uptear
> Th'Oppressor's dungeon from its deepest base;
> High o'er the towers of Pride undaunted rear
> Resistless in your might the herculean mace
> Of Reason; let foul Error's monster race
> Dragged from their dens start at the light with pain
> And die; pursue your toils, till not a trace
> Be left on earth of Superstition's reign,
> Save that eternal pile which frowns on Sarum's plain.   (541–49)

Error still has her Spenserian guise of superstition; it is the false face of gothic institutions that the knights of truth must annihilate. "Towers of pride" is a phrase vague enough to permit the widest definition, but certainly it would include a number of the erections that Wordsworth would later memorialize. He allows Stonehenge, the most venerable of ruins, to remain standing as a harmless memento of the bad old days; all other traces of superstition must be blotted out.

Wordsworth's rhetoric is revolutionist but essentially pacifist as well. Almost always the I-think prevails over the I-will. In the passage above, the herculean mace in line four turns in line five to the mace "Of Reason." The same technique reappears in his sonnet on Lowther where the sword in line six becomes the sword "Of ancient honour." He could not bear to consider violence, except as a means of defense against a foreign enemy. Violence against the Crumps and Flemings was unthinkable, for they held the very property rights he believed to be a bulwark against the democratic torrent. And violence against the torrent itself he could not bear to support, and never did. Wordsworth is always the Arab rider running before the flood, and

never (after Waterloo) the militarist, the Cuchulain taking arms
against the sea. Throughout his life he surprised his conservative
friends by recommending milder courses of action, given his terrors,
than they expected. Walter Savage Landor, for example, called for
harsher measures of repression against the Irish than did
Wordsworth, who, despite a sympathetic reading of Spenser's *Vewe
of the Present State of Ireland*, could not join his predecessor in the belief
that rebellious counties must be put to the sword.

But Wordsworth had no personal stake in Ireland; he could afford to be tolerant. Whenever the winds of change blew across the
Lake District the morbid fears of *The Tuft of Primroses* resumed their
sway in his imagination. When the railroads threatened to construct a
line through Kendal to Lowwood on Windermere, Wordsworth actively and successfully propagandized against the proposal. His sonnet on the railway was one of the last poems he wrote on any public
matter; it records in by now familiar terms his fear that the landscape
would be annihilated by the forces of improvement:

> Is then no nook of English ground secure
> From rash assault? Schemes of retirement sown
> In youth, and 'mid the busy world kept pure
> As when their earliest flowers of hope were blown,
> Must perish;—how can they this blight endure?
> And must he too the ruthless change bemoan
> Who scorns a false utilitarian lure
> 'Mid his paternal fields at random thrown?
> Baffle the threat, bright Scene, from Orrest-head
> Given to the pausing traveller's rapturous glance:
> Plead for thy peace, thou beautiful romance
> Of nature; and, if human hearts be dead,
> Speak, passing winds; ye torrents, with your strong
> And constant voice, protest against the wrong. (PW, III, 61–62)

He opposes the railroad not because of some mystical hatred of
technology or modern inventions; his praise of these in the sonnet
Steamboats, Viaducts, and Railways (1833) is perfectly sincere. Rather,
he censures the proposal on the grounds of taste outlined earlier. He
fears two things: first, that the railway will overrun hallowed spots in
the Lakes, including groves and places of retirement, and second,
that it will bring "imperfectly educated classes" into the Lakes where
their inability to appreciate properly the scenery before them—and it
is in this sense that they are uneducated—will cause them to abuse
the places they visit.[11] Good taste, Wordsworth insists, is not divinely
implanted in mankind. It must be developed through long and inti-

mate experience with natural forms, a participation in their unique
life. In a letter to the *Morning Post*, Wordsworth relates an anecdote
which illustrates his opinion:

In the midst of a small pleasure-ground, immediately below my house, rises a
detached rock, equally remarkable for the beauty of its form, the ancient oaks
that grow out of it, and the flowers and shrubs which adorn it. "What a nice
place this would be," said a Manchester tradesman, pointing to the rock, "if
that ugly lump were but out of the way." Men as little advanced in the
pleasure which such objects give to others are so far from being rare, that they
may be said fairly to represent a large majority of mankind. (*Prose*, III, 343)[12]

Critics of Wordsworth have looked in many places for the
sources of his political conservatism, particularly at his accumulation
of property in Westmorland and his friendship with members of the
peerage. But from this vantage we can estimate how strongly his fear
of change is based on his identification of self with landscape and
landscape with nation. Though he rebuked Mathetes for misgivings
about the destiny of the modern world, his own doubts increased in
the later part of his life and contribute to the analysis of nineteenth-
century English society we associate with Hazlitt's *Spirit of the Age*,
Southey's *Colloquies on the Progress and Prospects of Society*, and Carlyle's *Past and Present*.

In *Natural Supernaturalism*, M. H. Abrams remarks on "Wordsworth's assumption... that if life is to be worth living there cannot be a blank unreason or mere contingency at the heart of things;
there must be meaning (in the sense of a good and intelligible
purpose) in the occurrence of both physical and moral evils." The
evils of change and loss, Abrams demonstrates, are surmounted in
The Prelude by Wordsworth's "recognition that all process entails loss,
and that there can be no creative progress except through the painful
destruction, however unmerited, of the preceding stage." The
threatened destruction of Grasmere and its neighboring vales, in my.
opinion, cannot be incorporated into this dialectic of good and evil
because Grasmere is itself the symbolic alpha and omega of
Wordsworth's circuitous journey; it is the unitary source and end of
the poet's pilgrimage. Natural supernaturalism is neither cancelled
nor mocked by threats to Grasmere; Wordsworth would never have
retracted the central beliefs of his visionary poetry. But Grasmere *is*
an outpost of spiritual progress, a test case of Wordsworth's belief
that, in Abrams's words, "in our life in this actual world, with its
ineradicable evil, and suffering, lies the possibility and the only possibility of achieving a paradise which serves [Wordsworth], as it did

Milton, to justify the evil of our mortal state."[13] Suffering, or any deep distress, does fit into Wordsworth's scheme of salvation by humanizing the soul and taming its love of mastery. But if Grasmere, like Milton's Eden, falls to the enemy what strategy in the secular world can defend any landscape against annihilation? Here there is no intervening Christ, only the embattled poet of nature who must by tract and sonnet "redress the rigours of the inclement clime." At issue is the survival of an originating power, a center, a home, without whose existence the poetic imagination would itself vanish beneath an unrelenting doom.

But Wordsworth's agony has a happier issue than that of most poets, for his pleading did much to preserve the paradise he once claimed for his spiritual center. The Lake District has not been overwhelmed or desolated; visiting Grasmere or Rydal we do not, like Goldsmith at Leasowes, perceive the Genius loci as a scythe-wielding God of Time. Wordsworth's poetry made something happen; it awakened the moral conscience of posterity to the value of places which bear a habitual resemblance to Eden, our profound dream of harmony and joy. And our own joy owes much of its body to Wordsworth's recollections of his feeling in those places. Magical presences haunt the sites of Hawkshead, or Esthwaite Water, or the daffodils of Gowbarrow Park because Wordsworth felt and articulated their character. What he foresaw as a ruin—the trampled field of all his hopes and loves—we enjoy as his memorial. In his later life he had narrowed his optimism to the conventional compliment to immortal poesy:

> Communities are lost, and Empires die,
> And things of holy use unhallowed lie;
> They perish;—but the Intellect can raise,
> From airy words alone, a Pile that ne'er decays. (PW, IV, 197)

He was too modest. The tower of words, a displaced emblem of the vale, does certainly endure, but so does the vale.

11 The Wordsworthian Child

The beginning is like a god which as long as it dwells among men saves all things.
—Plato, Laws

The Child of Revolution

IN THE PRECEDING SURVEY of Wordsworth's engagement with historical events I have tried to account for the recurrence of highly charged images, symbols, and themes in his poetry. Often celebrated as the "soothing voice" of Arnold's memorial verses, teaching his audience to put by the cloud of mortal destiny, Wordsworth is also a minute chronicler of the age of revolutions, a man who boasted that he had given twelve hours of thought to the conditions and prospects of society for one to poetry.[1] Nothing is more typical of Wordsworth than his decision in 1804 to lengthen his autobiographical poem, *The Prelude*, so that public events like the French Revolution could be absorbed into his self-definition.

Wordsworth's whole canon rests on the assumption he declares explicitly in the Simplon Pass episode of *The Prelude*, that "our being's heart and home, / Is with infinitude, and only there" (VI.604–05). Infinitude is a term he sometimes but not always uses interchangeably with immortality. It refers to a limitless comprehension of unknown modes of being. We see everywhere in Wordsworth's poetry how spiritual expansion of this kind occurs also in response to historical events. When he re-creates his feelings about the French Revolution in *The Prelude*, he has a grammar ready at hand:

> and aware, no less,
> That throwing off oppression must be work
> As well of License as of Liberty;
> And above all—for this was more than all—

> Not caring if the wind did now and then
> Blow keen upon an eminence that gave
> Prospect so large into futurity;
> In brief, a child of Nature, as at first,
> Diffusing only those affections wider
> That from the cradle had grown up with me,
> And losing, in no other way than light
> Is lost in light, the weak in the more strong.   (XI.161–72)

In John Dyer's *Grongar Hill*, ascendancy allowed the poet a vantage on ruin and shadow; it taught the vanity of worldly aspirations. But here the prospect is of glorious infinitude, realized as a succession of historical days and nights in which the "god-like hours" of childhood maintain the "majestic sway" attributed to them in an earlier book of *The Prelude* (III.194–95). The cradle becomes in this Pisgah-sight the point of origin and of terminus, a companion symbol of the revolutionary birth.

Futurity, in this construction, comprises a universal fellowship, a humanity which has overcome all restraints on its natural desire for light and love. Wordsworth's affirmative rhetoric of imperialism is a perfect fit to his intuitions about the creative powers he inherited from his childhood. When he describes his first recognition of creative power, he draws together the public and private languages:

> I had inward hopes
> And swellings of the spirit, was rapt and soothed,
> Conversed with promises, had glimmering views
> How life pervades the undecaying mind;
> How the immortal soul with God-like power
> Informs, creates, and thaws the deepest sleep
> That time can lay upon her; how on earth,
> Man, if he do but live within the light
> Of high endeavours, daily spreads abroad
> His being armed with strength that cannot fail.   (IV.162–71)

Wordsworth completed the *Ode: Intimations of Immortality* immediately after Book IV, from which this passage is taken. We recognize in the passage the movement of mind which informs the uplifting conclusion of the *Ode*. The light of high endeavors, diffusing as it does in the direction of futurity, glows intensely enough to thaw even the deepest sleep of mortal experience. The last line is apt because the individual vision will have to struggle for sovereignty in a world oppressed by false prophets and false kings. Each high endeavor must be a new beginning, a revolutionary birth.

The rhythm of Wordsworth's major poems is not mournful, though the theme of loss, as I have shown, became an obsession. Wordsworth's fundamental vision assumes that vicissitude will impair the prophetic task, that God-like power will fluctuate, but he never concludes without a convincing *O altitudo* of rededication. Of no poem is this more true than the *Ode,* and the reluctance of some readers to follow Wordsworth through the dark passages of the poem has given it an undeserved reputation as the epitome of ruins literature, a lamentation in the tradition of Cowper, Goldsmith, and Gray. But a reading of the poem that sees it as, say, one more version of Gray's *Ode on a Distant Prospect of Eton College* confuses the prospects from two entirely different eminences. Gray begins by hinting of a "second spring" that overtakes him when he considers childhood joy, but as he watches the "little victims" at play his nostalgia enthralls him and the winter of age settles on his spirit. Wordsworth's *Ode* is armed with strength that cannot fail; it does not submit to nostalgia but progresses toward consolation and rejoicing. A reading that does not see in its structure the evolution of Wordsworth's historical imagination, tested by the events he himself described and interpreted, will always find it wanting. His praise of the "philosophic mind" will seem nothing more than a desperate rebuttal of Gray's conclusion, "where ignorance is bliss, / 'Tis folly to be wise." David Perkins, for example, remarks of the final stanzas, "It is as though the poet himself could scarcèly conceive or know exactly what he was talking about."[2] I think Wordsworth knew perfectly well what he was talking about, but his expression relies on a broader set of assumptions than even the capacious *Ode* can articulate.

The *Ode* is not a political poem, but written as it was in the midst of social and political turmoil it necessarily reflects the poet's agitation in its own activity. The circumstances which create the *Ode* have its own intricate pattern. If anything, Wordsworth's first years in Grasmere offer a more compelling drama than the timely utterance he distilled from them. In the *Ode* his constant touchstone is the child, whereas in his life the source of his "master light" has a more protean set of shapes and figures, and the progress of that light a more complex fate.[3] The *Ode,* spanning two years in composition, is a microcosm of the lifelong tensions I have sketched in the preceding three chapters. My purpose in this chapter is not to provide another close reading of the *Ode* but to survey the landscape of events from which it emerges, a secondary world, and reveal its conformation to the whole.

The place to start is by noting once again the symbolic character of the child in Wordsworth's historical writings. Though children are

real beings, and Wordsworth was at all times capable of describing
them with the condescension of a Montaigne, they offer to his dramatic purposes an obvious figure for beginning, or potentiality. Children emblematize infinitude because they can become anything, they
can realize themselves in the most heroic mode their parents can
imagine. Wordsworth's child is, like Blake's, an infant of the French
Revolution, and makes its first significant appearance in Wordsworth's work in that radical guise:

> Yet, yet rejoice, tho' Pride's perverted ire
> Rouze Hell's own aid, and wrap thy hills in fire.
> Lo! from th' innocuous flames, a lovely birth!
> With it's own Virtues springs another earth:
> Nature, as in her prime, her virgin reign
> Begins, and Love and Truth compose her train.
>
> (*Descriptive Sketches*, 1793 version, 780–85)

Nature here is a fiery babe, a phoenix, like the figure in the second
cycle of Blake's *The Mental Traveller:*

> Till from the fire on the hearth
> A little Female Babe does spring
> And she is all of solid fire   (43–45)

Just as Blake's babe drives out "the aged Host," the decayed spiritual
form of a once vital Christian tradition, so Wordsworth's symbolic
birth sweeps away those archaic persons and institutions which resist
the process of transformation.

In *Descriptive Sketches*, "Nature" is clearly human nature and not
only the external universe that Wordsworth wishes to marry with the
mind of man in the conclusion of *Home at Grasmere.* His later reconstruction of this period, in Book VI of *The Prelude,* recalls "France
standing on the top of golden hours, / And human nature seeming
born again" (340–41). As he returns to the era in memory he shifts to
figures of masculine power in order to chart the rise and decline of
revolutionary enthusiasm. His essential point is that the Revolution
could only become more powerful by becoming less. The first breaking of fetters, the first conquests, would require the most boldness,
strength, and even cruelty. After those successes the light carried
from the primal fire must fade into the greater enlightenment of the
whole human race. A reborn human nature, he felt, had the privilege
of license, though it would have to find the limits of its godlike power
before it became incapable of any social action not absolute in its
effect. This self-extinguishing, itself an imitation of organic life,

Wordsworth would have recognized as the cycle of powerful mythic figures about whose childhood tales of wonder-working tend to accumulate.

Describing the attack of the Allies on the revolutionary state, for example, Wordsworth figures the new birth as a "Herculean Commonwealth" which "throttled with an infant godhead's might / The snakes about her cradle" (X.391–93). Later in the same book the revolutionaries are criticized for their attempt to wash the Augean stables of inherited corruption with "a river of Blood" (583–86). Using the same classical figure of Hercules, he adeptly chastises the Jacobins for clinging to violence rather than assuming the rites of compassion which characterize maturity. If the first comparison recalls Milton's description in the *Nativity Ode* of the infant Jesus overcoming the pagan gods ("Our Babe, to show his Godhead true, / Can in his swaddling bands control the damned crew"), the second comparison measures the failure of the new birth to grow into the most enlightened conception of parental rule. This Hercules is not doing his father's work but his evil stepmother's; he does not imitate Jupiter Lucetius, lawgiver, holder of the scales of justice, but implacably obeys a tyrant who has carried the violent fantasies of childhood into adult life.

In one of the least discussed of his "child" passages, Wordsworth transfers mythic associations to the commonplace child by a bold conceit. He is describing the "domestic carnage" of the Reign of Terror in vivid detail, when suddenly there is this passage:

> They found their joy,
> They made it proudly, eager as a child,
> (If light desires of innocent little ones
> May with such heinous appetites be compared),
> Pleased in some open field to exercise
> A toy that mimics with revolving wings
> The motion of a wind-mill; though the air
> Do of itself blow fresh, and make the vanes
> Spin in his eyesight, *that* contents him not,
> But, with the plaything at arm's length, he sets
> His front against the blast, and runs amain,
> That it may whirl the faster.   (X.363–73)

The parenthetical comment shows Wordsworth's own surprise at his analogy, and yet he remained true throughout all revisions of *The Prelude* to the revolutionary spirit of his early writings as it is re-created in this passage. The comparison attempts to establish the basis by which the Terror is to be judged: as an impulsive restoration of nature's majestic sway. The child's toy has a natural force as its mainspring and his pleasure in the toy increases when he turns to confront the wind and struggles against it. The language is reminiscent of the passage quoted earlier in which the wind blows keen upon the child of nature. Here the child's windmill toy is like the eolian harp, stirred into more resounding life by the natural force to which it is an audible tribute.

Wordsworth deliberately did not compare the Terror to a calculated and destructive act like the ravage of his poem, *Nutting*. Revolutionary energy, in its originating phase, is preservative of nature, at one with nature. (And here we must remember, as a qualification, that nature includes earthquakes, storms, and unending predation, the very imagery of *The Prelude*'s revolutionary books.) The revolutionary birth consumes the ruins of human institutions and social habits because its primary goal is an imperial expansion of its own capacity for solitary pleasure. The polis would then be reconstructed according to each person's deepest yearning, what Wordsworth in *Michael* calls "A pleasurable feeling of blind love, / The pleasure which there is in life itself" (76–77). Volney spoke for the spirit of the age when he prophesied in *The Ruins* that the human race would forsake its solitary and competitive pursuit of unsatisfying luxury and evolve into "one and the same family, governed by the same spirit and the same laws, and participating all the felicity of which human nature is susceptible."[4] The new birth of the French Revolution, then, contrasts to the Whig values triumphant in the Glorious Revolution of 1688, hailed by its admirers also as a phoenix birth ushering in a golden period of Saturnian peace. Golden it was, but as we have seen the gold was Roxana's object of conquest, not the pastoral dream of productive work and peace. The gold of that glorious revolution accumulated by a pillage of nature that itself initiated new oppression. "The central feature of the industrial revolution," Asa Briggs points out, "was not mechanization but the successful attempt to master natural forces which hitherto had mastered man. . . . Opening the door of Nature in workshop, factory, mine and forge was the great technical achievement of the eighteenth century."[5] Wordsworth might have said of this transformation, as Beaupuy of the hunger-bitten child, " 'Tis against *that* / That we are fighting" (IX.517–18). The essential spirit of Wordsworth's revolution is a return to simplicity, a use of natural forces (the windmill) and not an exploitative conquest of them.

Intelligent use, however, assumes a degree of calculation. Windmills are not made by children. Wordsworth's task is to balance the *sine qua non* of the child's self-intoxication with the less exciting

190

but no less essential development of social concern. He has recorded in several poems (placed by him together in his *Poems Referring to the Period of Childhood*) the conflict of these two conditions. *We Are Seven* and *Anecdote for Fathers* have been much analyzed by critics; more pertinent to the passage from *The Prelude* and the *Ode* is a Grasmere poem, *The Idle Shepherd Boys* (1800). The poem begins:

> The valley rings with mirth and joy;
> Among the hills the echoes play
> A never never ending song,
> To welcome in the May.

Like the mountain raven's baby birds which leave the nest to search for food, or fly "in very wantonness of heart," two idle shepherd boys, ignoring their duties, make music on pipes and "wear the time away" in games and chases. Their heedless pleasure is the spirit of the season:

> Along the river's stony marge
> The sand-lark chants a joyous song;
> The thrush is busy in the wood,
> And carols loud and strong.
> A thousand lambs are on the rocks,
> All newly born! both earth and sky
> Keep jubilee, and, more than all,
> These boys with their green coronal.

These images, which anticipate lines 36–40 of the *Ode,* gather the boys into their joy, so much so that the boys fail to notice that a lamb has slipped into the stream and become trapped within the "black and frightful rent" of a pool. A wandering poet rescues the lamb and presents it to the boys, who have already spied it in the pool and were on their way to help. The poem concludes:

> And gently did the Bard
> Those idle Shepherd-boys upbraid,
> And bade them better mind their trade.

Like *We Are Seven* and *Anecdote for Fathers* this poem conjoins two irreconcilable points of view. The adult Bard is right to upbraid the boys for not minding their trade; the boys are right in not minding their trade. Neither can nor ought to do otherwise. The poet's reproach owes its gentleness to his understanding of this fact, his sympathy for the boys' pure enjoyment of the season. He is, after all, the

same poet who chastises himself in Book I of *The Prelude* for trying to
compose verses on a splendid evening:

> 'Be it so,
> It is an injury,' said I, 'to this day
> To think of any thing but present joy.'
> So like a Peasant I pursued my road
> Beneath the evening sun, nor had one wish
> Again to bend the sabbath of that time
> To a servile yoke.   (1805 version, 107–13)

The poet believes in constructive work, in calculations of rule and law,
but in 1800 (the date also of this passage), sensual pleasure has the
greater claim. To deny Pan would be to join those industrialists who
would bend the Godhead to a servile yoke. The poet must, like the
shepherd boys, abandon work and join the universal jubilee.

The darker implications of the poem remain clear, however. The
boys' heedless play can and will have destructive consequences for
the flock. Here the pastoral is hedged by several providential accidents: the lamb is spared by the flood, the boys happen to see it, the
Bard happens to see it. But under other circumstances the lamb will
be lost, sacrificed to their indulgence, the "heinous appetites" of the
Prelude passage quoted earlier. An adult reader ought to feel two
ways about the boys' play, as he ought to (helped by the comparison
of guillotine to toy) about the Terror. A recognition of the selfish
claims of childhood, its need for majestic sway, endorses the necessity and rightness of heedless play. Sooner murder an infant in its
cradle than nurse unacted desires.[6] But the reader must also as an
adult join the Bard's apt admonishment and understand the rightness
of preserving the flock from the antisocial instincts of its supposed
protectors.

Wordsworth's child is very recognizably a "modern" child,
achieving its humanity at the occasional expense of its fellow creatures. What happens when the child fails to grow up Wordsworth
witnessed in the history of the French Revolution. The child's self-
centeredness makes it by nature imperial; "the whole world is his
unfolding," says Kerenyi.[7] The absolutism of the sansculottes and
later of Bonapartism enacts the lust for power which Wordsworth
dramatizes in the childhood card games in Book I of *The Prelude*.
Playing at lu and whist, the schoolmates substitute "plebeian cards"
for "the persons of departed Potentates." The revolution authorized
by the game is called by the poet "cheap matter ... to boyish wit"
(529). Wordsworth contrasts these dangerous games with the solitary

ecstasy depicted in the "spots of time" passages, an ecstasy to which
he is everlastingly obligated. In Wordsworth's scheme it is childhood's unknowing function to create the garden into which the adult
can retire and share with the other sons and daughters of the father-
ing child. Grasmere and native fields like it represent an earned immortality. The child must not be allowed to destroy, heedlessly if
joyfully, the very conditions of its own future existence. Wordsworth
makes this point in another Grasmere poem, *Foresight* (1802), in
which an older child admonishes a younger:

> That is a work of waste and ruin—
> Do as Charles and I are doing!
> Strawberry blossoms, one and all,
> We must spare them—here are many:
> Look at it—the flower is small,
> Small and low, though fair as any:
> Do not touch it! summers two
> I am older, Anne, than you.

Innocence will blithely pluck the bud and cause its own and others'
starvation. The speaker and Charles have reached a desirable age of
natural wisdom. They tell Anne that she can pluck all the primroses,
daisies, and violets she wants, since these will wither very shortly
anyway and revive the next spring. The strawberry flower, however,
promises pleasure and nourishment in the coming summer months.
The typology of Eden is visible in the commandment to Anne not to
bring "waste and ruin" by plucking the one flower to which "God has
given a kindlier power." The highest sensual pleasures are reserved
for the obedient heart.

　　In poems like *Foresight,* Wordsworth reminds himself of the precarious condition of his bliss. Having regained paradise he must not
allow the impulsive goadings which nourished his homesickness and
turned his steps back to the Lakes to drive him restlessly into the
troubled world again. He must not seek new worlds to conquer but
rather "fit" his mind to the particular location he has chosen to inhabit.
The "spousal verse" of *Home at Grasmere* disowns by means of the
marriage metaphor the primacy of feeling with which in his earlier
"spots of time" passages he had credited the child. A passage in the
original draft of *Home at Grasmere,* later cancelled, goes as far as he
ever dared in this regard:

> What once was deem'd so difficult is now
> Smooth, easy, without obstacle, what once

> Did to my blindness seem a sacrifice,
> The same is now a choice of the whole heart
>
>   . . . .
>
> The unappropriated bliss hath found
> An owner, and that owner I am he.
> The Lord of this enjoyment is on Earth
> And in my breast. What wonder if I speak
> With fervour, am exalted with the thought
> Of my possessions, of my genuine wealth
> Inward and outward, what I keep, have gain'd,
> Shall gain, must gain, if sound be my belief
> From past and present, rightly understood,
> That in my day of Childhood I was less
> The mind of Nature, less, take all in all,
> Whatever may be lost, than I am now.
> For proof behold this Valley, and behold
> Yon Cottage, where with me my Emma dwells. (PW, V, 315–16)

In lines preceding these he addresses himself as "thou Sun in its meridian strength, / Thou flower in its full blow, thou King and Crown." The majestic sway of sheer physical existence intoxicates him; like Adam he is Lord of the creation. The knowledge of joy provides greater unity with nature than in childhood, and he looks back on his failure to understand this fact as a "blindness." Now vision emanates from him, a sun god, as the light of a new truth.

And what of the child? We see him only in the opening two paragraphs of the poem, his early visit to the "verge" of Grasmere reported in third person, a deliberate estrangement. The portrait is very curious:

> Alone and devious from afar he came;
> And, with a sudden influx overpowered
> At sight of this seclusion, he forgot
> His haste, for hasty had his footsteps been
> As boyish his pursuits; and sighing said,
> "What happy fortune were it here to live!
> And, if a thought of dying, if a thought
> Of mortal separation, could intrude
> With paradise before him, here to die!"
> No Prophet was he, had not even a hope,
> Scarcely a wish, but one bright pleasing thought,
> A fancy in the heart of what might be
> The lot of Others, never could be his.
>
> The Station whence he look'd was soft and green,
> Not giddy yet aerial, with a depth

> Of Vale below, a height of hills above.
> For rest of body, perfect was the Spot,
> All that luxurious nature could desire.   (6–23)

When he imagines a figure who has traveled "alone and devious from afar," who attains a prospect of fair fields identified as paradise, a perfect terrestrial spot, Wordsworth is clearly recalling Milton's description of Satan's visit to Eden in Book IV of *Paradise Lost*. The allusion serves Wordsworth's thematic purposes in several ways. It allows him to contrast the youthful visitor who cannot possess the vale to "the Lord of this enjoyment" and his Emma (Dorothy) who can. The borrowing in this phrase is from Milton's description of Adam and Eve:

> Two of far nobler shape erect and tall,
> Godlike erect, with native Honor clad
> In naked Majesty seem'd Lords of all,
> And worthy seem'd for in thir looks Divine
> The image of thir glorious Maker shone,
> Truth, Wisdom, Sanctitude severe and pure,
> Severe, but in true filial freedom plac't;
> Whence true autority in men.   (IV.288–95)

Milton's figures are free, but their freedom is conditional; it is "true filial freedom." Satan alone possesses what Wordsworth credits to the child in line 37 of *Home at Grasmere*, "unfettered liberty." Satan is free to rise against the source of his own being ("Nay curs'd be thou; since against his thy will / Chose freely"), and having done so he can never reenter heaven except as an adversary. In the soliloquy that precedes his entrance into Eden he considers the possibility of submitting to "true filial freedom" by renewed worship of God but rejects this sacrifice of his own ambition. From such spiritual blindness only destructive action can follow, the extension of his empire through false promises.

As a symbol of infinite potentiality, the child possesses a power of desolation that knows no limits. *Home at Grasmere*, like the revisitation itself, attempts to establish those limits and bring that unfettered liberty under control. Wordsworth explicitly identifies such liberty with the I-will, the desire to achieve triumphs of the spirit by historical action. In this poem, years after his disillusionment with political solutions, he confesses:

> Yea to this hour I cannot read a tale
> Of two brave Vessels matched in deadly fight,

> And fighting to the death, but I am pleased
> More than a wise man ought to be. I wish,
> Fret, burn, and struggle, and in soul am there;
> But me hath Nature tamed, and bade to seek
> For other agitations, or be calm.   (721–27)

Had nature not tamed Wordsworth (with the aid of Dorothy and Coleridge, we learn in *The Prelude*), he might in body as well as in soul be on the barricades, a happy warrior. Had Wordsworth not drawn in his freedom, contained it within the embracing perimeter of a self-sufficient vale, he might have enacted the Satanic destiny symbolized by the child. Self-restraint, which Wordsworth admitted "did [once] to my blindness seem a sacrifice," finally proved to be a deliverance. He adopted the prophetic responsibility which the child ("no Prophet was he") lacks, for he had learned from his own feelings no less than from Milton that where there is no vision, Eden must perish.

Ode: Intimations of Immortality

Wordsworth's belief in the necessity of outgrowing the sublime state of childhood is rooted in the prophetic faith which envisions history as having human form and divine guidance. The child evolves joyfully into the marriageable youth, like Ololon in Blake's *Milton*. In Blake's revolutionary phase he too conceived the child as a new birth of nature, under whose godlike sway Father Time and his imperial cycles would cease. Like Wordsworth, Blake altered his vision to accommodate the course of events, giving increasingly to the father (Los) the prophetic responsibilities which in earlier works, like *America*, had been performed by the son (Orc). Blake is the purest type of the prophet whose Jerusalem has its native home in the mind.[8] Lacking native fields inhabited by semidivine presences, Blake could more easily abandon the child as a preferred symbol of imaginative sovereignty. It is one of the coincidences of history that Blake's "second birth," like Wordsworth's, occurred in the year 1800 upon removal to an Edenic place far from London, Felpham on the English coast. Home at Felpham, he discovered, as Wordsworth did, the task awaiting him:

And Now Begins a New Life, because another covering of Earth is shaken off. I am more famed in Heaven for my works than I could well concieve [sic]. In my Brain are studies & Chambers fill'd with books & pictures of old, which I wrote & painted in ages of Eternity before my mortal life; & those works are the delight & Study of Archangels. Why, then, should I be anxious about the riches or fame of mortality. The Lord our father will do for us & with us according to his Divine will for our Good.[9]

At Felpham, Blake had his great vision recorded in *Milton* of the triumph over Satan, a state of being he associated by 1800 with the failure of the revolutionary birth.

As Felpham aided Blake, so Grasmere, paradoxically, recalled Wordsworth to the ages of eternity before his mortal life and educated him in the providential necessity of passing time. But there has never been a stronger resistance to the prophetic responsibility; the demurs of Moses and Jeremiah are nothing compared to Wordsworth's foot-dragging on the path to his epic of "the growth of a poet's mind." In his first year in Grasmere, he collected the "spots of time" he had composed in the 1790s, organized them into Books I and II with lengthy additions, began Book III, and then stopped. It is not difficult to appreciate his poignant dilemma in 1801, and in fact the *Ode* dramatizes it explicitly. He had made his Adamic deliverance dependent upon a proud distinction of childhood from adult being; in *Home at Grasmere* he had affirmed that "I was less / The mind of Nature, less, take all in all, / Whatever may be lost, than I am now." But the very poem he projected as a testimony of his powers seemed to belie his statement of faith. For *The Prelude* in its early form demonstrates that childhood entirely creates the conditions by which Adam is to enjoy his lordship of nature. Was it not true, then, that the child is the real "King and Crown" and the adult man his vassal? Wordsworth begins to see himself and not the child as the ungrateful rebel; if the child is father to the man a prophetic poem with the claims of *Home at Grasmere* would be a disowning of the "true filial freedom" which even the lords of creation owe to their Creator.

Wordsworth's emotional crisis has this dilemma as its foundation. His renewed envy of the child derives from the lack of enriching experience, of challenge, in his paradise. Despite Dame Nature's assurances in *Home at Grasmere,* Wordsworth began to suffer from a want of aspirations. *The Prelude* took on the character of a lengthy epitaph, a memorial *d'outre-tombe.* Work on it became an unwelcome duty, an injury to the day. He had anticipated such feelings by the languid metaphors and phrases of *Home at Grasmere* two years earlier. "Smooth, easy, without obstacle," he writes of his coming days, and he extends the passage about being tamed by nature with the figure of a turbulent stream "whom she leads / Through quiet meadows, after he has learnt / His strength, and had his triumph and his joy." This is a portrait postmortem. Grasmere has all the elements of Spenser's Bower of Bliss, a pleasure spot that can waylay the Knight from his crusade against the Serpent. Blake's lines in *Jerusalem* capture Wordsworth's feelings of 1802:

> I know I am Urthona keeper of the Gates of Heaven
> And that I can at will expatiate in the Gardens of bliss. (82:81–82)

David Erdman's comment on these lines applies to Wordsworth as well: "'At will'—but Orc must supply the will; the prophet without the rebel is impotent."[10] Sundered from the child's unfettered liberty by his belief in self-restraint, but impotent without the child's yearning and the child's energy, Wordsworth finds near the midpoint of his earthly journey that the "growth" of the mind may only be a delusion, a transfer of power from Urthona to Urizen, a self-imprisonment.

   In 1802, then, Wordsworth veers back to the belief that the child is in fact more the mind of nature than is the adult. Rather than lose energy entirely he consolidates it again in the mythic child. Now the child is the "Mighty Prophet" and the erstwhile lord of enjoyment a ruin of time. Freighted with Wordsworth's doubts the child becomes an endangered being. One poem, written the same year as the opening stanzas of the *Ode*, will serve as the best approach to the more complex masterpiece. I will quote it in full.

TO H. C.
SIX YEARS OLD

O thou! whose fancies from afar are brought;
Who of thy words dost make a mock apparel,
And fittest to unutterable thought
The breeze-like motion and the self-born carol;
Thou faery voyager! that dost float
In such clear water, that thy boat
May rather seem
To brood on air than on an earthly stream;
Suspended in a stream as clear as sky,
Where earth and heaven do make one imagery;
O blessèd vision! happy child!
Thou art so exquisitely wild,
I think of thee with many fears
For what may be thy lot in future years.

   I thought of times when Pain might be thy guest,
Lord of thy house and hospitality;
And Grief, uneasy lover! never rest
But when she sate within the touch of thee.
O too industrious folly!

O vain and causeless melancholy!
Nature will either end thee quite;
Or, lengthening out thy season of delight,
Preserve for thee, by individual right,
A young lamb's heart among the full-grown flocks.
What hast thou to do with sorrow,
Or the injuries of to-morrow?
Thou art a dew-drop, which the morn brings forth,
Ill fitted to sustain unkindly shocks,
Or to be trailed along the soiling earth;
A gem that glitters while it lives,
And no forewarning gives;
But, at the touch of wrong, without a strife
Slips in a moment out of life.   (PW, I, 247)

Here is Wordsworth's version of Blake's Thel—an insubstantial, vulnerable spirit imagined in a state preceding Generation. In this poem H. C. (Hartley Coleridge) is the furthest thing from the revolutionary child secure in its materiality, the "child of Nature." H. C. is ill-fitted to be trailed along the "soiling earth"; he must voyage on streams of air, fated like all dew-drops to evaporate after morning.

Wordsworth, in the manner of graveyard psychology, sees the child's very strengths as monitors of decay. Possession summons loss, exuberant life clings by the hooks and eyes of the poet's despondency to the terror of onrushing death. He is accustomed to killing off his literary children—Lucy being the foremost victim—but never in his poetry has the motive been so starkly spelled out. H. C. is condemned by the poet's own fears for the future, and though there are a few lines of hope for the preservation of his innocence in adult life they are not seriously intended. The only "Lord" in this poem is Pain, and H. C.'s demon lover, in this mockery of the spousal verse Wordsworth had projected, is Grief. H. C. cannot survive because Wordsworth is unwilling to connect the advantages the child enjoys in his state of blessedness with the continuation, however changed, of those advantages. The self-born carol is not attached to the poetic power; the "exquisitely wild" play must remain infantile, for Wordsworth fears the adult version of untamed spirits. H. C., then, is like the stone and shell of the Arab dream, the endangered lamb of The Idle Shepherd Boys, the strawberry flower of Foresight, and, looking ahead, the tuft of primroses in the poem of that title. All of these are frail vessels threatened by radical change, emblems of the poet's spiritual center in Grasmere.

It is in this context that we can speak of the Christian myth of the child. One historian of childhood, Horace Scudder, points out that the child in early English ballads and legendry most often represents an idealized and sentimental Christian spirit opposed to the brutality and violence of the northern temperament. The Christian child endures wrong and converts his tormentors by the example of forebearance and forgiveness. The late eighteenth century found this view preferable to that of the revolutionary child, the godhead strangling serpents in its cradle. Scudder remarks that "in the conception of French sentiment of the Rousseau and St. Pierre type, the child is a refuge from present evil, a mournful reminiscence of a lost Paradise. If only we could keep it a child! is the cry of this school,—keep it from knowing this wicked, unhappy world!"[11] Wordsworth, as Scudder points out, struggled to overcome this sentiment in himself. His philosophy of nature is a means of celebrating incarnation, and his quest for a worldly Eden is an affirmation that the adult man can regain his status, his "King and Crown," from the heavenly model:

> Our childhood sits,
> Our simple childhood, sits upon a throne
> That hath more power than all the elements.
>
> (*Prelude*, V.507–09)

In 1802, however, Wordsworth tries to keep the incarnation of the heavenly spirit from taking place. H. C. is suspended between heaven and earth, waiting, as it were, for Wordsworth to resolve his doubts about history before receiving permission to enter the sphere of earthly influence.

At this hopeless juncture Wordsworth sees only two alternatives once the heavenly child has descended. Either its light will fade into the light of common day, the progress of the *Ode*, or it will be willfully given up to history, as political light, to help create the greater enlightenment of the future. Neither alternative attracted the poet in 1802. In retrospect, he seems to be drawing together the various clues left by his own experience and his observation of real children in order to construct a model of absolute glory, in case he has some further use for it. The "Child of Joy" in the *Ode* (34) is a figure of potentiality held in reserve (literally in the poet's desk for two years) until its light is needed to overcome one of those obstacles which, Wordsworth later warned Mathetes, might send the stream of life backward for many miles before it could once again advance.

As a symbol of potentiality the "Child of Joy" is an abstract figure derived from realistic situations that Wordsworth narrates elsewhere. He is a "happy Shepherd-boy" at a "jubilee," but Wordsworth here omits the social responsibilities that make the child's heedless joy a danger to the flock in *The Idle Shepherd Boys*. The children are culling May flowers in the valleys but we are not told whether the strawberry flower falls victim with the rest. In short, the first stanzas of the *Ode* give us what the eighteenth century called "ideal property," a pastoral scene immune from danger. The scene is a reverie of fairyland, to use a term popular with the Wordsworth circle. Fairyland is a place in which celestial and terrestrial reflections make one imagery, where enchanted beings act their desires. "Shadowy recollections" preserve in the adult the magical capacity to reenter this garden of potentiality.

Coleridge depicts this capacity in *The Eolian Harp*, where such recollections, urged on by the "witchery of sound" emanating from the harp, draw his reveries out of their earthly source until he too is like a bird of paradise, footless, feeding on dew and nectar. His playful reveries are "wild and various" like the "self-born carol" of H. C. This capacity is the fond dream of the Romantic poets, the fundamental tenet of all their hopes for human happiness. In his essay, "On Life," Shelley wrote that "there are some persons who ... are always children. Those who are subject to the state called reverie feel as if their nature were dissolved into the surrounding universe, or as if the surrounding universe were absorbed into their being."[12] Unfortunately, the unfettered freedom of reverie the poets celebrate is constantly brought short by the "true filial freedom" endowed upon man as a condition of living in Eden. Coleridge is admonished in this poem by his dear Sara, "meek Daughter in the family of Christ." Sara's Christ is Milton's, the incarnated revolutionary, the light-bringer and not the dweller in shadows.

The "Child of Joy," even in a crowd of children, is always self-absorbed, a creature of its own reverie. In *Characteristics of a Child Three Years Old*, Wordsworth remarks that "this happy Creature of herself / Is all-sufficient; solitude to her / Is blithe society, who fills the air / With gladness and involuntary songs." Dorothy's descriptions of the Coleridge children have the same theme. Sara Coleridge, age three, is "an object of pure delight. She is as quick as a Fairy." The same year (1804) she writes, "such a little Fairy! a spirit! a thing that hardly seems to touch the earth as she skims along." The language is that of Wordsworth's poem on Hartley, who, two years older, is now described by Dorothy, in the same letter, in elegiac phrases: "Hartley is grown taller; he is still exceedingly slender, and there is so much thought and feeling in his face that it is scarcely possible for a person with any tenderness of mind and discrimination to look at him with indifference. It seemed to me that all that was left of the *Child* was wearing out of his face" (*Letters*, I, 482, 494).[13] Thought and feeling involve a recognition of other things and other people, and a discriminating valuation of them. They are qualities necessary to humanity but they decay the self-absorption in which the fullest experience of bliss occurs.

Fairyland exerts a powerful influence over the *Ode* of 1802, which, according to Mark L. Reed's *Chronology*, very possibly includes all of stanzas i–viii. Wordsworth realizes the state of immortality but only by setting it at odds with earthly life. By a series of poignant contrasts, these stanzas bring the poem to its lowest point of despair; they show the growing child yoked by the years to custom and bending under a weight "heavy as frost, and deep almost as life!" The last word is spit out as an insult because it expresses Wordsworth's present dissatisfaction with life in Grasmere. In attributing the impression of immortality to a symbolic and abstract child, a figure of potentiality, he is realizing a truism—that timelessness surrounds those incognizant of time. The disconnection between "life" and "Immortality" must have disturbed Wordsworth enough to prevent him from finishing the poem or considering it finished.

From our comfortable distance, Wordsworth seems blindly with his blessedness at strife. 1802 is the year of his marriage, a year of peace with France, a time preceding the depredations of Grasmere recorded in the last chapter and preceding the death of friends and family. His melancholy cannot help but resemble that of Rasselas in Samuel Johnson's tale. "I can discover within me no power of perception which is not glutted with its proper pleasure, yet I do not feel myself delighted," Rasselas complains in chapter 3. Rasselas pleads with his old instructor to give him aspiration, something to desire:

The old man was surprized at this new species of affliction, and knew not what to reply, yet was unwilling to be silent. "Sir," said he, "if you had seen the miseries of the world, you would know how to value your present state." "Now," said the prince, "you have given me something to desire; I shall long to see the miseries of the world, since the sight of them is necessary to happiness."

"Life," which Wordsworth had identified with his "Centre," his "whole without dependence or defect," could only be revalued under the pressure of some external stimulus. The smooth and easy course of his recent life needed an obstacle so that his original sources of strength could regather.

Rasselas had to leave the Happy Valley in order to confront the miseries of the world, but Wordsworth in 1803 had only to pick up the newspaper. In 1803 the treaty of Amiens collapsed and England again declared war on France. Napoleon, now "consul for life," vowed to

invade England and destroy it. David Erdman describes the mood of
the nation:

Not since the days of the Spanish Armada and not again till 1940 has England
suffered such an invasion alarm as in the autumn and winter of 1803. Napoleon was known to be assembling thousands of flat-bottomed gunboats and
rafts to embark a vast army with ten thousand horses and a prodigious four
hundred pieces of cannon.... Printing presses were busy, not with Sublime
Allegories but with handbills rousing Britons to "Seize the Musket, grasp the
Lance," and slay "the Hell-born Sons of France!" Prophetic writings? To
prove that Bonaparte was the genuine Apocalyptic Beast, an eater of human
flesh and poisoner of the sick.... Even candy was being made in the shape of
"Boney's Ribs" for children to crunch on.[14]

I have discussed Wordsworth's alarmed reaction to these threats in
chapter nine. Of special relevance to the *Ode*, which Wordsworth
returned to in the winter of 1803–04, is the way he turned during this
crisis to the figure of Milton as a model for the poet overtaken by
events. Milton's Eden had served him as the type of Grasmere and
his lordly place in it; now Milton's example was needed for the preservation of the same paradise.

   Wordsworth's sonnets of this period, themselves imitations of
Milton's trumpet blasts, laud the Puritan spirit as a continuing source
of political light. "Milton! thou shouldst be living at this hour" is the
most famous of these, but more to our purposes is the following:

> Great men have been among us; hands that penned
> And tongues that uttered wisdom—better none:
> The later Sidney, Marvel, Harrington,
> Young Vane, and others who called Milton friend.
> These moralists could act and comprehend:
> They knew how genuine glory was put on;
> Taught us how rightfully a nation shone
> In splendour: what strength was, that would not bend
> But in magnanimous meekness. France, 'tis strange,
> Hath brought forth no such souls as we had then.
> Perpetual emptiness! unceasing change!
> No single volume paramount, no code,
> No master spirit, no determined road;
> But equally a want of books and men!   (PW, III, 116)

This poem, published in 1807, probably antedates the invasion
threats, but it belongs to the same spirit. It is a response to Napoleon's invasion of Switzerland in October of 1802, and the war fever
that swept England in subsequent months. The poem is distinguished by the association of "moralists" and "genuine glory," a

linkage that Wordsworth had forged in his revolutionary period but abandoned after his return to the Lakes in the 1790s. Now, again, a nation shines in righteous splendor. His praise of the moralists who knew what strength was and would not bend under affliction sounds like a chastisement of his own recent waverings and despair. The memory of such great men, who rose to the challenge of historical necessity, stimulates him to another defense of the light he believes worth preserving. This defense he conceives as a rebellion against imperialism, this time the "unceasing change" that France desires to consummate in the world. He is again rebel and prophet both; the child's energies are drawn back into Grasmere where they are needed. *The Prelude* and the *Ode*, both of them resumed in 1804, begin to chronicle a renewed association between "Immortality" and "life."

The turn which Wordsworth gives to the *Ode* in 1804 was certainly implicit in the stanzas of 1802, though he could not bring himself to compose it. Stanza ix begins:

> O joy! that in our embers
> Is something that doth live,
> That nature yet remembers
> What was so fugitive!
> The thought of our past years in me doth breed
> Perpetual benediction.

The child's light, illumined in years of ecstatic solitude, remains a potential source of power for the adult, who, though dependent upon thought and fellow-feeling for pleasure, can extend the light he receives from "the imperial palace whence he came" throughout the community he loves. In a late addition to *Home at Grasmere* Wordsworth elaborated on the saving remnant of the master light he recognized in himself:

> I would stand clear, but yet to me I feel
> That an internal brightness is vouchsafed
> That must not die, that must not pass away.
> Why does this inward lustre fondly seek,
> And gladly blend with outward fellowship?
> Why do *they* shine around me whom I thus revere?
>   . . . .
> Possessions have I that are solely mine,
> Something within which yet is shared by none,
> Not even the nearest to me and most dear,
> Something which power and effort may impart,
> I would impart it, I would spread it wide,
> Immortal in the world which is to come.   (674–80, 686–91)

So long as Wordsworth kept his eye on the child, on Hartley Coleridge or even himself, he was fated to see only waste and ruin. But
the light itself he rediscovered in everything that had been preserved
by its original power: in Grasmere, in the wisdom of great men, in
love, and in his own poetic genius. "We in thought will join your
throng," he says to the children who pipe and play, meaning, I take
it, that thought itself, the philosophic mind, need not and should not
cease from play. The light of the mind, whether "wild and various" in
its twilight reveries or perfectly ordered in the cadences of verse and
prose, compensates for the eye's loss of glory by "inward lustre."

Wordsworth changes the controlling metaphor in stanza ix, but
the prospect on futurity remains the same:

> Hence in a season of calm weather
>   Though inland far we be,
> Our Souls have sight of that immortal sea
>   Which brought us hither,
>   Can in a moment travel thither,
> And see the Children sport upon the shore,
> And hear the mighty waters rolling evermore.

The sea is the Imperium Pelagi of the Arab Dream, but like the mythic
child who emerges from it into earthly being it can represent salvation
instead of annihilation. The sea is destroyer and preserver both, like
Shelley's west wind. The shell of the Arab Dream becomes implicitly
in the *Ode* and explicitly in *The Excursion* the shell of "the universe
itself" which in Book IV(1132–46) "a curious child" applies to his ear,
and hears "Authentic tidings of invisible things; / Of ebb and flow,
and ever-during power; / And central peace, subsisting at the heart /
Of endless agitation." Wordsworth makes a point of the child's dwelling "upon a tract / Of inland ground," like the adult writer and reader
of the *Ode*. The "central peace" of the passage may recall *Home at
Grasmere* but here Wordsworth does not cling to the still water of
Grasmere Lake as a refuge against the gathering deluge; in his
greatest works after the *Ode*, and *The Excursion* is certainly one, he
turns to the "mighty waters" which all can hear by the shell of poetry,
the shell of childhood, the shell of the universe itself—all fused in his
lucent imagination.

The *Ode*, then, though an entirely nonpolitical poem, reflects the
education of Wordsworth's imagination in a period of "Perpetual
emptiness! unceasing change!" His determination to uphold the
philosophic mind in the midst of his afflictions rather than be conquered by despair represents a heroic engagement with the forces of

mutability. Wordsworth knew that the outcome of such a struggle would be as precarious as the *Ode* itself, a wavering balance between mortality and the "shadowy recollections"

> Which neither listlessness, nor mad endeavour,
>   Nor Man nor Boy,
> Nor all that is at enmity with joy,
> Can utterly abolish or destroy!

He saw clearly that the imperial power could and did destroy its believers by overwhelming their reason. He fears the "mad endeavour" that overtook poets like Chatterton and Collins, and he fears that the master light, projected into the future as political light, will deceive civilized men into exchanging their arduous work for anarchy, for heedless play. Coleridge drew the several dangers together in an essay he wrote for *The Friend* in 1809:

Doubtless, to act is nobler than to think: but as the old man doth not become a child by means of his second childishness, as little can a nation exempt itself from the necessity of thinking, which has once learnt to think. Miserable was the delusion of the late mad Realizer of mad Dreams, in his belief that he should ultimately succeed in transforming the nations of Europe into the unreasoning hordes of a Babylonian or Tartar Empire, or even in reducing the age to the simplicity, (so desirable for tyrants) of those times, when the sword and the plough were the sole implements of human skill. Those are epochs in the history of a people which having been can never more recur. Extirpate all civilization and all its arts by the sword, trample down all antient Institutions, Rights, Distinctions, and Privileges, drag us backward to our old Barbarism, as beasts to the den of Cacus—deemed you that thus you could re-create the unexamining and boisterous youth of the world, when the sole questions were—"What is to be conquered? and who is the most famous leader!"[15]

"Unexamining... unreasoning," these are the bugbears of the philosophic mind, which defends from annihilation what the "mad Realizer of mad Dreams" threatens by the force of primitive feelings. It is no coincidence that the greatest conservative voices after Burke were those of former primitivists.

It is certainly true that Wordsworth dwindled to the ruin of Jupiter Lucetius, the lost leader of Shelley's *Prometheus Unbound* whose majestic sway is comprised of restrictive laws and morbid philosophy. A glance at one of Wordsworth's later poems of childhood, like *The Longest Day*, reveals him importing the assumptions of graveyard literature in order to deny the value of a second birth. Immortality is no longer the transfiguration of essential life in this world but only a ghostly continuance beyond the beckoning grave. Against the somber background of his later years, when his heart, like Peele Castle, was "cased in the unfeeling armor of old time," the humane sentiments of the *Ode* seem both more disturbing and more consoling.

The mention of *Prometheus Unbound* reminds us that Wordsworth's prophetic claims for the majestic sway of the symbolic child found their most complete dramatization not in his own later work but in the masterpiece of his younger contemporary, Shelley. *Prometheus Unbound* is a work redolent with echoes from the *Ode* and other of Wordsworth's poems; it owes as much to him as to its more obvious classical influences. In Shelley's work, as in Wordsworth's, the whole force of the poetic imagination operates to transform human time into a joyful measure, the mercy of eternity. The embodiment of this transformation, though not the cause of it, is the Wordsworthian child, the Spirit of the Earth who embraces the contrary qualities of power and frailty. The newborn Spirit begins his sway when humanity, imaged as Prometheus, exorcises from its own haunted mind the depraved imperialism Shelley associated with all commanding hierarchies. Prometheus awakens from his nightmare by announcing his forgiveness of Jupiter, by understanding that usurpation of power ungoverned by love imprisons humanity in the cycles of ruin that mortals know as history. Jupiter is destroyed by his "child," Demogorgon (III.i.54), whose own self-extinction preserves the universe of love.

Shelley, then, urges the necessity of growth as insistently as does Wordsworth. The Spirit of the Earth is a mutable child. It says to its mother, Asia, a figure of the fulfilling love required by humanity, "Mother, I am grown wiser, though a child / Cannot be wise like thee, within the day" (III.iv.33–34). The prolific sexual imagery which follows his appearance reminds us that the child symbolizes bodily joy. Shelley willingly accepts the condition of mutability and death, though he diminishes their potency by expanding the life of humanity to *almost* unlimited proportions. Immortality is achieved by an imperial overwhelming of physical symbols which restrain man from complete self-realization. The great vision of cosmic harmony in Act IV casts out all that is mortal but not human:

> The beams flash on
> And make appear the melancholy ruins
> Of cancelled cycles; anchors, beaks of ships;
> Planks turned to marble; quivers, helms and spears,
> And gorgon-headed targes, and the wheels
> Of scythed chariots, and the emblazonry

> Of trophies, standards, and armorial beasts,
> Round which death laughed, sepulchred emblems
> Of dead destruction, ruin within ruin!   (287–95)

The paraphernalia of empire is swept away by the power of Shelley's revolutionary imagination, but it is replaced by "self-empire, and the majesty of love" (II.iv.42). As Wordsworth proclaimed in *Home at Grasmere*, where there is self-empire the child does not become a haunting threat to Adamic pleasures. In Shelley's pastoral dream as well, man and woman are the lords of enjoyment.

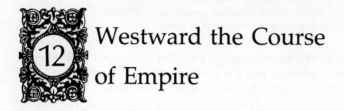

Westward the Course
of Empire

*The soul is not twin-born but the only begotten, and though revealing itself as a child
in time, child in appearance, is of a fatal and universal power, admitting no co-life.*
—*Emerson*, Experience

The Old and New Worlds

PROBABLY THE MOST FAMOUS expression of the ruin sentiment in
English literature is Lord Byron's lines on the Roman Colosseum and
Forum in *Childe Harold's Pilgrimage.* His stanzas made their way into
textbooks of rhetoric, school orations, and the common parlance so
that even in the New World their phrases echoed on the stage, in the
Congress, and, if we believe Eugene O'Neill's *A Touch of the Poet,* in
everyman's privacy at the mirror. They convey a profound *amor fati,* a
willingness, in Byron's words, "to meditate amongst decay, and
stand / A ruin amidst ruins" (IV.217–18).[1] They pay tribute to glory
without blinking at the absolute loss inescapable from the honor of
glorious achievement, and by doing so summarize complex attitudes
handed down from artist to artist since the Renaissance. Byron's
eloquence is not only a reflection of his own *mal de siècle* but a motivat-
ing cause of elegiac meditations in subsequent generations. When
Matthew Arnold turns his attention to the triumph of Alaric, or
Dorothea Brooke visits the ruins of Rome in *Middlemarch,* or Thomas
Cole begins his designs for a series of mammoth paintings on *The
Course of Empire,* Byron's spirit weighs upon them with the force of
centuries.

Byron is the bard of civilization, mournful that imperial power
could not perpetually sweep over nations with its trumpet call to
freedom, noble aspiration, and heroic action. In Canto II, Harold sits
in the temple of Jupiter watching the blithe Athenians pass unstirred
by the ruined ideal which Jupiter represents. Harold knows better

than they how the pursuit of divine light led to the formation of a democratic state, the flowering of art and philosophy, the architectural marvel of the Parthenon itself. It is this power which Byron praises in an adaptation of *Prometheus Bound*, in his earliest volume:

> Great Jove, to whose almighty throne
> Both gods and mortals homage pay,
> Ne'er may my soul thy power disown,
> Thy dread behests ne'er disobey.
>
>   . . . .
>
> My voice shall raise no impious strain
> 'Gainst him who rules the sky and azure main.

The Athenian Empire, not Eden or Arcadia, is Byron's perpetual and most cherished myth. When he praises other imperial civilizations—Naples, Venice, Rome—he has in mind always that "land of lost gods and godlike men" (II.802) which was the cradle of liberty. Robert Gleckner argues, in *Byron and the Ruins of Paradise*, that Byron's whole work, including the satires, can be profitably seen as a cry against the injustice of mankind's growing up, its descent from the place of its first perfect self-realization. Haunted by images of perfection preserved in art and history, modern man confronts only the diminished shadows of past greatness.[2] In the modern world Pericles yields to "bastard Attilas" like Napoleon and Ali Pasha, and the treasures of Athens to spoilers like Lord Elgin who would rather transfer glory than re-create it.[3] Harold found it "a worthless world to win or lose" when he came to judge Napoleon's fall, making it clear that he claimed no loyalty to the Europe preserved from conquest. Byron almost always exposed the illusion of new beginnings as tragic, futile, or stupid, even though people like himself often chose to die for it.

Byron, like Shelley, tends to depict England as the fallen form of Jupiter Lucetius, as a place of corruption needing yet suppressing new light from its rebellious spirit. England is another "Sea-Sodom" like Venice in *Marino Faliero*, which a providential act of history may soon humble and reform. And yet it would be a mistake to infer that Byron wishes such an overthrow. If he is the fire-breathing author of *Prometheus*, he is also the panegyrist of Voltaire and Gibbon in *Childe Harold's Pilgrimage*; he holds fast to the judicious humanism that resists the Promethean energies of the democratic spirit as he saw it in France and America. Byron's imagination is not apocalyptic; it values discipline and hierarchy, it clings to even the shadow of Jupiter's majestic sway. For this reason he could not countenance the extreme

form of revolutionary sentiment that proclaimed, quite simply, that
the Old World was irredeemably ruined. Philip Freneau's prophetic
utterance is typical of this charge:

> From Europe's realms fair freedom has retired,
> And even in Britain has the spark expired—
> Sigh for the change your haughty empire feels,
> Sigh for the doom that no disguise conceals!
> Freedom no more shall Albion's cliffs survey;
> Corruption there has centered all her sway.[4]

Democracy had omnipotent power in readiness, appealing as it did to
the largest multitude, and in America it possessed a new homeland
with seemingly unlimited space and resources. In Byron's view, the
very self-confidence of American democracy, its proud disowning of
the parent civilization, would cause it to recapitulate the model of
oppression. He saw in the institution of slavery the first omen of
premature ruin for the United States.

Byron preferred a corrupt state in vital touch with the glory of
Greece to a deracinated state intellectually defenseless against its own
craving for power. He rebuked a friend for his admiration of Robes-
pierre and Marat by exclaiming: "Why, our classical education alone
should teach us to trample on such unredeemed dirt as the *dis*-honest
bluntness, the ignorant brutality, the unblushing baseness of these
two miscreants, and all who believe in them."[5] Byron probably has in
mind the orations of Cicero against Catiline; his moral imagination,
when confronted with an absolutist rhetoric like Freneau's, becomes
highly combative. His recorded opinions on America seem to depend
on his audience: laudatory of the freedom and moderation of the
American government when speaking to Americans, patronizing of
American vulgarity when addressed to his inner circle. He delivered
one of his most sustained comments on America to William Parry in
Missolonghi, shortly before his death:

They are children who profit by the knowledge of their parents, but who are
at the same time the victims of their prejudices. They have a fresh country to
work on, and the civilization and knowledge of Europe to work with. They
have carried with them, however, some of the worst vices of European society, and they have been heightened in the Southern states by a voluptuous
climate, and by the facility the people once had of procuring slaves. Though I
think the government of America good, because it is the government of the
whole people, and adapted to their views, I have no love for America. It is not
a country I should like to visit. The Americans, they say, are great egotists. I
suppose all the people of young countries are so. Man must have something

to be vain of, and when he has no ancestors in whose fame he may exult, he must talk and boast of himself.[6]

Byron shows his aristocratic prejudice in the remark about "ancestors in whose fame he may exult," but there is more than personal snobbery; he has in mind the antiquity of the country for which he was sacrificing his fortune and, though he did not know it, his life. Not only his ancestral estate, Newstead Abbey, but the Temple of Jupiter looms over his condescension toward America.

These remarks of 1824, however, should be taken less as a reasoned critique and more as a commonplace of the period, enforced and reinforced by reports from travelers returning from the New World. These reports agreed as if by conspiracy on the notion of "youthful decay." America had been ruined from the start by the superimposition of European vices on the primitive condition of the Indian tribes. The impure mixture, as European visitors saw it, contained too much of the poisonous to effect the radical goals either of the first settlers or the Founding Fathers. Byron's friend and biographer, Thomas Moore, put the case succinctly in a preface to his *Odes, Epistles and Other Poems* (1806), published shortly after a visit to the eastern states and Canada:

The rude familiarity of the lower orders, and indeed the unpolished state of society in general, would neither surprise nor disgust, if they seemed to flow from that simplicity of character, that honest ignorance of the gloss of refinement, which may be looked for in a new and inexperienced people. But, when we find them arrived at maturity in most of the vices, and all the pride, of civilization, while they are still so remote from its elegant characteristics, it is impossible not to feel that this youthful decay, this crude anticipation of the natural period of corruption, represses every sanguine hope of the future energy and greatness of America.[7]

Moore's tour of the states divided neatly into a visit to the seaboard estates and cities, where he could appreciate the genteel imitations of classical style, and inland to Niagara Falls, where he could experience the Sublime. This became a standard arc in the American version of the Grand Tour, a circular odyssey by which the meaning of America could be formulated. America had already failed as a civilization, and so one passed through its communities as mere way stations on the road to the essential locus, the landscape whose beauty has terror in it. The view of Niagara, like Wordsworth's prospect from Mount Snowdon in *The Prelude*, or Shelley's vision of Mont Blanc, returned man to the source of life itself, the primal energy from which man had become estranged but yearned to return. Wilderness America excited

Moore, and, in a kindred imagery to his, drew from Byron his most extended praise of the New World.

In *Don Juan* Byron devotes seven stanzas to Daniel Boone, praising the frontiersman as a spirit who kept in front of the civilization he himself brought into being. The stanza which introduces the series on Boone uses the ruin sentiment to make its point:

> 'God made the country, and man made the town,'
> So Cowper says—and I begin to be
> Of his opinion, when I see cast down
> Rome, Babylon, Tyre, Carthage, Nineveh,
> All walls men know, and many never known;
> And pondering on the present and the past,
> To deem the woods shall be our home at last.   (VIII.474–80)

The speaker's whimsical sallies in *Don Juan* usually have a serious point and this one is no exception. Boone enjoys a "home" in nature, "even in age the child / Of Nature," which the troubled Juan is toiling all his life to find. The equivalent of Boone's virgin land in Juan's experience is Haidée, the containing form of Juan's dream of perfect union. Their idyll together in the cave is a timeless refuge from the world of action and high endeavor. They conceive there the child, "a second principle of life" (IV.554), which realizes the human dream of perpetuating unity of being. As a narrative poet, however, Byron is faithful to Jupiter, and will not turn his great poem, as Shelley did *Prometheus Unbound,* into a celebration of the redeeming child, the Spirit of the Earth. Byron kills off Haidée and the second principle with her, for Juan can have no legitimate successors. Boone, the pioneer, leaves behind him "a sylvan tribe of children of the chase," whom Byron describes as "tall, and strong, and swift of foot were they, / Beyond the dwarfing city's pale abortions." Here again are the two Americas: pale copies of a parent culture, "abortions" because they suffer from premature ruin, and the Wordsworthian child who must, like Boone, keep aloof from urban hegemony in order to thrive. Haidée dies because her father, Lambro, opposes his tyrannical will to her desires; in America Lambro is the city itself, aborting its time-bound conceptions.

After the sylvan interlude devoted to Boone, Byron turns the poem back to its essential theme:

> So much for Nature:—by way of variety,
> Now back to thy great joys, Civilisation!
> And the sweet consequence of large society,
> War, pestilence, the despot's desolation,
> The kingly scourge, the lust of notoriety.   (VIII.537–41) —

Byron's true home as a creative artist is this fallen world in which power usurps the place of continuity; when he turns from Boone, Byron moves on to a lengthy description of the annihilation of Ismail. This movement of mind can be found everywhere in Byron's verse. If he summons a fairyland, like Venice in *Childe Harold's Pilgrimage,* he watches it give way to a prospect of ruin, her glory "whelm'd beneath the waves" of successive invasions (IV.115). He is like his own Sardanapalus, an idle dreamer who is nevertheless a descendant of Nimrod, and rises to the opportunity of a rousing battle. The paradises he conceives are therefore always lost in advance, doomed by the poet's own sense of historical inevitability. It is Boone's children whom Byron (of all people) criticizes as egotistical in his remarks to Parry. Byron, like Boone, must move further west toward the frontier of his imagination until, in *The Island,* he reaches the "infant world" (IV.420) of Toobonai in the Pacific. Toobonai is a paradise but Fletcher Christian, the mutineer who leads his party into the perfect spot, brings Satanic vices with him. Christian's senseless murder of a comrade, as he himself is dying, foreshadows the violence which time and trade will bring to the island. The mutineer Torquil and the native girl Neuha hope to enjoy "happy days" in their sanctuary, "Neuha's Cave," but like Juan and Haidée they are living on borrowed time. In this demonic version of *Pilgrim's Progress,* the presence of Christian turns a heaven into hell, and Christian's defiling act at the conclusion of the poem carries the promise of more wanton destruction. The infant world must grow up and receive its inheritance from the ages.

Byron is content to gaze upon America with hopeless pity, and then turn back to his chronicles of the original civilization, the parent power. Wordsworth, in keeping with his suspicion of all "unfettered liberty," expresses a greater degree of scorn for the New World. He derived his knowledge about American landscape from travel literature, which emphasized the wild beauty and seclusion of Edenic spots. Before his revisitation of Grasmere, he read William Bartram's *Travels* (1792) and the lyrical passion of Bartram's descriptions inflamed his, no less than Coleridge's, yearning to locate and settle in a secluded vale. In Bartram's rapturous language we hear the voice of Wordsworth's later poetry of praise:

What a beautiful retreat is here! blessed unviolated spot of earth, rising from the limpid waters of the lake: its fragrant grove and blooming lawns invested and protected by encircling ranks of Yucca gloriosa. A fascinating atmosphere surrounds this blissful garden! . . .

How happily situated is this retired spot of earth! What an elysium it is! where the wandering Siminole, the naked red warrior, roams at large, and after the vigorous chase retires from the scorching heat of the meridian sun.

Here he reclines, and reposes under the odoriferous shades of Zanthoxylon, his verdant couch guarded by the Deity; Liberty, and the Muses, inspiring him with wisdom and valour, whilst the balmy zephyrs fan him to sleep.[8]

Coleridge and Southey actually planned to establish an ideal community, a Pantisocracy, on the banks of the Susquehanna River. But Wordsworth, a Lord Elgin of the spirit, preferred to transfer the new beginnings represented by America to English soil. Bartram's America appears most significantly in Wordsworth's poetry about Grasmere. A beautiful passage from Jonathan Carver's *Travels through the interior parts of North-America* (1778), describing how the transparency of a lake seems to suspend a boat between earth and heaven, is imported (with a note for credit) into the poem, *To H. C.* Wordsworth cherishes the English child in the English landscape and reserves for him the optical effect of glorification.

The Wordsworth who sought a refuge in the 1790s, as I have shown, is the Adamic Wordsworth, the "Lord of enjoyment" who prefers maturity to childhood. Like the conceivers of Pantisocracy, Wordsworth wanted to be a founder of civilization and not what Byron calls Daniel Boone, "the man of Ross run wild." The America of Bartram is the naked force of unlimited potentiality, the primal source. For this very reason Wordsworth fears its destructive lure, its overabundance of life. "So much of earth—so much of heaven" is his description of the young American suitor's upbringing in the narrative of *Ruth* (1799). In that poem, Wordsworth's most extensive meditation on the meaning of America, the suitor, not himself an Indian, is depicted roaming with "vagrant bands / Of Indians in the West." From these companions—and here Wordsworth echoes Bartram very selectively—the youth receives the vices of lawlessness and self-indulgence:

> His genius and his moral frame
> Were thus impaired, and he became
> The slave of low desires:
> A Man who without self-control
> Would seek what the degraded soul
> Unworthily admires.   (151–56)

The suitor unsurprisingly proves a failure at conjugal love and deserts Ruth for the wilderness. When *Ruth* is set beside another poem of this period, *The Complaint of a Forsaken Indian Woman* (1798), a pattern of condescension seems to emerge. The Indian woman is left to die by her companions because she is too ill to travel with them. Slaves of necessity, the Indian tribes cannot afford compassion; they must practice human sacrifice to preserve the whole of the tribe. Wordsworth's scorn for the Indian way of life is seen again in *The Excursion*, where the Solitary relates his quest for "Primeval Nature's child" after the new birth of the French Revolution failed his expectations. The Solitary tells how he migrated to America, and, after being put off by the vulgarity of the eastern seaboard, plunged into "the unviolated woods" to find the noble savage:

> But that pure archetype of human greatness,
> I found him not. There, in his stead, appeared
> A creature, squalid, vengeful, and impure;
> Remorseless, and submissive to no law
> But superstitious fear, and abject sloth.   (III.951–55)

The Solitary returns to England, and to a "little lowly vale" where he settles down. When the narrator of the poem describes the vale we recognize its lineaments at once as Grasmere's:

> were this
> Man's only dwelling, sole appointed seat,
> First, last, and single, in the breathing world,
> It could not be more quiet: peace is here
> Or nowhere.   (II.361–65)

In England, not America, lies the true center of the world man imagines for his future happiness.

Many English writers, then, perceived America as young but old, like Hardy's fatal child, Father Time, in *Jude the Obscure*. The weight of ages had descended upon America, heavy as frost, and congealed the freshness which Renaissance explorers had praised as the certain evidence of America's real identity, Eden. As a symbolic rebirth of human nature America had undergone the process of degeneration that historians had described in classical models; it presented a well-mapped stretch of psychohistory. For our purposes, the syndrome of events that resulted in the ruin of America's natural landscape needs to be isolated and exemplified, for from the beginning the meaning of America lay in its wilderness.

The earliest Renaissance explorers firmly established the New World as a bountiful garden reserved by Providence for man's everlasting delight. The report of Florida by Jean Ribaut in 1562 may be cited as representative: the country seemed to him "the fairest, frutefullest and pleasantest of all the worlde, habonding in honney, veneson, wildfoule, forrestes, woodes of all sortes... and to be shorte it is a thing inspeakable, the comodities that be sene there and shalbe founde more and more in this incomperable lande, never as yet broken with plowe irons, bringing forthe all thinges according to his first nature, whereof the eternall God endued yt."⁹ The nakedness of the Indians reminded Europeans that their own iconography of the unfallen soul equated nudity with angels and our first parents; the idealized portraits of Indians in this period associate the noble savages with paradise's only children. The new world, as Ribaut emphasizes, was unbroken by the plow; here man did not have to earn his nourishment by the sweat of his brow or the artificial technology which testified to weakness. Food was plentiful and because nature profusely offered universal remedies for all diseases—such was the early claim—life was long and happy.

Wordsworth's remark on Thomas Gray's rapturous description of Grasmere may be cited again in this context: "It might have been hoped that these words, indicating how much the charm of what *was* depended upon what was *not* . . . would have secured scenes so consecrated from profanation" (*Prose*, II, 208). In fact, the new Eden posed one question to the European mind: *what shall we do with it?* Although the Indians could and did teach the first colonists how to cope in the New World, the new farmers, traders, and missionaries assumed that the civilization they transplanted excelled the native customs they discovered. The Indians were taught the redemptive value of cultivation and labor so that they could share in the "improved" paradise. Settlers convirtced the natives that by submitting to a new control, principally a self-control, they would gain more than they would lose—law instead of anarchy, true faith instead of superstition, tribal communion instead of tribal warfare. The iron plow was imported, the straight furrows laid out in the land. Chateaubriand's account in *Atala* conveys the visionary dream of the Europeans. In that novel the converted Indian, Chactas, describes the founding of a stable society:

Surveyors with long chains went to measure the land. Arbitrators were setting up the first properties. The bird gave up its nest, and the lair of the wild beast was changed to a cabin. Forges were rumbling. Blows of the ax, for the last time, made reverberate echoes which died away like the trees. . . . I stood in awe of the triumph of Christianity over primitive life. I saw the Indian becoming civilized through the voice of religion. I was attending the primal marriage feast of man and earth: man by this sacred contract, yielding to the earth the fruit of his sweating; the earth, in return, agreeing to bear faithfully man's harvests, his sons and his ashes.¹⁰

The death of the Indian maiden, Atala, corresponds to the passing of the Indian way of life. Chateaubriand makes it clear that Christian succession is a good thing, and, in fact, could have saved Atala's life by abolishing the superstition that causes her suicide. But there is an undercurrent even in Chateaubriand of profound disquiet over the conformity of all social designs to the same model.

The ruin of the Indian culture remained a common and complex theme as the course of empire moved westward. In English literature the Indian became a locus for all the virtues of uncorrupted human nature. In popular literature, particularly, the Indian served as effectively in the role of distressed innocence as the pursued maiden of Gothic melodrama or the abused child. Byron's Neuha is the culmination of a long line of primitive American figures who civilize the civilizers by converting them to the religion of nature. In one poem, *The Injured Islanders, or the Influence of Art upon the Happiness of Mankind*, the queen of Otaheite (Tahiti) makes an appeal to the English explorer, Captain Wallis:

> far remove, if Vengeance be forgot,
> These Injur'd Isles to some sequester'd Spot,
> Some placid corner of the boundless Main,
> Unmark'd by Science, unexplor'd by Gain,
> Where Nature still her Empire safe may hold
> From foreign Commerce, Confidence, and Gold,
> From foreign Arts—from all that's foreign free,
> Save Wallis only—if approv'd by Thee.

American writers like Cooper and Parkman spoke to this subject a century later. They justified the usurpation of Indian land but not without sincere expressions of nostalgia for the simplicity of life which had been superseded by their own well equipped and future oriented society.[11]

The myth of progress and improvement by which the New World was colonized received an influx of support from America's second birth into republicanism. The revolutionaries, using the language and figures of prophecy against the parent power, absorbed the missionary responsibility into themselves and became the patriarchs of a new Jerusalem. Their task, as the title of an American epic puts it, was *The Conquest of Canaan*. In that poem of 1785, Timothy Dwight proclaimed, "Here Empire's last, and brightest throne shall rise; / And Peace, and Right and Freedom, greet the skies!" (X.556–57). The doctrine of manifest destiny is implicit in such millennial thinking, for clearly there can be no peace until antagonists are either converted or destroyed. A generation later we find William Cullen Bryant asking in *The Ages*, "Who shall place / A limit to the giant's unchained strength, / Or curb his swiftness in the forward race?"[12]

Bryant in 1822, like Wordsworth in 1793, exults in an imperial destiny for which he consciously adopts a language of limitless expansion. He concludes the stanza just quoted:

> On, like the comet's way through infinite space,
> Stretches the long untravelled path of light,
> Into the depths of ages; we may trace,
> Afar, the brightening glory of its flight
> Till the receding rays are lost to human sight.   (xxxiii)

The American empire, Bryant affirms in the final stanza, is indisputably immortal ("thou, my country, thou shalt never fall") and will carry into perpetuity the undying hope and dreams of the human mind. Against the decay of Europe, writers like Bryant and Emerson set this adamantine optimism.

American egotism rested securely on the same historical forces that alarmed and depressed European moralists. Democracy, said Tocqueville, is an "irresistible revolution which has advanced for centuries in spite of every obstacle and which is still advancing in the midst of the ruins it has caused."[13] These ruins are not just armies but ideas, and principally the idea of civilization as Byron sarcastically defined it in the passage from *Don Juan* already quoted. To the American democrat the old civilization is properly emblematized by ruins, for the worship of power, the reign of tyranny, the division into class and caste, all of these produced the vainglorious relics that distinguish the European, as opposed to the American, landscape. The American democrat loves the here and now, and would no more worship at the temple of Jupiter than at the foot of the Sphinx. Thoreau writes in his journal:

What though the traveller tell us of the ruins of Egypt, are we so sick or idle that we must sacrifice our American and to-day to some man's ill-remembered and indolent story? Carnac and Luxor are but names, or if their skeletons remain, still more desert sand and at length a wave of the Mediterranean Sea are needed to wash away the filth that attaches to their grandeur. Carnac! Carnac! here is Carnac for me.[14]

The annihilating flood that Thoreau would send over the ruins of time, like Hawthorne's imagined obliteration of the past in *Earth's Holocaust*, represents an apocalyptic expansion of the solitary American soul. American democracy preaches that man creates his spiritual self by meaningful work; that when hindering traditions are set aside he can, if he is able, realize his ideal conceptions by industry. Democracy seeks practical knowledge which will give it absolute power over

natural things and therefore power over its future. The first impulse
of the democrat is to build something—a cabin, a city, a railroad,
more stately mansions—to become by doing rather than thinking.
Progress toward an egalitarian community of satisfied workers was
the ideal from the first moment of the American Revolution, if not
before. It is John Dyer's vision of a "mighty brotherhood" participating in commercial exchange that nourishes the first poets of the Revolution. Philip Freneau repeats the dream of Dyer's *Fleece* in *American
Liberty* (1775):

> The time shall come when strangers rule no more,
> Nor cruel mandates vex from Britain's shore;
> When Commerce shall extend her shorten'd wing,
> And her free freights from every climate bring;
> When mighty towns shall flourish free and great,
> Vast their dominion, opulent their state.   (*Poems*, I, 152)

And Joel Barlow, who translated Volney's *Ruins*, celebrates in *The
Columbiad* the community that cooperation rather than oppression
will create in the New World. A Spirit shows Columbus in a vision of
the future how his discoveries will result in man's future happiness:

> Now see, my son, the destined hour advance;
> Safe in their leagues commercial navies dance,
> Leave their curst cannon on the quay-built strand
> And like the stars of heaven a fearless course command.
>   The Hero lookt; beneath his wondering eyes
> Gay streamers lengthen round the seas and skies;
> The countless nations open all their stores,
> Load every wave and crowd the lively shores;
> Bright sails in mingling mazes streak the air,
> And Commerce triumphs o'er the rage of war.[15]

   That improvement through labor is the gospel of America may be
seen in Timothy Dwight's popular poem, *Greenfield Hill*. The second
part, "The Flourishing Village," is a direct answer to Goldsmith's *The
Deserted Village* and especially to its critique of "trade's unfeeling
train." Dwight begins like his model by isolating one perfect spot of
bliss: "Fair Verna! loveliest village of the west." (Goldsmith's poem
begins "Sweet Auburn, loveliest village of the plain.") Dwight explains in the poem that industry and constant labor preserve the joys
of Verna and save it from the stagnation he attributes to the impro-
gressive Orient. Verna is fortunate that "in falling forests, Labour's axe
resounds" (693); she gains from these daily efforts a just competency.

Dwight attacks luxury as severely as does Goldsmith and matches the English poet's dislike of large landholders who tend to squeeze out the able yeomanry. But these yeomen, like the Farmer of Part VI, are introduced only to espouse the philosophy of work, not because they have a life that transcends labor. They are given no character in the poem, only precepts:

> And first, *industrious* be your lives;
> Alike employ'd yourselves, and wives:
> Your children, join'd in labour gay,
> With something useful fill each day.   (31–34)

The desire for improvement is the wealth of nations, and Dwight confidently concludes his poem with a vision of the new heaven and new earth proceeding from the peaceful strife of commerce. It is easy to point out in retrospect that his prescription for happiness threatens the pastoral Eden he imagines as the result of incessant building. Writing by the glorious light of the French Revolution, in 1793, the poet understandably ignored the hard social and economic realities which underlie Goldsmith's work. In any case, they must have seemed irrelevant to the largely unsettled world of early America.

Bryant, writing more than thirty years later, has less excuse for the buoyant optimism of his poem, *The Ages*. He knows this, and prefixes to his bright prospect of the future, as a counterbalance, a survey of doomed empires. He revisits the ruins of Greece and Rome to point a conventional moral, that imperialism thwarted the national goals of each civilization. He tries to resolve the apparent contradiction between their fate and his own support for America's imperial destiny by insisting on the necessity of maturity and self-control. The giant must rein in his gargantuan powers and exchange old fetters for new. The new America can thrive only by evolving within the governing discipline of familial protection and love. Bryant repeats the same hope in his poem, *The Conjunction of Jupiter and Venus*, in which he imagines the occupation of the American continent guided by the best principles and policies "born of the meeting of those glorious stars." The astronomical conjunction unites emblems of power and love (specifically in this, an epithalamion, conjugal love). He attaches to manifest destiny, then, the same qualification of "true filial freedom" that Milton enjoined upon Adam and Eve in the garden.

Despite his qualifications, *The Ages* is a confused expression of Bryant's, and his entire generation's, attitude toward the westward movement. In the body of the poem he blames the rapaciousness of extinct empires for their decline, yet when he spurs his own people on toward the Pacific his very encouragement acknowledges that expansion is impossible without destruction. One simile, especially, is worth noting in the context of this discussion: "The full region leads / New colonies forth that toward the western seas / Spread, like a rapid flame among the autumnal trees." These lines precede the stanza on "the comet's way" quoted above; they make us wonder about this young poet, in his mid-twenties, who must have watched his beloved forests burn and yet summoned the idealism to see that fire as the origin of a wonderful light whose "brightening glory" would continue into futurity, forever. Bryant would live to rue this imperial enthusiasm, though he never retracted it. He dedicates his later work to a plea for the forethought and self-adjustments that earlier poems had only suggested. In 1865, after watching the American landscape fall victim unremittingly to the axe, he writes a pathetic essay "with a view of preventing the destruction of trees which is so rapidly proceeding." *The Utility of Trees* argues that since the American people cannot restrain themselves from denuding the land, perhaps the federal government ought to create a forest service to conserve the remaining vegetation. In the essay he quotes his own poem, *An Indian at the Burial-Place of His Fathers*, which puts into the deracinated Indian's mouth the melancholy lines, "The realm our tribes are crushed to get / May be a barren desert yet." In the poem, though not in the essay, Bryant elaborates on this point:

> They waste us—ay—like April snow
>   In the warm noon, we shrink away;
> And fast they follow, as we go
>   Toward the setting day—
> Till they shall fill the land, and we ·
> Are driven into the Western sea.
>
> But I behold a fearful sign,
>   To which the white men's eyes are blind;
> Their race may vanish hence, like mine,
>   And leave no trace behind,
> Save ruins o'er the region spread,
> And the white stones above the dead.

America had been much attacked, by Thomas Moore for example, as a place of "barrenness in intellect, taste, and all in which *heart* is concerned," but fears about the transfiguration of its great forests into deserts were a new and traumatizing development.[16]

As Bryant came to understand, however, barrenness in taste has its consummation in barrenness of landscape. The worship of nature typical of his early poems yields to a mode of graveyard literature in which all lasting beauty and joy is projected beyond the tomb. In one of his last poems, *The Flood of Years*, he looks backward upon the overwhelming power of time, which defeats all human efforts:

> Lo! wider grows the stream—a sea-like flood
> Saps earth's walled cities; massive palaces
> Crumble before it; fortresses and towers
> Dissolve in the swift waters; populous realms
> Swept by the torrent see their ancient tribes
> Engulfed and lost; their very languages
> Stifled, and never to be uttered more.

Though the language is deliberately general we recognize at once that the "populous realms" which watch their ancient tribes drown in the deluge are the United States and that the fate they see is the fate they bring to the victims. The horror is increased by the cyclical character of this overthrow, for when Bryant laments the death of Indian languages he is also thinking of his own language. The function of poetry, in his hands, becomes that of Wordsworth's shell in the Arab Dream of *The Prelude*, to utter a blast of prophecy and warn the people of destruction near at hand. Bryant's poem continues:

> Sadly, I turn and look before, where yet
> The Flood must pass, and I behold a mist
> Where swarm dissolving forms, the brood of Hope,
> Divinely fair, that rest on banks of flowers,
> Or wander among rainbows, fading soon
> And reappearing, haply giving place
> To forms of grisly aspect such as Fear
> Shapes from the idle air—where serpents lift
> The head to strike, and skeletons stretch forth
> The bony arm in menace.

The serpent in the garden, as in Byron's tale of *The Island*, is the European lust for unlimited power; when America became its own parent in the Revolution, it incorporated the menace of Fletcher Christian into its daily life.

The Utility of Trees: Cooper and Cole

Any number of works could be cited from this period to demonstrate how Bryant's fears became the foundation of an adversary literature in America, a counterrevolutionary epicycle (to change the metaphor) within the accelerating wheel of American fortunes. James Fenimore Cooper's novel, *The Pioneers* (1823), grapples with these matters directly and lucidly. The time of the novel is 1793; the Reign of Terror casts its light (or darkness) over the central debates concerning the game laws, or more precisely over the disputes about all law, natural and man-made alike. At first glance the frontiersman, Natty Bumppo, seems to be the complete child of nature and Judge Temple the figure of civilization, extending his ambition like a rapid flame among trees. But Cooper has written a more complex novel than such a melodramatic division suggests. It would be more accurate to say that Cooper invites us to establish that division, by scenes like the first one in which Temple's accidental wounding of Natty's young companion (later revealed as Oliver Effingham, the dispossessed English heir) shows how little Temple's woods and guns are deserved property. We make a firm association of the American Eden with Natty and its misuse with Temple.

Shortly afterward, however, we must change our perspective. Temple enters his mansion for a dinner party which his cousin, Richard Jones, has overseen. There follows this scene:

An enormous mirror in a gilt frame hung against the wall, and a cheerful fire, of the hard or sugar maple, was burning on the hearth. The latter was the first object that struck the attention of the Judge, who, on beholding it, exclaimed rather angrily, to Richard:

"How often have I forbidden the use of the sugar maple in my dwelling! The sight of that sap, as it exudes with the heat, is painful to me, Richard. Really, it behooves the owner of woods so extensive as mine to be cautious what example he sets for his people, who are already felling the forests as if no end could be found to their treasures, nor any limits to their extent. If we go on in this way, twenty years hence we shall want fuel."

"Fuel in these hills, cousin 'duke!" exclaimed Richard, in derision— "Fuel! Why, you might as well predict that the fish will die for the want of water in the lake.... But you are always a little wild on such subjects, Marmaduke."

"Is it wildness," returned the Judge, earnestly, "to condemn a practice which devotes these jewels of the forest, these precious gifts of nature, these mines of comfort and wealth, to the common uses of a fireplace?"[17]

The situation resembles that of Wordsworth's poem, *Foresight*, in which a child is warned that she may pluck any spring flower but the strawberry flower, lest she annihilate the means of her own future welfare. In this scene Judge Temple plays the part of the older child whose practical knowledge makes him a leader in the community. Temple becomes the true lawgiver, Jupiter Lucetius, restraining the revolutionary child, Richard, from the heedless destruction that is also self-destruction.

Richard, and the Herculean strongman Billy Kirby who executes all orders to cut down the trees, speak for an absolute democracy. "This is a free country," Billy says, "where a man is privileged to follow any calling he likes." When Judge Temple tries to reason with Billy on the wisdom of foresight, the woodcutter answers, "I know you calkilate greatly on the trees, setting as much store by them as some men would by their children, yet to my eyes they are a sore sight at any time, unless I'm privileged to work my will on them. . . . Now, I call no country much improved, that is pretty well covered with trees" (pp. 344, 232). Children and trees symbolize the potentiality from which the future draws its life, but Billy's vigorous will, in Emerson's phrase, "is of a fatal and universal power, admitting no co-life." Billy believes that trees are nothing more than gross matter whose divinely appointed end is realized by human improvement. He does not intentionally try to annihilate the future, but his ignorance of the ecological facts of life makes his prejudice against trees a real danger to posterity.

In Cooper's new politics, Billy's violent action upon nature links him to Caesarism, or as it will soon be known in its modern incarnation, Bonapartism, the reign of the rebel-tyrant. Billy, after leveling the trees, would "light the heaps of timber, and march away under the blaze of the prostrate forest, like the conqueror of some city, who, having first prevailed over his adversary, applies the torch as the finishing blow to his conquest" (p. 191). Natty, by contrast, represents the ideal maturity of a child of nature, his natural piety intermingled with the still, sad music of humanity in whose measure he has enjoyed lifelong tranquillity. As Richard is Billy's mentor, so Indian John is Natty's. John, we are told, is called by the white man's name because the name of Mohegan "recalled the idea of his nation in ruins" (p. 78). John is a memento whose constant presence has given Natty a moral conscience, an intuitive sense of God's plan for his suffering creatures. When Bryant eulogized Cooper after the novelist's death he was careful to make just this point about Natty, that "in him there is a genial blending of the gentlest virtues of the civilized man with the better nature of the aboriginal tribes."[18] Natty possesses more self-control than Judge Temple, and the irony of their culminating dispute over the game laws is that Temple's policies are attempts to preserve the wilderness Natty loves from total ruin. Natty deplores the "wasty ways" he sees in Templeton, the pigeon-shoot, the fish-haul, the decimation of forests; Temple, admitting Natty's point, promises to put an end to the wanton destruction. In fact, only

Temple can do so, for Natty's practice of abandoning his former haunts when they are overpopulated, makes him an undependable arbiter of social needs.

Cooper's obsession with the rights of property arises from his rejection of Richard and Billy, not of Natty. Equality of condition was abhorrent to him; he saw absolute democracy as a bill of rights for spoilers. In this he resembles Wordsworth, who wrote to Lord Lonsdale that "the People are already powerful far beyond the encrease of their information, or their improvement in morals" (*Letters*, III, 508).[19] Cooper's prescription for controlling the flood centered on figures who valued information and were able to use it to design a liveable future. Judge Temple, as a character, has an informed heart but he is flawed by ambition and a love of property as wealth. Cooper relates Temple's unflattering history as a land-grabber in great detail in the novel's opening chapters. Temple does not escape the censure, by implication, that Cooper directs at the Timons and Roxanas of his day in *The American Democrat*. "A people that deems the possession of riches its highest source of distinction," he writes, "admits one of the most degrading of all influences to preside over its opinions."[20]

Because Temple has lived by expediency, knowing the Good but not always serving it, he is not the ideal protector of his republic. The guaranteed accession of Oliver Effingham to power, by his marriage to Temple's only child, secures the stability of property laws and forests alike. Oliver's grandfather, Major Effingham, had been adopted as a son by Mohegan (Indian John) in former times, and Oliver had hunted with John and Natty long enough to learn much of the woodlore that Temple lacks. Oliver's stoic patience, his refusal to seek revenge upon Temple in the Jacobin manner, and his susceptibility to love and sympathy for Elizabeth Temple, make him the proper executor of the laws. He alone in the novel can restore a civilization which is neither degraded by excess of luxury nor endangered by the impulse to move westward. In a later novel, *Home as Found,* Cooper shows us Templeton after the Effinghams have exerted their influence for a generation, and the change is admirable, a more cultivated and not a ravaged community.

Cooper's later fiction, however, is not on the whole optimistic. In *The Prairie,* which follows Natty westward, and dramatizes his final adventures, the premonition of ruin for America is underscored heavily. The Bush family, whose dullness and predatory character foreshadow the Snopes clan in Faulkner's work, seems to be the type of humanity destined to inherit the new earth. It is no coincidence that a long debate between Natty and Dr. Bat in chapter 22 turns on the cycle-of-empires theme and its relevance to America. And in *The*

Crater, Cooper composes a tale of the Pacific which, like Byron's *The Island,* submits the paradise myth to elegiac scrutiny. Significant also is Cooper's great admiration for the painter Thomas Cole, whom he called "the highest genius this country has ever produced," and whose series of paintings, *The Course of Empire,* he proclaimed "one of the noblest works of art ever wrought."[21] Cooper undoubtedly saw in Cole's rendering of the stages of empire the very painting of his own fears for America, which by 1836, when Cole completed his work, had greatly increased.

Cole's canvases are distinguished by a certain neutrality; they seem to invite the viewer to make judgments, but their genre quality prevents him from abstracting a moral or seizing upon one stage of mankind's development as Cole's ideal of perfection. The first canvas, *The Savage State,* has all the morning freshness of the new found land, "as though nature were just springing from chaos," Cole wrote of it. The hunter stalking his prey in the forest mist cannot help but recall Natty as Deerslayer. Cole put into this landscape his own youthful love of the wilderness, chronicled in poems, letters, journals, and obvious in his landscapes. There is something of the demi-savage, as Cooper calls Natty, in Cole's ecstatic wanderings through mountains and woods, and in his rapturous worship of their presiding spirit. In an early poem he wishes for artistic talent so that he may "call from crumbling fanes my fellow-men / To kneel in nature's everlasting dome" (*Life,* p. 40). Bryant had popularized this religious imagery in nature writing, particularly in *A Forest Hymn,* whose opening line is "The groves were God's first temples" and in *The Prairies* where he describes the western land as "Fitting floor / For this magnificent temple of the sky." In this painting, Cole's religious enthusiasm is crossed with Salvator Rosa's chiaroscuro effects for a conventional expression of the Sublime.

The second scene, *The Arcadian or Pastoral,* also appeals to the viewer by representing forms endeared to mankind by millennia of artistic reproduction. In the foreground a philosopher traces geometric abstractions with a stick, a shepherd plays on his pipe, and a child etches a design on stone. The Arcadian surroundings give to these achieved visions a tone of serenity that seems providential.

And yet the third canvas, *The Consummation of Empire,* speaks to our recognition that independent visions require application if the circuit of thought and action is not to atrophy. Cole had located the drawing child in the lower right foreground; the *Consummation* shows us a marvelous fountain in the same spot, the product of enterprise like the child's. The geometry too has its application in the order of temples, palaces, colonnades, and domes abundantly illustrated in the later scenes. Here, in classical terms, is the realization of the revolutionary dream: the "opulent state" of Freneau, and, in the trading ships that crowd the bay, the "commercial navies" of Barlow's epic. A mountain which looms in the background of all five canvases is here almost effaced, as man's control over nature reaches its apex. The "gaud and glitter" (Cole's words) of the *Consummation* is just pompous enough to remind us that we are looking at the ruins of Arcadia, that by keeping the location constant Cole has interpreted national progress as a process of renewal through self-ruin. Meyer Abrams cites Hegel on the unfolding of the historical spirit as just such a phoenixlike renewal: "The harmoniousness of childhood is a gift from the hand of nature: the second harmony must spring from the labour and culture of the spirit."[22]

Cole's use of this idea, however, is thoroughly ironic. The next canvas, *The Destruction of Empire,* adapts motifs from the first, but as an implied criticism of labor and culture alike. The solitary hunter and deer are replaced by thousands of combatants, aided by nautical technology in their mutual slaughter for the sake of luxury. The mists of morning become here the smoke rising from annihilating fires. The smoke obscures the architectural marvels and in the foreground dead bodies choke the fountain and bridges. The headless statue of a gladiator symbolizes the absurd culmination of this civilization— power purchased by the overthrow of intellect.

Finally, *The Desolation of Empire* reveals nature reassuming its sway. Ivy crawls up a ruined column in the foreground, on whose top we see a family of herons. The immaculate mountain looms as before, in the sunset. The scene is ready for Childe Harold's appearance.

Cole preferred repose to action in his landscapes because the introduction of human endeavor vitiated the spiritual glow of permanent forms. Where people are present in his paintings they are often diminished, set in the far distance so that the viewer comes upon them as incidental figures of small importance amid the mountains and woods. Except for Cole's own devotion to art we might surmise that the wilderness state attracted him more than any other, but his later canvas, *Dream of Arcadia* (1838), with others completed after *The Course of Empire,* suggests that Cole found the pastoral most appealing. He seems to believe that in the evolutionary cycle of human consciousness man's one reprieve from predation is the discovery of new truths in the arts and sciences. The play of intellect, majestic and happy in its solitary sway but limited in social effect by the simplicity of rustic life, becomes corrupted when it extends outward and creates pyramids and temples by means of wealth extracted from empire.

His sentiments fed on historical causes, and he was not slow to

The Destruction of Empire, by Thomas Cole. Courtesy of the New-York Historical Society.

recognize his own moment in the cycle of empire. Like his contemporaries he was pursued by sounds of the axe. "They are cutting down all the trees in the beautiful valley on which I have looked so often with a loving eye," runs one letter, "maledictions on all our dollar-goaded utilitarians." A letter written two days later moderates his curse in a curious manner:

After I had sealed my last letter, I was afraid that what I had said about the tree-destroyers might be understood in a more serious light than I intended. My "maledictions" are gentle ones, and I do not know that I could wish them any thing worse than that barrenness of mind, that sterile desolation of the soul, in which sensibility to the beauty of nature cannot take root. One reason, though, why I am in so gentle a mood is, that I am informed some of the trees will be saved yet. Thank them for that. If I live to be old enough, I may sit down under some bush, the last left in the utilitarian world, and feel thankful that intellect in its march has spared one vestige of the ancient forest for me to die by.   (*Life*, pp. 160–61)

"Intellect in its march" proceeds from "barrenness of mind," an apparent but not a real contradiction. Like Wordsworth in his *Guide to the Lakes,* Cole equates true intelligence with taste or sensibility, and the lack of it with destruction of whatever in the external world has value. If groves are God's first temples, the rightful replacement in modern belief of a decayed orthodoxy, then the utilitarian spirit ("intellect") which tries to improve on them by making and building represents a false belief engendering a false taste—the serpent in the garden. The desecration-of-nature theme becomes the latest ectype of the ruined abbey theme so popular in the eighteenth century. In this genre, horror results from the absolute denial of the future to man, from the extinction of some worldly emblem of immortal life. Cole's vision of the last remaining bush corresponds to Bryant's of the universal desert; both are secular versions of the Last Day motif, but the more hopeless because detached from images of resurrection.

Cole's most ambitious poem, *The Complaint of the Forest,* applies to American landscape the set of historical assumptions underlying *The Course of Empire,* and in so doing recapitulates the conventional ruin piece in every feature. The poem opens in a natural amphitheater made by mountains rising above a serene lake. Cole's imagination converts the scene to the sublime remains of giants' handiwork, the giants themselves having been destroyed in the Flood. "It yet remained / A ruin more sublime than if a thousand / Roman colloseums had been pil'd in one," he writes. By a train of associations aided no doubt by his extensive reading in ruins literature, he follows his identification with a vision of "groaning multitudes—to gratify / Imperial pomp and pride." From an ecstatic view in the opening lines, in which his enchanted mind mingled and communed with all the elements, the poet has been drawn downward, as in Dyer's description of the Colosseum, into the lowest pit of despair and death. His naturalized imagination, displaced into time, has been desolated by its own sense of the past.

At this point "the voice of the great Forest" arises, a spirit of place, in order to call attention to its own melancholy plight. As Verulam had lamented the loss of her domes and towers in Spenser's poem, so the Forest expresses regret for the oncoming march of that very civilization represented by Verulam's glory. Once, she recalls, amid the madness and fury of destruction that humans call history,

> there was one bright virgin continent
> Remote, that Roman name had never reached;
> Nor ancient dreams in all their universe—
> As inaccessible in primal time
> Unto man's thought and eye, as far Uranus
> In his secret void.

The terrestrial paradise had existed as a dream of peace, located beyond the fierce whirlpools and terrible monsters of the Western seas. This place was man's dream of Eden, and like Adam he awoke to find it true. Eventually he discovered the New World and its promise of limitless joy. "O peace primeval! Would that thou hadst staid!" the Forest cries. But there is no preserving Eden once it has been uncovered. "The axe—the unresting axe / Incessant smote our venerable ranks" and even the "shelter'd vales" began to undergo radical change. The Forest knows that her complaint is futile and that the religion of progress will erect its shrines upon her ruins: "Our doom is near... / Each hill and every valley is become / An altar unto Mammon." In a "few short years," she concludes, the rivers will be polluted or dry, the ground be denuded of trees, and the deer and squirrel be driven from their home. All will vanish beneath an unrelenting doom. [23]

It should be no surprise that Cole, like Wordsworth, gradually abandoned his exclusive worship of nature. Like the mariners in the *Complaint,* he conceived an ideal property beyond the troubled seas around him, but one that could not be overrun in mortal life. Cole never lost his wonder at the beauty of natural forms but increasingly his journals and letters tend to locate the highest peace and joy in the immortal paradise secure beyond the grave. "What a harsh and cruel climate," he remarks typically in 1837, "But are not all earthly climes imperfect, and bearing some evil?" (*Life*, p. 181). One of Cole's last paintings was a *Prometheus Bound* in which the chained figure of a suffering Humanity is watched over by the morning star, specifically identified by Cole as Jupiter. The price of his release, and reconciliation with the god, is not in doubt.

Bryant, Cooper, and Cole each perceived the sorrow of the human situation in the same way: that man is not only fated to destroy Eden but to want its destruction as a proof of his manifest destiny. Every American generation has recognized some part of itself in Milton's description of Satan standing at the rim of Eden, momentarily remorseful at the change which his intrusion will shortly effect. The early and middle nineteenth century perceived its place in Cole's scheme as just such a prospect, the transition between Arcadian and imperial glory. At such a crossroads, wavering in loyalty between the primal utopia behind and the technological one ahead, both the Old and New World paused long enough to question its united destiny in the coming century. A recent commentator on Cole very aptly cites Tocqueville's moving passage from *Democracy in America* as a document of this ambivalence:

It's this idea of destruction, this conception of near and inevitable change which gives in our opinion so original a character and so touching a beauty to the solitudes of America. One sees them with melancholy pleasure. One hastens in a way to admire them. The idea of this natural and wild grandeur which is to end mingles with the superb images to which the march of civilization gives rise. One feels proud to be a man, and at the same time one experiences I know not what bitter regret at the power God has given us over nature. The soul is agitated by these ideas, these contrary sentiments. But all the impressions it receives are great and leave a deep mark.[24]

 Conclusion

The desire of Man being Infinite the possession is Infinite & himself Infinite.
— Blake, There Is No Natural Religion

A LAMENT like Tocqueville's for the ruin of wilderness places not yet seen or lived in by man seems in retrospect a unique sorrow of the human spirit. Regret for the annihilation of wilderness speaks to a nostalgia that may be said to precede and encompass all other conditions, a yearning for the potentiality embodied in the precivilized, Eden before Adam. This development in the spiritual life of mankind attests more than anything else to man's disappointment with the powers he inherits, as an individual or nation, once he evolves into adult life and is charged by necessity with action.

To identify a natural paradise as Eden is to see it as part of a vanishing possibility for man, because Eden, unlike Arcadia, belongs to a mythology that insists on exile as a permanent condition. The most extreme ruin sentiment assumes that worldly action of any sort, beginning with the first willful aspiration in the Garden, must be futile and self-destructive. The more this futility is disguised as high endeavor the more delusory and destructive it becomes.

Ernest Becker's recent and widely acclaimed book, *The Denial of Death*, restates this position using the vocabulary and insights of psychoanalytic theory. According to Becker, man has overlaid his fears of death through the ages by a belief in some divinity that grants immortality in exchange for homage. When natural law usurped the power of superstition it enforced on man an inextirpable despair. The teleology of organic nature is death, so that whenever a person meditates on his creaturely condition he achieves a prospect on the ruins of time. There can be evasions but no successful escape from this beckoning ruin. If a person or nation refuses to recognize the inherent limitations of its condition it will only rage against an enemy projected from its own inner despair. Becker uses the contemporary issue of the Vietnam War as an example of doing to another nation what we would like to do (but cannot) to the real enemy, the proverbial last enemy, death.

In this argument, man destroys whatever potentiality exists, natural wilderness and civilization together, because whatever *can* be ruined is a hated simulacrum of his own mutable self. Becker concludes that "men are doomed to live in an overwhelmingly tragic and demonic world"[1] and criticizes as romantic those contemporary thinkers, like Norman O. Brown, who appreciate the grounds for pessimism but still hold out the possibility of new beginnings. Needless to say, Becker respects very few poets or novelists, since these more than any other class of humanity argue for the spiritual resources that he considers delusory. In so arguing, he joins other recent authors whose interest in anxiety and despair has led to compelling and gloomy conclusions about the human condition. The immediate father of this new pessimism, as its disciples attest, is Freud, especially the Freud of *Reflections on War and Death, Group Psychology and the Analysis of the Ego,* and *Civilization and Its Discontents,* his major reassessments of personality and culture after the Great War.

This is no place for an exposition of Freudian thought. I would, however, like to point out one aspect of Freud's, and Becker's, theory of civilization relevant to my studies of English and American artists. Freud attempts to trace the continuity of self from the infant child to the adult. He identifies the power that adults wield as the primal energy, limitless and polymorphous, of the child in his imperial palace. Freud in his later work calls this "the instinct of destruction" which the adult no less than the child must satisfy upon person or thing, even if the object is himself. Against this principle of force, Freud opposes the process of self-control I have represented in this study as Jupiter Lucetius, the lawgiver and guardian of public morality. "Replacement of the power of the individual by the power of a community constitutes the decisive step of civilization," he writes, and adds, "the first requisite of civilization . . . is that of justice."[2] Sublimation of the instinct of destruction into constructive endeavor remains an essential part of the sane society, but outright repression of desire, with all its baneful aftereffects, cannot be avoided.

Freud approves of the exchange, godlike power for the possibility of a wise and virtuous social organization, but with so many elegiac misgivings that even those of his followers who reject civilization as a bad deal for mankind may be said to derive their most telling arguments from the master. In Freud's mature conception justice often resembles the Jupiter of *Prometheus Unbound* rather than Jupiter Lucetius. Prolonged contact with his patients made him feel vindictive toward a perverse Humanity writhing unhappily in its chains. "I have found little that is 'good' about human beings on the whole," he wrote in a letter. "In my experience most of them are trash, no matter whether they publicly subscribe to this or that ethical doctrine or none at all."[3] Self-gratification and self-preservation, Freud acknowledged, almost always usurp the inclination to preserve anything or anyone else. Without elaborate social engineering civilization could not effectively protect itself from destruction, and the apostles of such engineering would almost certainly bring a cure worse than the disease, as Europe was to learn in the decade following the publication of *Civilization and Its Discontents.*

Can there be such a thing as a civilization untainted by the ravaging power of childhood impulse, willing to settle for a conditional happiness? The problem of utopian philosophers since Plato has been the construction of a just society in which the governed assent to their own predetermined happiness. One carefully articulated plan for community perfection in our time is B. F. Skinner's *Walden Two.* Skinner's utopia attempts to cancel the power of instinct by removing the external supports of egotistical desires. As in Plato's *Republic,* children are trained to not involve their affections with people, places, and things. Weaned from the desire for attachment and possession, they will also lose the desire for domination. "The fact is," the spokesman at Walden Two explains, "it's very unlikely that anyone at Walden Two will set his heart on a course of action so firmly that he'll be unhappy if it isn't open to him. That's as true of the choice of a girl as of a profession."[4] Nobody will die for love, or kill for it, or have any cause to mourn the loss of an Auburn or Grasmere. The tragic quality of life posited by Freud and Becker, one that has all of history as evidence, is negated by a wholehearted commitment to utilitarian goals grounded in self-control.

For that control to be effective the community must deny its members the ultimate desire of the ego, immortality. Here is the relevant exchange between the founder of Walden Two, Frazier, and his critics, Professor Castle and the narrator, Professor Burris:

"The whole thing runs counter to a lot of modern psychology," I said. "Personal domination is a powerful motive."

"In a competitive world," said Frazier.

"But of great men, at least, in other respects. The geniuses—"

"Only the geniuses who have been great in the field of personal domination. The rest of us—" Frazier caught himself but it was too late and he let it stand. . . . "The rest of us—have other motives, equally powerful and better adapted to a successful social structure. The last step in the long evolution of government is to employ unselfish motives where personal domination has always seemed ideally suited even if always fatal. . . .

"When I die," he went on hastily but in a dramatic manner, "I shall cease to exist—in every sense of the word. A few memories will soon follow me into the crematorium, and there will be no other record left. As a personal figure, I shall be as unidentifiable as my ashes. That's absolutely essential to the success of all the Waldens. No one has ever realized it before."   (P. 240)

The society preserves itself from ruin by institutionalizing the necessity of oblivion. Frazier is correct in claiming uniqueness for this view. Though in many ways Walden Two reminds us of the utopias conceived after the model of Bacon's *New Atlantis*—materialistic, technocratic, perpetuated by an internalization of the spirit of the laws—it is distinguished by making no appeal to posterity on the part of its founders or servants. It erects no statues, keeps no books. It abolishes memory as an instrument of policy.

Though Becker's and Skinner's books seem polar opposites, they share a disbelief in the access to new light that poets like Blake and Wordsworth have described as essential to a full humanity. Both Becker and Skinner urge a mechanistic view upon the reader, and necessarily so since each must construct a screen to keep out the polluting influence of the other. Walden Two is secure from the consciousness of death; it has yet to descend into the dying process which renews the zest for life. For this reason its social organization seems immature, remote from the full complexity of human experience which must be the model for societies in which humans are to live. The most superficial comparison with Thoreau's original makes the blithe inhabitants of Walden Two look spectral, bodiless, passionless. Moreover, Skinner's utopia has not built into its design the proper safeguards against the nameless supervisors who, for the good of the community, will suppress new ideas and new impulses of compassion and love. In this sense, *Walden Two* of necessity joins the other utopias of world literature, for the impulse to social engineering, however well-intentioned, carries with it an intolerance of disequilibrium.

If Skinner has taken the celestial railroad directly to paradise, Becker has never quite escaped the inferno. Becker dismisses new beginnings as mysticism and offers skepticism as a modern alternative to high endeavor. Modern heroism, he writes, adapting Paul Tillich, should be measured by "the absorption of maximum meaninglessness into oneself." A kind of cosmic pity stirs in Becker

when he defines what Blake calls the human abstract, finding ruins
on every side. The last sentence of his book offers a proposition that
has behind it the mocking laughter of the gods: "The most that any
one of us can seem to do is fashion something—an object or
ourselves—and drop it into the confusion, make an offering of it, so
to speak, to the life force" (pp. 280, 285). Here is Blake's natural
religion in its cruelest form. The life force is removed from each single
life, idolized. Man does not recover new life from it; it extracts life by
human sacrifice. As with Skinner, the question here is not whether
Becker is right or wrong, but whether his understanding of the
human condition is complete or partial.

In this book I have discussed a literary tradition that values the
ruin sentiment, the vicarious experience of dying and rising, as a
necessary ordeal in the regaining of self-mastery, and through self-
mastery, joy. Writers like Wordsworth achieve direct experience of
the life force and sustain a symbiotic relation to it. Speaking of
Wordsworth's *Ode*, G. Wilson Knight remarks, "Immortality is an
extension, or expansion of life itself; there can be no other starting
point in any profitable analysis."[5] To believe with Freud and Becker
that death is all metaphors causes a despair in which the legitimate
desire for immortality is denied in favor of an exclusive conception of
man as a waste product ("most of them are trash"). Wordsworth saw
the task of a great writer as the correction of such despondency by
means which expanded the capacity to think and feel. The endorsement of a capacious imagination necessarily brought Wordsworth
into conflict with schemes like Frazier's which imprison the imaginative spirit in mazes of moral instruction. Wordsworth defended the
child-victim against the utilitarian masters:

> For this unnatural growth the trainer blame,
> Pity the tree.
>
>   . . . .
>
>   but how escape?
> For, ever as a thought of purer birth
> Rises to lead him toward a better clime,
> Some intermeddler still is on the watch
> To drive him back, and pound him, like a stray,
> Within the pinfold of his own conceit.   (*Prelude*, V.328–36)

The importance of Romantic literature, from its own generation to
ours, has been that it provides texts and case histories distinguished
by the expansion of individual life. Wordsworth's poetry has long

been recognized as a source of light capable of bringing thoughts of purer birth to those who despair of the future. John Stuart Mill, in his *Autobiography*, credits Wordsworth's poems for his recovery from a mental crisis; a century later Paul Goodman, after suffering "an event too hard to bear" turned to the same poems for inspiration.[6]

I would like to conclude, however, by citing another model of the evolved imagination, one in which even death is subsumed into a comprehensive vision. My example is William Blake's residence in Felpham from 1800 to 1803, a change of scene which illustrates in its effects the fruitful interaction between natural landscape and the human spirit.

During the 1790s Blake underwent a period of intense despair in London. He had looked with penetrating clarity at the creaturely condition of man as Freud and Becker describe it, and he suffered a loss of faith in the utopian schemes of which Walden Two is the latest ectype. The depths of his despair, if we trust his letters and *The Four Zoas*, represented Blake's dark night of the soul. "I begin to Emerge from a Deep pit of Melancholy, Melancholy without any real reason for it," he wrote in a letter of 1800, "a Disease which God keep you from & all good men" (*Letters*, p. 37). Blake dramatized the power of this despair in *The Four Zoas* and his later work in the figure of the Spectre. The Spectre is the selfhood in everyone, the corporeal ego locked in time and space. Depending on its senses for the "ideas" posited by empirical epistemology, the Spectre sees all of life enclosed by mutability and death:

> O that I could cease to be! Despair! I am Despair,
> Created to be the great example of horror & agony; also my
> Prayer is vain. I called for compassion: compassion mock'd;
> Mercy and pity threw the grave stone over me, & with lead
> And iron bound it over me forever. Life lives on my
> Consuming, & the Almighty hath made me his Contrary
> To be all evil, all reversed & for ever dead: knowing
> And seeing life, yet living not; how can I then behold
> And not tremble? how can I be beheld & not abhorr'd?
>
> (*Jerusalem*, 10:51–59)

As each person has a Spectre, so the collective selfhood of England, the giant being whom Blake calls Albion, is possessed by its Spectre, Satan. Satan's work in England is symbolized by Stonehenge and Avebury, the Druid places of human sacrifice: "The Spectre of Albion frown'd over the Nations in glory & war. / All things begin & end in Albion's ancient Druid rocky shore" (*Milton*, 6:24–25). By the end of the 1790s, when all revolutionary hopes had forfeited, it appeared that Satan had irrevocably subdued Albion and his prophets.[7]

In 1800 Blake was invited by the popular man of letters, William Hayley, to spend a few years in retirement with him at Felpham, a lovely seacoast town, and execute designs for projects Hayley had in mind. Blake's first letter from Felpham, immediately upon arrival in September, describes it as "more spiritual than London." I have quoted part of the letter before but it is worth repeating:

> Heaven opens here on all sides her golden Gates; her windows are not obstructed by vapours; voices of Celestial inhabitants are more distinctly heard, & their forms more distinctly seen, & my Cottage is also a Shadow of their houses....
>   ... And Now Begins a New life, because another covering of Earth is shaken off. I am more famed in Heaven for my works than I could well concieve.... Why, then, should I be anxious about the riches or fame of mortality. The Lord our father will do for us & with us according to his Divine will for our Good.   (*Letters*, pp. 41–42)

The natural beauty of Felpham is responsible for the increase in nature images in *Milton* over *The Four Zoas*. Felpham is in Blake's own experience the Beulah he describes in Book II of *Milton*, which surrounds the fiery Eden on all sides. In order to reach the center of creative life the artist moves into "a pleasant lovely Shadow" to separate himself from the sordid world of generation. There, in Beulah, he sleeps, as Blake went through a "three years' Slumber" in Felpham, but the repose is in actuality a time of intensely creative work.[8]

This work, as his letter above suggests, is a matter of listening to voices and seeing the forms of angels who can awaken him from the dream of fallen life which is human history. Because the city is the work of historical forces it tends to obscure these divine voices and forms by what Wordsworth calls "the press / Of self-destroying, transitory things" (*Prelude*, VII.769–70). Blake had realized this, and admitted to a friend:

> One thing of real consequence I have accomplish'd by coming into the country, which is to me consolation enough: namely, I have recollected all my scatter'd thoughts on Art & resumed my primitive & original ways of Execution in both painting & engraving, which in the confusion of London I had very much lost & obliterated from my mind.   (*Letters*, p. 55)

Felpham provided Blake with time to compose his true self in the autobiographical *Milton* after the disintegrating years in London. He had immortal prospects in Felpham. His first biographer, Alexander

Gilchrist, cites reports that Blake loved to recall how he would gaze out his cottage windows at the sea, and how he enjoyed strolling through the spacious fields. Once he heard a young laborer call to his father, "The Gate is Open" and Blake took this as a sign that his entrance to fresh woods and pastures new was also unimpeded (*Letters*, p. 43).[9] A famous letter to Thomas Butts in October 1800 shows that Blake achieved distinct views of the spirit world immediately. In the enclosed verses he records a vision of Los, the prophetic spirit, who addresses inspiring words to the poet at the seashore. In *Milton* Blake acknowledges that his removal to Felpham was Los's strategy to overcome the Spectre:

> For when Los join'd with me he took me in his fi'ry whirlwind:
> My Vegetated portion was hurried from Lambeth's shades,
> He set me down in Felpham's Vale & prepar'd a beautiful
> Cottage for me, that in three years I might write all these Visions.
> (*Milton*, 36:21–24)

Blake began work on his brief epic, *Milton*, in order to transcend the sorrowful vision of *The Four Zoas*. The superseded poem had imitated the movement of mind in Young's *Night Thoughts*, even to its division into nine Nights, but the new work reached further back in literary history for a model, the Milton of *Paradise Regained*. In *Milton*, the prophetic imagination triumphs over Satan as Christ does in Milton's brief epic. In the poem's conclusion the spirits of John Milton and William Blake draw together as each confronts the terror of history, the deep backward abysm revealed in Satan's breast as the fiend stands before them in the garden at Felpham. Satan relies on the proven effectiveness of ruins images to force the two prophets into despair of life:

> I also stood in Satan's bosom & beheld its desolations:
> A ruin'd Man, a ruin'd building of God, not made with hands:
> Its plains of burning sand, its mountains of marble terrible:
> Its pits & declivities flowing with molten ore & fountains
> Of pitch & nitre: its ruin'd palaces & cities & mighty works:
> Its furnaces of affliction, in which his Angels & Emanations
> Labour with blacken'd visages among its stupendous ruins,
> Arches & pyramids & porches, colonades & domes,
> In which dwells Mystery, Babylon.   (38:15–23)

When Milton recognizes his Spectre, his Emanation, Ololon, joins him in an act of self-annihilation. Their historical selves overcome, they are now visible as Jesus and Jerusalem, preparing by means which include the poem Blake has written for the awakening of Albion. Blake gives to natural beings, those which have become in his own life the emblems of his adopted vale, the initiating role in England's resurrection:

> Immediately the Lark mounted with a loud trill from Felpham's Vale,
> And the Wild Thyme from Wimbleton's green & impurpled Hills,
> And Los & Enitharmon rose over the Hills of Surrey:
> Their clouds roll over London with a south wind; soft Oothoon
> Pants in the Vales of Lambeth, weeping o'er her Human
> > Harvest.   (42:29–33)

Blake does not claim that he alone, because of a private vision, will liberate England from its captivity. He does believe that "every honest man is a Prophet"[10] and that recourse to a tradition of sacred writing would aid each in his quest of the vital truth. Blake had turned to Milton, others would turn to Blake.

In his vision as in his work, Blake insured that the power which Freud identified as the instinct of destruction would serve and not overmaster him. He wrote in a letter after returning to London from Felpham, "O Glory! and O Delight! I have entirely reduced that spectrous Fiend to his station, whose annoyance has been the ruin of my labours for the last passed twenty years of my life. He is the enemy of conjugal love and is the Jupiter of the Greeks, an iron-hearted tyrant, the ruiner of ancient Greece.... He is become my servant who domineered over me, he is even as a brother who was my enemy" (*Letters*, pp. 106–07).[11] Blake enacted the compassionate triumph of Prometheus over Jupiter in Shelley's verse drama, *Prometheus Unbound*, and by so doing preserved what he describes in *Milton* as the "real and immortal Self" (15:11), the self which actively participates in the life force.

Blake, Shelley, Wordsworth—these are names not found in Becker's book, nor would they be allowed or understood in Walden Two. Skinner has admitted that even his inclusion of Bach in the utopian community was a mistake; nobody with the right upbringing could make sense of either the agony or joy of the Mass in B Minor.[12] This is less than humanity deserves. An age of traumatizing events, of nostalgia and future shock, requires from history models of control, artists who have blinked at nothing but kept their confidence and vision amid universal ruin until, in Shelley's phrase, "Hope creates / From its own wreck the thing it contemplates."[13] A person or nation which preserves and expands that power in itself has made the most valuable use of the ruins of time.

Notes

Index

 Notes

A list of the editions cited throughout the text will be found on pp. xiii–xiv.

Chapter 1. Introduction

1. From her essay, "On the Supernatural in Poetry," quoted in the introduction to *The Mysteries of Udolpho*, ed. Bonamy Dobrée (London: Oxford University Press, 1966), p. xi.

2. Trans. Walter Leaf. *The Oxford Book of Greek Verse in Translation*, ed. T. F. Higham and C. M. Bowra (Oxford: The Clarendon Press, 1938), p. 619.

3. Trans. Edward Morgan. Quoted in Rose Macaulay, *Pleasure of Ruins* (1953; rpt. New York: Walker, 1967), p. 10.

4. *The Looker-On*, 3, 25.

5. Trans. A. J. Butler. *Oxford Book of Greek Verse in Translation*, p. 618.

6. *The Heavenly City of the Eighteenth-Century Philosophers* (New Haven: Yale University Press, 1932), p. 129.

7. See the discussion in Michael Felmingham and Rigby Graham, *Ruins: A Personal Anthology* (London: Country Life Books, 1972), pp. 59–93.

8. Cited in Jonathan Schell, *The Time of Illusion* (New York: Knopf, 1976), p. 160.

9. *The Works of Thomas Love Peacock* (London: Constable, 1927), VI, 154–55.

10. *Wordsworth: A Re-Interpretation* (London: Longmans, Green, 1956), pp. 39–40.

Chapter 2. Immortal Longings and The Ruines of Time

1. *The Prose of Sir Thomas Browne*, ed. Norman Endicott (New York: New York University Press, 1968), pp. 284, 293. All references in the text are to this edition.

2. The reappearance of an almost certain pastiche, the "Fragment on Mummies," in the latest printing of Geoffrey Keynes's edition of Thomas Browne, proves that an author's oeuvre may sometimes expand with his influence. The much-admired "Fragment" first appeared in the Wilkin edition of Browne (1836) and was based on a handwritten reproduction by James Crossley of a Browne manuscript Crossley claimed to have discovered in the British Museum, copied, and then lost. It was removed from subsequent editions until that of Keynes. A debunking of the "Fragment" can be found in the *Review of English Studies*, 9 (1933), 266. The "Fragment" is not considered in this chapter as Browne's work.

3. *The Book of the Dead: The Papyrus of Ani*, ed. E. A. Wallis Budge (New York: G. P. Putnam's Sons, 1913), II, 463–64.

4. *The Sermons of John Donne,* ed. George R. Potter and Evelyn M. Simpson (Berkeley and Los Angeles: University of California Press, 1959), IV, 52–53.

5. *A Dialogue of Comfort Against Tribulation,* ed. Leland Miles (Bloomington: Indiana University Press, 1965), p. 23. See pp. 157–58 for More's commentary on the vainglory of empire.

6. *The Advancement of Learning,* ed. G. W. Kitchin (London: Everyman's Library, 1965), p. 59. A full discussion of the Renaissance concern with immortality can be found in Russell A. Fraser, *The Dark Ages and the Ages of Gold* (Princeton: Princeton University Press, 1973).

7. Quoted in Malcolm Letts, *Sir John Mandeville: The Man and His Book* (London: The Batchworth Press, 1943), p. 58. Though Mandeville relates stories of this kind—including one of a tree whose fruit provides such balm the local inhabitants live for four or five hundred years—he does show some skepticism. He narrates an anecdote concerning Alexander the Great's triumphal entrance into one territory where the people hungered for enduring life. They asked the conqueror to make them immortal with his great power, and when he answered he could not "they asked him why he was so proud and so fierce, and so busy for to put all the world under his subjection, right as thou were a God, and hast no term of this life." *Travels of Sir John Mandeville* (London: Macmillan, 1923), p. 194.

8. *The Anatomy of Melancholy,* ed. Floyd Dell and Paul Jordan-Smith (New York: Tudor, 1927), p. 75.

9. *A Relation of a Journey begun An: Dom 1610. Foure Books. Containing a description of the Turkish Empire, of Aegypt, of the Holy Land, of the Remote parts of Italy, and lands adjoining* (London, 1615), p. 127. Later in the century, Thomas Flatman calls the Pyramids "eternal symbols of pride and sin" in his *Ode Made in the Time of the Great Sickness, 1665.* See *Minor Poets of the Caroline Period,* ed. George Saintsbury (Oxford: The Clarendon Press, 1921), III, 16.

10. *Selected Prose,* ed. Helen Gardner and Timothy Healy (Oxford: The Clarendon Press, 1967), p. 79.

11. In *Spenser's World of Glass: A Reading of "The Faerie Queene"* (Berkeley and Los Angeles: University of California Press, 1966), Kathleen Williams identifies the Blatant Beast as "that impulse of pleasure in negation and in pulling down of good achievement, that inability to believe in any motive but the lowest, which is a permanent element in human society" (p. 194). Jane Aptekar considers the role of the Blatant Beast in Book V of *The Faerie Queene* in *Icons of Justice* (New York: Columbia University Press, 1969), pp. 201–14.

12. Cited in J. E. Neale, *Essays in Elizabethan History* (London: Jonathan Cape, 1958), p. 34.

13. Gerard de Malynes, *The Center of the Circle of Commerce* (1623; rpt. Clifton, N.J.: A. M. Kelley, 1973), p. 139.

14. The identification of Israel and England is discussed in William Haller, *The Elect Nation* (New York: Harper and Row, 1963), and Harold Fisch, *Jerusalem and Albion* (New York: Schocken Books, 1964). In *Essays,* Neale cites an Elizabethan navigator's claim: "There is no doubt but that we of England are this saved people, by the eternal and infallible presence of the Lord predestinated to be sent into these Gentiles in the sea . . . there to preach the peace of the Lord; for are not we only set upon Mount Zion to give light to all the rest of the world; . . . It is only we, therefore, that must be these shining messengers of the Lord, and none but we" (p. 29).

15. *Anatomy of Melancholy,* p. 82.

16. *Works,* IX, 149. A full context for the *Vewe* is provided by Pauline Henley's *Spenser in Ireland* (1928; rpt. New York: Russell & Russell, 1969).

17. J. L. Stampfer, "The Cantos of Mutabilitie: Spenser's Last Testament of Faith," *University of Toronto Quarterly*, 21 (1952), 141–44. C. Litton Falkiner relates the dispute of Mutabilitie and Dame Nature directly to Spenser's ambivalent feelings about "the system of selfish, unprincipled and purposeless methods of government which had lasted through the poet's Irish career." *Essays Relating to Ireland* (London: Longmans, Green, 1909), pp. 3–31.

Chapter 3. John Dyer in the Eternal City

1. For the 1811 remark, *Letters*, II, 521; For the 1829 remark, *The Letters of William and Dorothy Wordsworth: The Later Years*, ed. Ernest de Selincourt (Oxford: The Clarendon Press, 1939), p. 346. In a letter to Horace Walpole, Thomas Gray wrote, "Mr. Dyer (here you will despise me highly) has more of poetry in his imagination, than almost any of our number; but rough and injudicious." *Correspondence of Thomas Gray*, ed. Paget Toynbee and Leonard Whibley, 3 vols. (Oxford: The Clarendon Press, 1935), I, 295–96.

2. Johnson's most serious error, which even George Birkbeck Hill let pass in his edition of *Lives of the English Poets*, is his statement that Dyer "travelled to Italy, and coming back in 1740 published *The Ruins of Rome*." Johnson at least did not, like some later commentators, confuse John with Samuel Dyer, a member of Johnson's Literary Club. A modern and carefully researched biography is Ralph M. Williams, *Poet, Painter, and Parson: The Life of John Dyer* (New York: Bookman Associates, 1956).

3. *Silence in the Snowy Fields* (Middletown, Conn.: Wesleyan University Press, 1968), p. 46.

4. *The Prose of Sir Thomas Browne*, ed. Norman Endicott (New York: New York University Press, 1968), pp. 343, 335.

5. *The Subtler Language* (Baltimore: The Johns Hopkins University Press, 1959), p. 73. The identification of the stag as Strafford has been generally accepted. Brendan O Hehir, in *Expans'd Hieroglyphics: A Study of Sir John Denham's "Cooper's Hill" with a Critical Edition of the Poem* (Berkeley and Los Angeles: University of California Press, 1969), argues that the stag must be Charles I, but his view is a minority one.

6. *English Taste in Landscape in the Seventeenth Century* (Ann Arbor: University of Michigan Press, 1955), pp. 138–39. Richardson, undoubtedly, would have introduced Dyer to works like Henry Peachum's popular treatise, *Graphice: or the Most Auncient and Excellent Art of Drawing and Limning*, which recommends "the ruines of Churches, Castles and c." as an effective addition to natural landscapes. See ibid., p. 44. Elizabeth Mainwaring surveys the influence of Claude and Salvator Rosa in *Italian Landscape in Eighteenth Century England* (New York: Oxford University Press, 1925). Paul Zucker's *Fascination of Decay* (Ridgewood, N.J.: The Gregg Press, 1968), traces the vogue of ruins in painting throughout modern (Western) history.

7. Williams, *Life*, p. 71.

8. Robert Willmott, ed., *The Poetical Works of Mark Akenside and John Dyer* (London, 1855), p. 115.

9. Addison, in his *Letter from Italy*, line 12.

10. See Cohen's essay, "Interrelations of Literary Forms," in *New Approaches to Eighteenth-Century Literature*, ed. Phillip Harth (New York: Columbia University Press, 1974), p. 41. Paul Fussell, whose discussion of architectural imagery in eighteenth-century works has aided me in approaching Dyer, remarks that "the constant excavation of classical antiquities during the eighteenth century, not in Rome only but also in such sites as Herculaneum and Pompeii, guaranteed that the ruins of Rome would occupy something like the center of the imagination." *The Rhetorical World of Augustan*

Humanism (Oxford: The Clarendon Press, 1965), p. 293. The compelling power of Roman ruins, however, lay in their conformity with the ruins of all empires, and not until the eighteenth century (if then) did the English public begin to realize the enormity of those vanished civilizations by means of travel literature. Works like Henry Maundrell's *Journey from Aleppo to Jerusalem* (1703), Richard Pococke's *A Description of the East* (1745), Robert Wood's *The Ruins of Palmyra* (1753), and Richard Chandler's *Travels in Asia Minor* (1765) expanded and deepened the abyss of historical retrospection.

11. Willmott, ed., *Poetical Works*, p. vii.

12. From Bowden's poem, *Antiquities and Curiosities in Wiltshire and Somerset* (1733). Quoted in Robert Arnold Aubin, *Topographical Poetry in Eighteenth Century England* (New York: Modern Language Association, 1936), p. 198. Bowden compares the ruins in Wiltshire to the Pyramids, a not uncommon analogy because of the pyramidal shapes of the ruins at Avebury. Poets who wished to import the symbolic significance of Egyptian remains (treated in my second chapter) into a poem about England were always willing to stretch an architectural point. The word "dome" for example, could be applied to the Pyramids under the Latin usage for home or mansion, and then used to cinch the comparison by reference to the hemispherical structures of London. John Ogilvie in *The Day of Judgement* (1762) refers to "Th'Aegyptian pyramid, majestic dome! / Where Kings exchang'd the scepter for the tomb" in conjunction with the final purging of London's sins: "To aid the fire Britannia's domes combin'd, / Nor left one trace of all their pomp behind." *Poems on Several Subjects to which is prefix'd An Essay on the Lyric Poetry of the Ancients* (London, 1762).

13. Frank H. Ellis, ed., *Poems on Affairs of State: Augustan Satirical Verse, 1660–1714*, VI (New Haven: Yale University Press, 1970), 12–25. The treatment of William III recalls that of Charles II upon his restoration. Some poets, like Dryden, imagined Charles as a heaven-sent salvation from the "sad ruines" of Puritan oppression (*To His Sacred Majesty*, 25). Other writers foresaw worse ruins as a result of the Stuart triumph. See Steven N. Zwicker, *Dryden's Political Poetry* (Providence: Brown University Press, 1972), pp. 71–77.

14. *The Prose Works of Alexander Pope*, ed. Norman Ault (Oxford: Blackwell, 1936), I, 143–44.

Chapter 4. The Fleece *and the World's Great Age*

1. Jacques Choron, *Death and Modern Man* (New York: Collier Books, 1964), p. 106. Freud writes, "It is indeed impossible to imagine our own death; and whenever we attempt to do so we can perceive that we are in fact still present as spectators. Hence the psycho-analytic school could venture on the assertion that at bottom no one believes in his own death, or, to put the same thing in another way, that in the unconscious every one of us is convinced of his own immortality." *The Standard Edition of the Complete Psychological Works of Sigmund Freud*, ed. James Strachey (London: The Hogarth Press, 1964), XIV, 289.

2. Frank H. Ellis, ed., *Poems on Affairs of State: Augustan Satirical Verse, 1660–1714*, VI (New Haven: Yale University Press, 1970), 391, 484.

3. *The History of the Decline and Fall of the Roman Empire*, ed. J. B. Bury (London: Methuen, 1914), III, 357.

4. I use here the edition of Plato's *Republic* translated and edited by F. M. Cornford (London: Oxford University Press, 1971), pp. 61, 125.

5. James Boswell, *The Life of Samuel Johnson*, ed. George Birkbeck Hill, rev. L. F. Powell (Oxford: The Clarendon Press, 1934–50), II, 453.

6. *At the End of the Open Road* (Middletown, Conn.: Wesleyan University Press,

1964), p. 55. The line of Whitman is from *Song of the Exposition,* a manifesto-poem honoring common trades and occupations.

7. Quoted and discussed in O. H. K. Spate's essay, "The Muse of Mercantilism," *Studies in the Eighteenth Century: Papers Presented to David Nichol Smith Memorial Seminar* (Toronto: University of Toronto Press, 1969), p. 126.

8. *The Compleat English Gentleman* (London: David Nutt, 1890), pp. 176–77, 212. Defoe is here following the lead of the Royal Society, which recommended the new knowledge of natural philosophy and practical arts as a means to revitalize poetry as well. Thomas Sprat, the historian of the society, wrote in 1667: "The wit that is founded on the arts of mens hands is masculine and durable: It consists of images that are generally observ'd, and such visible things which are familiar to mens minds. This therefore I will reckon as the first sort [of wit in writing] which is still improvable by the advancement of experiments." See Dwight L. Durling, *Georgic Tradition in English Poetry* (New York: Columbia University Press, 1935), p. 19. John Chalker surveys the popularity of didactic poetry in this period in *The English Georgic: A Study in the Development of a Form* (Baltimore: The Johns Hopkins University Press, 1969).

9. Quoted in Ralph M. Williams, *Poet, Painter, and Parson: The Life of John Dyer* (New York: Bookman Associates, 1956), p. 98.

10. *English Literature in the Early Eighteenth Century, 1700–1740* (New York: Oxford University Press, 1959), p. 518.

11. Strain the Third, stanza 7. Richard Koebner, in *Empire* (Cambridge: Cambridge University Press, 1961), points out that the term "British Empire" was substantiated in the eighteenth century by the revenues from England's sea-borne trade. He traces the motif of an "empire of the sea" from Matthew Prior's *Carmen Seculare for the year 1700*—which includes high praise for woolen exports—through the poetry of John Dennis, Thomson, Dyer, and Young.

12. A definitive text is *"The Castle of Indolence" and Other Poems,* ed. Alan Dugald McKillop (Lawrence: University of Kansas Press, 1961). There seems to have been a vogue of poems forecasting an apocalyptic doom for England. Often they appeared under the guise of a poem about the Day of Judgment. John Ogilvie peered back at his own time in *The Day of Judgment:*

> Where now the nation, whose controuling law
> Rul'd every state, and held a world in awe?
> Say where, Britannia, thy remoter plain?
> Thy fields enrich'd with Plenty's welcome train?
> Thy fleets, to sound their dreadful fame afar,
> And rule the deep, the thunderbolts of war?
> Still in my thought thy happier days detain'd,
> When George, when Anna, when Eliza reign'd.

See his *Poems on Several Subjects to which is prefix'd An Essay on the Lyric Poetry of the Ancients* (London, 1762), p. 58. See also Pope's *Epistle to Bathurst,* 133–44.

13. *History of Economic Analysis* (New York: Oxford University Press, 1954), pp. 346–47.

14. *Studies in Iconology* (1939; rev. ed., New York: Harper Torchbooks, 1962), p. 73.

15. Thomson's contradictions are documented by R. D. Havens in "Primitivism and the Idea of Progress in Thomson," *Studies in Philology,* 29 (1932), 41–52. For more examples from the eighteenth century, enough to suggest a national blindness, see Lois Whitney, *Primitivism and the Idea of Progress in English Popular Literature of the Eighteenth Century* (Baltimore: The Johns Hopkins University Press, 1934).

16. Robert Willmott, ed., *The Poetical Works of Mark Akenside and John Dyer* (London, 1855), p. 41.

17. William Cobbett chronicled the degeneration of English workers in service of "Seigneurs of the Twist, sovereigns of the Spinning Jenny, great Yeomen of the Yarn." *Political Register*, 10 July 1824.

18. Cited by Samuel Johnson in his *Life of Dyer*.

19. Willmott, ed., *Poetical Works*, p. xvi.

Chapter 5. Roxana *and* Empire

1. In his essay, "On the Desire of Distinction," *The Prose Works of Alexander Pope*, ed. Norman Ault (Oxford, Blackwell, 1936), I, 20. "The Desire of Distinction," he writes, "was doubtless implanted in our Natures as an additional Incentive to exert our selves in virtuous Excellence." But he cautions, "This Passion indeed, like all others, is frequently perverted to evil and ignoble Purposes; so that we may account for many of the Excellencies and Follies of Life upon the same innate Principle, to wit, the Desire of being remarkable."

2. The West Indies comprised England's most important colonies during the eighteenth century, and Dyer's moral problem was complicated further by the insatiable need of the West Indian plantations for slaves. It was no secret that slaves were mistreated on a scale approaching genocide. One account is the following: "In Barbados in 1763 . . . the slave population stood at 70,000. Over the next eight years 35,000 more were imported yet the slave population rose to only 74,000—in those eight years 31,000 slaves died on the island. A complete turn-over of the slave population every twenty years or so was not considered unusual by West Indian planters." *The Horizon History of the British Empire*, ed. Stephen W. Sears (New York: American Heritage, 1970), p. 42. Though Dyer admits that "there are ills to come of crimes" he stops short of making the popular prediction that the slave trade would cause the eventual destruction of the English empire. His friend Richard Savage had made such a forecast in his poem, *Of Public Works* (1737), employing the familiar analogy to Rome:

> Why must I Afric's sable children see
> Vended for slaves, though form'd by Nature free,
> The nameless tortures cruel minds invent,
> Those to subject, whom Nature equal meant?
> If these you dare (albeit unjust success
> Empowers you now unpunish'd to oppress)
> Revolving empire you and your's may doom.
> (Rome all subdued, yet Vandal's vanquish'd Rome)
> Yes, empire may revolve, give them the day,
> And yoke may yoke, and blood may blood repay.

A survey of verse contributions to the debate on the slave trade may be found in Cecil A. Moore, *Backgrounds of English Literature 1700–1760* (Minneapolis: University of Minnesota Press, 1953), pp. 132–39.

3. *The Republic*, ed. F. M. Cornford (London: Oxford University Press, 1971), p. 55.

4. I have selected Defoe's terms and quotations from Maximillian E. Novak's discussion of Defoe's aesthetics in *Defoe and the Nature of Man* (New York: Oxford University Press, 1963), pp. 129–61. From my discussion it should be obvious that an approach like Ian Watt's, which insists that "all Defoe's novels are . . . ethically neutral because they make formal realism an end rather than a means," must seem overstated, especially in the case of *Roxana*. Watt's remark is from *The Rise of the Novel* (Berkeley and Los Angeles: University of California Press, 1957), p. 117.

5. *Roxana*, ed. Jane Jack (London: Oxford University Press, 1964), p. 161. All citations in the text are to this edition.

6. *The Rise of the Novel*, p. 114.

7. Defoe, *The Political History of the Devil* (1726; rpt. New York: AMS Press, 1973), pp. 53–54.

8. *Luxury and Capitalism* (Ann Arbor: University of Michigan Press, 1967), p. 60. Sombart links England's increasing wealth with the astonishingly large number of courtesans in eighteenth-century London. He notes that "one outgrowth of the new prominence of the elegant courtesan in social life was that bourgeois wives followed her example in style and taste" (p. 56).

9. This is one of the most controversial scenes in Defoe's fiction. In *Defoe and the Nature of Man*, Novak places Defoe on Amy's side of the argument. Defoe "regarded necessity as a force above all human morality or virtue" (p. 72), he concludes. Novak does identify those characters in Defoe's fiction who hypocritically claim necessity for actions which clearly spring from inclination, and he distinguishes their claims from the legitimate ones of characters facing starvation or certain death. Roxana's later career makes us wonder about the authenticity of her desperation. In his essay, "Sympathy v. Judgment in Roxana's First Liaison," G. A. Starr argues that "Defoe deliberately leaves the question open. Few readers can have given the landlord's brief such wholehearted assent as do Amy and Professor Novak; on the other hand, few readers can have dismissed it as summarily as does Roxana herself. . . . What matters is that we find both sides of the argument sufficiently plausible to ensure that, whatever Roxana finally chooses to do, we shall not condemn her." *The Augustan Milieu: Essays Presented to Louis A. Landa*, ed. Henry Knight Miller, Eric Rothstein, and G. S. Rousseau (Oxford: The Clarendon Press, 1970), pp. 64–65.

10. P. 269. Maximillian E. Novak remarks that "almost all of Defoe's heroes and heroines eventually confront Satan. Moll feels his presence when she thinks of murdering the little girl whom she entices into the alley; Crusoe feels his presence on the island; Captain Singleton dreams of him." "Crime and Punishment in Defoe's *Roxana*," *JEGP*, 65 (1966), 451.

11. Cited and discussed in Maximillian E. Novak, *Economics and the Fiction of Daniel Defoe* (Berkeley and Los Angeles: University of California Press, 1962), p. 33.

12. From *The True-Born Englishman*. See Frank H. Ellis, ed., *Poems on Affairs of State: Augustan Satirical Verse, 1660–1714*, VI (New Haven: Yale University Press, 1970), 287.

13. From Pope's *Epistle to a Lady*, 219–20. The subject of beauty has traditionally absorbed metaphors from the fields of diplomacy and power politics. A commentary pertinent to my discussion is offered by a London periodical called *The Lounger* (1787): "In the [female] sex, I confess I feel myself more inclined to make allowances for those rebels against time, who wish to extend the period of youth beyond its natural duration. The empire of beauty is a distinction so flattering, and its resignation makes so mortifying a change in the state of its possessor, that I am not much surprised if she who has once enjoyed it, tries every art to prolong her reign" (II, 148).

14. I use the following editions: *"Love and Honour" and "The Siege of Rhodes,"* ed. James W. Tupper (Boston: D. C. Heath, 1909), and *The Rival Queens*, ed. P. F. Vernon (Lincoln: University of Nebraska Press, 1970).

15. *Defoe: The Critical Heritage*, ed. Pat Rogers (London: Routledge & Kegan Paul, 1972), p. 81.

16. *The Monk*, ed. Howard Anderson (London: Oxford University Press, 1973), p. 306.

17. *Melmoth the Wanderer*, ed. Douglas Grant (London: Oxford University Press, 1968), p. 354. In modern times the existence of nuclear power has made apocalyptic

forecasts less melodramatic and incredible. In a modern novel like Norman Mailer's *The Deer Park* (New York: G. P. Putnam's Sons, 1955), Hollywood's demoralizing luxury, unregulated sexuality, and destructive willfulness seem to invite a "Blast of Heaven." Marion Faye's soliloquy in the desert resembles Melmoth's:

> So let it come, Faye thought, let this explosion come, and then another, and all the others, until the Sun God burned the earth. Let it come, he thought, looking into the east at Mecca, where the bombs ticked. . . . Let it come, Faye begged, like a man praying for rain, let it come and clear the rot and the stench and the stink, let it come for all of everywhere, just so it comes and the world stands clear in the white dead dawn.   (P. 161)

18. Defoe's own text is *Jure Divino*, Book VII.
19. *The Critical Heritage*, p. 5.

Chapter 6. Graveyard Literature: The Politics of Melancholy

1. *The Background of Gray's Elegy: A Study in the Taste for Melancholy Poetry, 1700–1751* (New York: Columbia University Press, 1924), p. 36. Eleanor M. Sickels extended Reed's survey into the later part of the eighteenth century in *The Gloomy Egoist* (New York: Columbia University Press, 1932).
2. *The Critical Works of John Dennis*, ed. Edward Niles Hooker (Baltimore: The Johns Hopkins University Press, 1939–1943), I, 183. A full discussion of Dennis's contribution to the tradition of melancholy literature may be found in David B. Morris, *The Religious Sublime: Christian Poetry and Critical Tradition in Eighteenth Century England* (Lexington: University Press of Kentucky, 1972), pp. 47–78.
3. *The Christian's Defence Against the Fears of Death, with Seasonable Directions How to Prepare our Selves to Die well* (London, 1701), p. 45.
4. See *Minor Poets of the Caroline Period*, ed. George Saintsbury (Oxford: The Clarendon Press, 1921), III, 413.
5. Cited in Reed, *Background*, p. 69.
6. Included in an omnibus volume of melancholia, *The Grave, To Which are added, Death, Evening Reflections Written in Westminster Abbey, and Night Thoughts Among the Tombs* (London, 1800), n. pag.
7. *Christian's Defence*, p. 29. Louis L. Martz surveys the seventeenth-century background to this attitude in *The Poetry of Meditation* (1954; rev. ed., New Haven: Yale University Press, 1962). Martz emphasizes particularly John Donne's *First Anniversary*, and its description of man's decline through sin:

> There is no health; Physitians say that wee,
> At best, enjoy but a neutralitie.
> And can there bee worse sickness, then to know
> That we are never well, nor can be so?
> Wee are borne ruinous
>
> . . . .
>
> For that first marriage was our funerall:
> One woman at one blow, then kill'd us all.   (91–106)

8. *The Poetical Works of Beattie, Blair, and Falconer*, ed. George Gilfillan (Edinburgh: James Nichol, 1854).
9. *Essays of George Eliot*, ed. Thomas Pinney (New York: Columbia University Press, 1963), p. 378.
10. *The Standard Edition of the Complete Psychological Works of Sigmund Freud*, ed. James Strachey (London: The Hogarth Press, 1961), XXI, 121.

11. *Meditations and Contemplations* (New York: Robert Carter, 1868), p. 61. All citations of Hervey in the text are to this edition.

12. Cowper's letter emphasizes the connection of darkness and grace in a vivid metaphor: "The heart is a nest of serpents, and will be such while it continues to beat. If God cover the mouth of that nest with his hand, they are hush and snug; but if he withdrew his hand, the whole family lift up their heads and hiss, and are as active and venomous as ever."

13. W. Sherlock, *A Practical Discourse Concerning Death* (London, 1713), p. 336.

14. "Memoirs of the Life and Writings of the Rev. James Hervey, A.M." in Hervey, *Meditations*, pp. 3, 6.

15. Martz discusses this tradition in *The Poetry of Meditation;* see especially the example of Robert Southwell, pp. 28–40. Young's line is from *The Last Day*, II, 370. George Eliot distinguishes Young from Cowper on this matter: "Young applauds God as a monarch with an empire and a court quite superior to the English, or as an author who produces 'volumes for man's perusal.' Cowper sees his Father's love in all the gentle pleasures of the home fire-side." *Essays*, p. 384.

16. For a discussion of the retirement myth see E. M. W. Tillyard, *Some Mythical Elements in English Literature* (London: Chatto & Windus, 1961), pp. 72–107. Cowper writes earlier in the poem that retirement calls man

> To regions where, in spite of sin and woe,
> Traces of Eden are still seen below,
> Where mountain, river, forest, field, and grove,
> Remind him of his Maker's power and love.   (27–30)

17. Letter of 26 October 1790. See *The Correspondence of William Cowper*, ed. Thomas Wright (1904; rpt. New York: Haskell House, 1969), III, 492–93.

18. For a review of this subject see Morton D. Paley, "Cowper as Blake's Spectre," *Eighteenth Century Studies*, 1 (1968), 236–52. The quotation in my last sentence is from an entry in Cowper's 1796 diary: "My Despair is infinite, my entanglements are infinite, my doom is sure." See "Cowper's Spiritual Diary," *London Mercury*, 15 (1927), 495.

Chapter 7. The Deserted Village: *The Politics of Nostalgia*

1. Ralph Harper, *The Sleeping Beauty* (New York: Harper & Brothers, n.d.), p. 20.

2. A convenient reprinting of Hill's poem, retitled *A Retrospect*, is *The Book of Georgian Verse*, ed. William Stanley Braithwaite (1809; rpt. Freeport, N.Y.: Books for Libraries Press, 1969), I, 199. Cowper's remark is quoted in David Cecil, *The Stricken Deer* (London: Constable, 1930), p. 284.

3. From *The Rambler*, no. 178. For an extended discussion of Johnson's opinions on remembrance and nostalgia, see Paul Fussell, *The Rhetorical World of Augustan Humanism* (Oxford: The Clarendon Press, 1965), pp. 110–35, and Walter Jackson Bate, *The Achievement of Samuel Johnson* (New York: Oxford University Press, 1955), pp. 63–91.

4. *The Collected Letters of Oliver Goldsmith*, ed. Katherine Balderston (Cambridge: The University Press, 1928), p. 28.

5. *Collected Letters*, p. 40.

6. *The Collected Works of Oliver Goldsmith*, ed. Arthur Friedman (Oxford: The Clarendon Press, 1966), I, 258. Citations in the text are to this edition.

7. In his essay, "The Family-Wanderer Theme in Goldsmith," Morris Golden argues, principally on the basis of *The Vicar of Wakefield*, that Goldsmith mixes his envy of a home situation with condescension: "The family has warmth, stability, comfort, innocence, mutual love. But . . . it is essentially a retreat from the world. Its concerns

are small and narrow, it has a certain selfishness, it achieves nothing of prominence because it is afraid of the unknown, and the unknown is the repository of glory and progress." *ELH,* 25 (1958), 193. Ricardo Quintana similarly believes that the theme of Goldsmith's novel is "We cannot go home and we are recompensed." *Oliver Goldsmith* (New York: Macmillan, 1967), p. 115.

8. *Letters, Speeches, and Tracts on Irish Affairs,* ed. Matthew Arnold (London: Macmillan and Co., 1881), p. 277. For Goldsmith's relation to Irish policy see R. W. Seitz, "The Irish Background of Goldsmith's Social and Political Thought," *PMLA,* 52 (1937), 405–11.

9. In his essay, "The Deserted Village and Goldsmith's Social Doctrines," Howard J. Bell, Jr., points out that Goldsmith formulates his defense of luxury as an improvement over the condition of savagery and not as an absolute good. Thus, Bell argues, there is no essential contradiction between a defense of luxury and an attack on its excesses. Bell's point is well taken, but by flattening Goldsmith's opinions into a platitude ("Goldsmith's attitude toward luxury can be summarized as a belief in the golden mean") Bell loses the tensions inherent in Goldsmith's unique personal situation. *PMLA,* 69 (1944), 747–72.

10. *Critical Essays on Some of the Poems of Several English Poets* (London, 1785), p. 278.

11. *The Search for Good Sense* (1958; rpt. New York: Macmillan, 1961), p. 328. Though enclosure for the sake of private pleasure gardens inflicted obvious damage upon the English peasantry (Goldsmith's term), and presented an easy target for critics, the more common goal of enclosure was a conversion of the traditional and supposedly inefficient system of open-field villages into more profitable farming units. Enclosure was an improvement recommended by many economists after the Restoration. Samuel Fortrey, for example, wrote in his pamphlet *England's Interest and Development* (1673): "How increase and plenty can depopulate, cannot well be conceived; nor surely do any imagine that the people which lived in those towns they call depopulated, were all destroyed, because they lived no longer there; when indeed they were only removed to other places, where they might better benefit themselves, and profit the publick." See *Early English Tracts on Commerce,* ed. J. R. McCulloch (1856; rpt. Cambridge; Economic History Society, 1954), p. 229. Raymond Williams argues in *The Country and the City* (London: Chatto & Windus, 1973) that enclosure must not be viewed as an isolated misfortune which befell a hitherto harmonious agricultural community but as a continuation of exploitation by other means:

> What really happened was that in the economically dynamic areas a capitalist social system was pushed through to a position of dominance, by a form of legalised seizure enacted by representatives of the beneficiary class. This is crucially important, and in the acreage it affected—a quarter of all cultivated land— it can be said to be decisive. But it cannot be isolated from the long development of concentration of landholding, from the related stratification of owners and tenants, and from the increasing number of the landless, which were the general consequences of agrarian capitalism.   (P. 98)

Ironically, Williams points out, some villages enjoyed more community spirit than they had mustered for centuries when they united in the nineteenth century to seek their political rights from landlords.

12. John Forster, in his biography of Goldsmith, calls attention to "one of the most subtle and curious remarks made by [Johnson] in almost the whole of *Boswell.*" The passage is from the entry for 20 September 1773 during the tour to the Hebrides: "Depend upon it, this rage of trade will destroy itself. You and I shall not see it, but the time will come when there will be an end on't. Trade is like gaming. If a whole

company are gamesters, it must cease, for there is nothing to be won. When all nations are traders, there is nothing to be gained by trade. And it will stop the soonest where it is brought to the greatest perfection. Then, only the proprietors of land will be the great men." *The Life and Times of Oliver Goldsmith* (London: Chapman and Hall, 1871), II, 116.

13. *The Political Writings of Dr. Johnson*, ed. J. P. Hardy (New York: Barnes & Noble, 1968), p. 76.

14. See also his discussion of "the natural rise and decline of kingdoms" in Letter XXV of *Citizen of the World*.

15. *The Horizon History of the British Empire*, ed. Stephen W. Sears (New York: American Heritage, 1973), p. 496. For a more sympathetic view see Lawrence Henry Gipson, *The Triumphant Empire*, Vol. IX of *The British Empire Before the American Revolution* (New York: Knopf, 1956), pp. 3–21.

16. In his *History of the Earth, and Animated Nature*, Goldsmith describes the life of birds in terms of their homing instinct, like the lark who sings ecstatically because it approaches the nest, "the spot where all its affections are centered, the spot that has prompted all this joy." His highest praise, significantly, is for birds which "though they are so well fitted for changing place with ease and rapidity, yet the greatest number remain contented in the districts where they have been bred, *and by no means exert their desires in proportion to their endowments*" (italics mine). See *The Works of Oliver Goldsmith*, ed. Peter Cummingham (New York: Harper & Brothers, 1881), pp. 421, 412.

17. *Miscellaneous Poems by Several Hands* (London, 1726), pp. 98–99.

Chapter 8. Wordsworth at Grasmere

1. *The History of the Decline and Fall of the Roman Empire*, ed. J. B. Bury (New York: Heritage Press, 1946), III, 2426–29 and II, 1224–25. Gibbon concludes his "General Observations" optimistically: "Since the first discovery of the arts, war, commerce, and religious zeal have diffused, among the savages of the Old and New World, these inestimable gifts: they have been successively propagated; they can never be lost. We may therefore acquiesce in the pleasing conclusion that every age of the world has increased, and still increases, the real wealth, the happiness, the knowledge, and perhaps the virtue, of the human race" (II, 1225). But see my later chapters for the precarious conditions, suggested even in this passage, of Gibbon's optimism.

2. *The Lounger: A Periodical Paper* (London, 1787), II, 121–22.

3. *Philosophical and Critical Observations on the Nature, Character and Various Species of Composition* (London, 1774), p. 233.

4. *Collected Works*, ed. P. P. Howe (London: J. M. Dent, 1930–34), VIII, 22. In *The Friend*, ed. Barbara E. Rooke (London: Routledge & Kegan Paul, 1969), II, 41, Coleridge wrote in a similar tone about recollections (italics mine):

> If men laugh at the falsehoods that were imposed on themselves during their childhood, it is because they are not good and wise enough to contemplate the Past in the Present, and so to produce by a virtuous and thoughtful sensibility that continuity in their self-consciousness which nature has made the law of their animal life. Ingratitude, sensuality, and hardness of heart all flow from this source. Men are ungrateful to others only when they have ceased to look back on their former selves with joy and tenderness. *They exist in fragments, annihilated as to the Past, they are dead to the future*, or seek for the proofs of it everywhere, only not (where alone they can be found) in themselves.

5. Cited in *The Prelude*, p. 547.

6. *The Collected Writings of Thomas De Quincey*, ed. David Masson, 14 vols. (Edinburgh: Adam and Charles Black, 1889–90), II, 246.

7. *The Landscape of Memory* (Lincoln: University of Nebrasks Press, 1965), p. 80. For examples of Wordsworth's "photographic and omnivorous memory" see F. W. Bateson, *Wordsworth: A Re-Interpretation* (London: Longmans, Green, 1956), pp. 163–64, 191. Karl Kroeber discusses the "somatic component of memory" in relation to *Home at Grasmere* in *Romantic Landscape Vision* (Madison: University of Wisconsin Press, 1975), p. 118.

8. *The Poetical Works of William Drummond of Hawthornden*, ed. L. E. Kastner (New York: Haskell House, 1968), II, 84.

9. The structure of *Tintern Abbey* allows repetition, at the conclusion, to usurp the place of honor given to recollection in the opening paragraphs. Kierkegaard's distinction is relevant: "Repetition and recollection are the same movement, only in opposite directions; for what is recollected has been, is repeated backwards, whereas repetition properly so called is recollected forwards. Therefore repetition, if it is possible, makes a man happy, whereas recollection makes him unhappy." *Repetition*, trans. Walter Lowrie (Princeton: Princeton University Press, 1941), pp. 3–4.

10. *Beyond Formalism: Literary Essays, 1958–1970* (New Haven: Yale University Press, 1970), p. 314. Alan D. McKillop discusses one aspect of the revisitation theme in "Local Attachment and Cosmopolitanism—The Eighteenth Century Pattern," in *From Sensibility to Romanticism*, ed. Frederick W. Hilles and Harold Bloom (New York: Oxford University Press, 1965), pp. 191–218. McKillop notes that "until well into the eighteenth century the force of the idea of an instinctive local attachment deeply rooted in human nature was checked both by a satirical and critical view of human nature itself and by the enduring tradition of classical cosmopolitanism" (p. 197). Goldsmith and Wordsworth are given the principal credit for the triumph of local attachment as a quasi-religious idea later in the century.

11. Wordsworth uses a composite "Vale" in many of his works. In her essay, "Wordsworth's Symbolic Vale as It Functions in *The Prelude*," Mary Lynn Woolley states that "such actual valleys as Grasmere, Esthwaite, and Windermere—almost never mentioned by name—cohere in one Vale having special significance for Wordsworth and for the "I" character who is his hero. From these various valleys, each of which is a self-sustaining universe sheltering the hero in his state of innocence or grace, emerges an archetypal Vale transcending the topography of the Lake District." *Studies in Romanticism*, 7 (1968), 176. Russell Noyes provides a good description of both the return to Grasmere and daily life there in *Wordsworth and the Art of Landscape* (Bloomington: Indiana University Press, 1968), pp. 101–11.

12. Wordsworth's lack of interest in Mary as a poetic subject is difficult to understand until one appreciates that the circuit of feeling between William, Dorothy, and Grasmere was already complete before their marriage in 1802. The one feature wanting is children, second selves when Wordsworth is gone, and for this reason Mary is welcome. In the only poem Wordsworth writes to or about Mary in the prolific year of 1802, titled *A Farewell*, he addresses the poem to Grasmere and tells the vale that "A gentle Maid . . . Will come to you; to you herself will wed; / And love the blessed life that we lead here" (*PW*, II, 24). It is more important that she be recommended to the vale than vice versa.

13. *The Prelude: Text of 1805* (London: Oxford University Press, 1960), p. x. In his essay, "On the Dating of *Home at Grasmere*: A New Approach," John Alban Finch concludes from a study of the manuscripts that "as late as June 1805, *Home at Grasmere* did not exist as a complete unit: parts of it had no doubt been written in 1800, but for Wordsworth himself the poem did not yet have a separate entity." As Finch admits, dating is problematic because manuscript portions of the text from the period after 1800 may be transcriptions or revisions of 1800 texts afterward destroyed. My assumption in this chapter is that all of the feelings described in *Home at Grasmere* belong to the first

year of Wordsworth's residence. It is clear from many texts that revisitation stimulated him into the writing of an ambitious long poem and that *The Prelude* was the result. Once Wordsworth decided that *The Prelude* should be published after *The Recluse*, however, it may have suited his purpose, as Finch suggests, to write a section of *Home at Grasmere* linking his earlier project with his later one. *Bicentenary Wordsworth Studies, in Memory of John Alban Finch*, ed. Jonathan Wordsworth (Ithaca: Cornell University Press, 1970), pp. 14–28.

14. *The Fane of the Druids* (London, 1787), p. vi.

15. *Collected Letters of Samuel Taylor Coleridge*, ed. E. L. Griggs (Oxford: The Clarendon Press, 1959), IV, 956. Herbert Lindenberger cites a passage from De Quincey which tries to account for Coleridge's own failure to return to the Lakes: "What might be his reason for this eternal self-banishment from scenes which he so well understood in all their shifting forms of beauty, I can only guess. Perhaps it was the very opposite reason to that which is most obvious: not possibly because he had become indifferent to their attractions, but because his undecaying sensibility to their commanding power had become associated with too afflicting remembrances, and flashes of personal recollections, suddenly restored and illuminated—recollections which will "Sometimes leap / From hiding places ten years deep," and bring into collision the present with some long-forgotten past, in a form too trying and too painful for endurance." Lindenberger notes that "the dialectic in which [De Quincey] accounted for Coleridge's absence shows his complete immersion in Wordsworth's theory of the restorative effects of memory." *On Wordsworth's "Prelude"* (Princeton: Princeton University Press, 1963), p. 183. The theme of return in Romantic art and philosophy is surveyed by M. H. Abrams in *Natural Supernaturalism* (New York: W. W. Norton, 1971). Abrams comments on *Home at Grasmere* on pp. 288–92.

16. In 1839 De Quincey wrote his "Recollections of Grasmere" for *Tait's Edinburgh Magazine*. Speaking of one "dependancy of Grasmere" named Easedale he comments: "I have thought that, if a scene on this earth could deserve to be sealed up, like the valley of Rasselas, against the intrusions of the world—if there were one to which a man would willingly surrender himself a prisoner for the years of a long life—this it is—this Easedale—which would justify and recompense the sacrifice." *Recollections of the Lakes and the Lake Poets*, ed. David Wright, p. 250.

17. *The Prelude*, p. 525.

18. A variant for lines 149–51 quoted in text (*PW*, V, 477). Abbie Findlay Potts compares Grasmere to John Bunyan's Heaven in *Pilgrim's Progress*, in *Wordsworth's "Prelude": A Study of Its Literary Form* (Ithaca: Cornell University Press, 1953), pp. 230–32.

19. Stephen Gill has reconstructed the text of the earliest draft in *The Salisbury Plain Poems of William Wordsworth* (Ithaca: Cornell University Press, 1975). See also Enid Welsford, *Salisbury Plain: A Study in the Development of Wordsworth's Mind and Art* (New York: Barnes & Noble, 1966).

Chapter 9. The Arab Rider

1. *The Salisbury Plain Poems of William Wordsworth*, ed. Stephen Gill (Ithaca: Cornell University Press, 1975), p. 110.

2. *Between Past and Future: Eight Exercises in Political Thought* (New York: Viking Press, 1968), pp. 162–63.

3. See John Alban Finch, "Wordsworth's Two-Handed Engine," *Bicentenary Wordsworth Studies in Memory of John Alban Finch*, ed. Jonathan Wordsworth (Ithaca: Cornell University Press, 1970), pp. 1–13.

4. *Père Goriot*, trans. Henry Reed (New York: New American Library, 1962), pp. 36, 72–73, 250. "Adequately treated," Balzac writes, "the poor student's struggles with Paris could provide one of the most dramatic themes in modern civilization" (p. 122).

5. *The Table Talk and Omniana of Samuel Taylor Coleridge*, ed. H. N. Coleridge (London: Oxford University Press, 1917), p. 189. A good discussion is Ford T. Swetnam, "The Satiric Voices of *The Prelude*," *Bicentenary Wordsworth Studies*, pp. 92–110.

6. *Confessions of an English Opium-Eater*, ed. Malcolm Elwin (London: Macdonald, 1956), p. 256. Throughout his sufferings in London, De Quincey yearned to join Wordsworth in Grasmere, where he did finally settle in 1809. "*That* is the road to the north, and, therefore, to Grasmere," he would tell himself while pent in the great city, "and if I had the wings of a dove, *that* way I would fly for rest" (p. 257).

7. *Between Past and Future*, pp. 111–12.

8. *The Ruins, or a Survey of the Revolutions of Empires* (Philadelphia: James Lyon, 1799), p. 191.

9. *The Poetical Works of Robert Southey* (Boston: Houghton, Osgood, 1880), I, 103.

10. *Poetical Works*, I, 360.

11. *An Historical and Moral View of the Origin and Progress of the French Revolution and the Effect It Has Produced in Europe* (1795; rpt. Delmar, N.Y.: Scholars' Facsimiles, 1975), p. 460. Carlyle's revolutionary says of Versailles: "Beautiful, if seen from afar, resplendent like a Sun; seen near at hand a mere Sun's-atmosphere, hiding darkness, confused ferment of ruin!" *The French Revolution* (New York: Modern Library, 1934), p. 177.

12. *Evidence for a Future Period of Improvement* (London, 1787), p. 20.

13. Southey, *Poetical Works*, I, 64. For the Miltonic influence on the Romantic poets' double vision of the sun, see Geoffrey H. Hartman, *Beyond Formalism: Literary Essays, 1958–1970* (New Haven: Yale University Press, 1970), pp. 124–50. Two excellent discussions of the apocalyptic element in revolutionary rhetoric are M. H. Abrams, "English Romanticism: The Spirit of the Age," *Romanticism Reconsidered*, ed. Northrop Frye (New York: Columbia University Press, 1963), pp. 26–72, and Carl Woodring, *Politics in English Romantic Poetry* (Cambridge, Mass.: Harvard University Press, 1970).

14. The *Letter to the Bishop of Llandaff* and pertinent selections from the appendix to Watson's pamphlet can be found in *Prose*, I, 29–66.

15. *The French Revolution*, pp. 467–68. The recognizable source of this sentiment is Rousseau's *Discours sur l'inegalité*.

16. *Reflections on the French Revolution*, ed. A. J. Grieve (London: J. M. Dent, 1955), pp. 36–37. Conservatives in France, like Burke, used the ruin sentiment against the Revolution just as Volney had employed it in the Revolution's defense. In a pamphlet of 1795, for example, the aristocrat Adrien Paul Francois Marie Lezay-Marnezia tells how he returns from a visit to the ruins of Greece when he hears of the new French Republic. "Une grande et heureuse révolution venoit, disait-on, de s'opérer dans l'Occident. Un peuple de héros, conduit par un peuple de sages, avoit réalisé les rêves de Platon," he writes sarcastically. In fact, he finds worse ruins in Lyons and Paris than in Athens, and desolation in the formerly prosperous villages. The Revolution, he claims, was not an experience of liberation: "S'il étoit vrai que ces torrens de sang dont ils ont inondé ses autels, eussent coulé en pure perte, et que tout ce que ce peuple a prodigué pour élever son temple eût été dépensé à lui forger des chaînes!" *Les Ruines ou Voyage pour servir de suite à celui de la Grèce*, 2nd ed. (Paris, 1795), pp. 2, 21.

17. David Perkins states his equation thus: "the Arab is the poet; the shell is the poem; the dreamer is the audience; and the sea is the reality from which the poem comes and to which it leads." *Wordsworth and the Poetry of Sincerity* (Cambridge, Mass.: Harvard University Press, 1964), p. 102. Geoffrey H. Hartman identifies the deluge as the imagination itself: "I shall propose that the dream is sent by Imagination to lead the

poet to recognize its power, and that what the dreamer desires and fears is a direct encounter with Imagination." *Wordsworth's Poetry, 1787–1814* (New Haven: Yale University Press, 1964), p. 229. Frank D. McConnell believes that Hartman's interpretation is self-contradictory, "since the book of apocalyptic poetry is also certainly an imagination symbol, and neither dream- nor poetic-logic seems to countenance the kind of doubling such an interpretation suggests." McConnell believes "that the sea in the dream represents the destructive power of the phenomenal world—and that power apprehended *under the aspect of the visual.*" *The Confessional Imagination: A Reading of Wordsworth's "Prelude"* (Baltimore: The Johns Hopkins University Press, 1974), pp. 132–33. Richard J. Onorato believes that "the impending Apocalypse... would be a revelation of a death behind [Wordsworth] in the past and of a desired life beyond it." He identifies the death as that of Wordsworth's mother. *The Character of the Poet: Wordsworth in "The Prelude"* (Princeton: Princeton University Press, 1971), p. 375.

18. *William Wordsworth: The Early Years, 1770–1803* (Oxford: The Clarendon Press, 1957), p. 250. The dating of a dream in a literary work is always hazardous. Jane W. Smyser has pointed out that the imagery of the dream owes a great deal to a dream recorded by Descartes. Wordsworth may have heard about this, from Coleridge most likely, and amalgamated Descartes's symbols into dreamworks of his own. See "Wordsworth's Dream of Poetry and Science: *The Prelude,* V," *PMLA,* 71 (1956), 269–75. Abbie Potts does not relate the dream to the French Revolution, but she does see it as an expression of anxiety about the state of English culture: "The deluge which threatens human culture looks like a Wordsworthian version of Pope's deluge of dullness and darkness which 'drown'd... Sense, and Shame, and Right, and Wrong' in *The Dunciad.*" *Wordsworth's "Prelude": A Study of Its Literary Form* (Ithaca: Cornell University Press, 1953), p. 51. Michael Ragussis points to classical descriptions of a civilization's overwhelming: Ovid's tale of the flood in *Metamorphoses* and Plato's account in the *Timaeus.* "Language and Metamorphosis in Wordsworth's Arab Dream," *Modern Language Quarterly,* 36 (June 1975), pp. 148–65.

19. In quoting from the dream in Book V, I have relied on the 1805 text of *The Prelude* because its language stays closer to Wordsworth's feelings in that period. His most significant alteration in the later text is the identification of the dreamer not as a friend but as himself.

20. *The Looker-On* (London, 1794), III, 31.

21. Commenting on the idolatry of Napoleon in a lay sermon of 1816, Coleridge writes, "Hope in which there is no Chearfulness; Stedfastness within and immovable Resolve, with outward Restlessness and whirling Activity; Violence with Guile; Temerity with Cunning; and, as the result of all, Interminableness of Object with perfect Indifference of Means; these are the qualities that have constituted the COMMANDING GENIUS! these are the Marks, that have characterized the Masters of Mischief, the Liberticides, and mighty Hunters of Mankind, from NIMROD to NAPOLEON. And from inattention to the possibility of such a character as well as from ignorance of its elements, even men of honest intentions too frequently become fascinated. Nay, whole nations have been so far duped by this want of insight and reflection as to regard with palliative admiration, instead of wonder and abhorrence, the Molocks of human nature." *Lay Sermons,* ed. R. J. White (London: Routledge & Kegan Paul, 1972), pp. 65–66.

22. The quotation is from Rabaud de St. Etienne, a member of the French Assembly. In her biography of Arthur Rimbaud, Enid Starkie surveys the tradition of apocalyptic rhetoric in France, including statements by Vico and Michelet similar to St. Etienne's, as the source of Rimbaud's poem, *Après Le Deluge,* the first of his *Illuminations.* In that poem Rimbaud calls for another flood to cleanse the world. *Arthur Rimbaud* (New York: New Directions, 1961), pp. 313–26.

23. Burke argues that an ahistorical philosophy like the revolutionists' is necessarily "abstract" and looks upon permanent things as obstacles to the general will. Wordsworth applauds Burke's contempt for "all systems built on abstract rights" in a passage added to *The Prelude* sometime after 1820 (VII.512–43). Burke's equation of liberty with the laws regarding real property is discussed by J. G. A. Pocock in *Politics, Language and Time* (New York: Atheneum, 1971), pp. 202–32. See also Donald W. Livingston, "Burke, Marcuse, and the Historical Justification for Revolution," *Studies in Burke and His Time*, 14 (1972–73), 119–31.

24. I have quoted a variant of stanza 52 written on the opposite verso of the manuscript. See *The Salisbury Plain Poems*, p. 103. Robert Southey, in his early poetry, uses Henry V of England as an imperial tyrant comparable to Wordsworth's Pizarro. Southey's obsession with the landscape of war may have influenced Wordsworth's later practice, for when he describes scenes of carnage in his period of militant patriotism he uses language remarkably similar to Southey's. If there is one single source for the desert scene of the dream in Book V, which I doubt, it might be Southey's passage in *Joan of Arc* beginning "Sad sight it was / To see so wide a waste" (*Poetical Works*, I, 106). The passage describes the wilderness of France after Henry V has completed his invasion. Shakespeare's model king became the arch-villain of Southey's revolutionary poetry because of his imperial designs on a neighboring nation; when Napoleon threatened England in later years Southey could claim consistency for his opposition.

25. *Meditations and Contemplations* (New York, 1868), p. 271.

26. See Victor Harris, *All Coherence Gone* (Chicago: University of Chicago Press, 1949), p. 182. See also the discussion by M. H. Abrams of Thomas Burnet's *The Sacred Theory of the Earth* (1689), which describes the earth after the deluge as overall "the Image or Picture of a great Ruin... the true Aspect of a World lying in Rubbish." *Natural Supernaturalism* (New York: W. W. Norton, 1971), pp. 99–102.

Chapter 10. The Auburn Syndrome: Change and Loss in Grasmere

1. *Reflections on the French Revolution*, ed. A. J. Grieve (London: J. M. Dent, 1955), p. 55.

2. Ironically, the Wordsworth family resided in the Crump house, Allan Bank, from 1808 to 1811.

3. "Spirit of the Wood" is from Wordsworth's poem, *Nutting*.

4. Maynard Mack, *The Garden and the City* (Toronto: University of Toronto Press, 1969), p. 28.

5. Thomson is the principal influence on the poetry of disassociation, in which "the hurried eye / Distracted wanders" from scene to scene (*Spring*, 518–19). See my discussion in chapter nine of Wordsworth's parodic use of the style.

6. *Observations, Relative Chiefly to Picturesque Beauty, Made in the Year 1776, On Several Parts of Great Britain; Particularly the High-lands of Scotland* (London, 1789), II, 161. Good discussions of the picturesque are Russell Noyes, *Wordsworth and the Art of Landscape* (Bloomington: Indiana University Press, 1968), and J. R. Watson, *Picturesque Landscape and English Romantic Poetry* (London: Hutchinson Educational Ltd., 1970).

7. Cited in Asa Briggs, *The Age of Improvement* (London: Longmans, Green, 1959), p. 48.

8. An incident in 1809 dramatized this fallen spirit perfectly. Two wealthy families abutting Nab Scar, opposite Rydal, disputed the rights to a grove of trees. Each disputant brought workmen in to clear the forest of its choicest timber. The Wordsworths were appalled at the frenzied and profitless destruction. Dorothy wrote, "Oh, my dear Friend! is not this an impious strife? Can we call it by a milder name? I cannot express

how deeply we have been affected by the loss of the trees (many and many a happy hour have we passed under their shade), but we have been more troubled to think that such wicked passions should have been let loose among them. The profits of the wood will not pay the expenses of the workmen on either side!!!" (*Letters*, II, 338).

9. Wordsworth's (and Coleridge's) fascination with architectural structures is discussed in G. Wilson Knight, *The Starlit Dome* (1941; rpt. London: Methuen, 1959), pp. 61–76. See also Donald Wesling, *Wordsworth and the Adequacy of Landscape* (New York: Barnes & Noble, 1970), pp. 72–73. James A. Butler argues that the narrative concerning St. Basil and the Grand Chartreuse attempts to balance the images of transcience in the poem with an architectural emblem of eternity. "Wordsworth's Tuft of Primroses: An Unrelenting Doom," *Studies in Romanticism*, 15 (Summer 1975), 237–48.

10. A contrast to his early view that "hereditary distinctions and privileged orders . . . counteract the progress of human improvement" (*Letters*, I, 123).

11. The railway issue must also be seen in the context of local history, especially the use of enclosures and the ruin of domestic industry which Wordsworth foresaw as one result of the industrial revolution. A good discussion is in Kenneth MacLean, *Agrarian Age: A Background for Wordsworth* (New Haven: Yale University Press, 1950), pp. 87–103.

12. Wordsworth told a similar story to Isabel Fenwick: "Strangely do the tastes of men differ according to their employment and habits of life. 'What a nice well that would be,' said a labouring man to me one day, 'if all that rubbish was cleared off.' The *rubbish* was some of the most beautiful mosses and lichens and ferns and other wild growths that could possibly be seen. Defend us from the tyranny of trimness and neatness showing itself in this way!" See *PW*, IV, 438.

13. *Natural Supernaturalism* (New York: W. W. Norton, 1971), pp. 95, 126, 116.

Chapter 11. The Wordsworthian Child

Note: The literature of this area is vast. Besides the works cited in the notes I have found the following to be useful discussions of the general subject: A. Charles Babenroth, *English Childhood* (New York: Columbia University Press, 1922); Peter Coveney, *Poor Monkey* (London: Rockliff, 1957); Gaston Bachelard, *The Poetics of Reverie* (Boston: Beacon Press, 1960); Morse Peckham, *Man's Rage for Chaos* (New York: Schocken Books, 1967); and the chapter on "The Romantic Revolutionary" in Northrop Frye's *A Study of English Romanticism* (New York: Random House, 1968). For my discussion of the *Ode* I benefited from two works which insist on the importance of Wordsworth's delay in completing the poem: Alan Grob, *The Philosophic Mind* (Columbus: Ohio State University Press, 1973), and Jared R. Curtis, *Wordsworth's Experiments with Tradition* (Ithaca: Cornell University Press, 1971). Though I reach somewhat different conclusions from their readings, I profited by David Ferry's study, *The Limits of Mortality* (Middletown, Conn.: Wesleyan University Press, 1959), and Harold Bloom's *The Visionary Company* (New York: Doubleday, 1961).

1. Wordsworth told this to an American visitor, Orville Dewey, in 1833. See Dewey's *The Old World and the New* (New York, 1836), p. 90.

2. *The Quest for Permanence* (Cambridge, Mass.: Harvard University Press, 1959), p. 80. Perkins charges that the lofty ethical sympathies of the two concluding stanzas are neither precisely defined nor logically derived from the basic premises of the poem.

3. I have been influenced in this view of the *Ode* by G. Wilson Knight's discussion in *The Starlit Dome* (1941; rpt. London: Methuen, 1968). Knight argues that "the child is to be equated with the Eden of Genesis" (p. 47), that is, with the most generalized symbol of beginning or potentiality. The child is thus a figure that Knight can compare

with Shakespeare's Marina or Dante's Beatrice. I have tried to follow Wordsworth's own lead in extending his symbols only to the boundaries of his own work and his own time. In a letter of 1814, for example, Wordsworth remarks that "the soul . . . may be re-given when it had been taken away." But the illustration in the next sentence is characteristically egotistical: "My own Solitary [in *The Excursion*] is an instance of this." Moreover, the Solitary is a recognizable projection of Wordsworth's own historical self. See *Letters*, III, 188.

4. *The Ruins, or a Survey of the Revolutions of Empires* (Philadelphia: James Lyon, 1799), p. 145.

5. *The Age of Improvement* (London: Longmans, Green, 1959), pp. 18–19.

6. William Blake, *The Marriage of Heaven and Hell*, 10:7.

7. C. G. Jung and C. Kerenyi, *Essays on a Science of Mythology*, rev. ed. (New York: Harper Torchbooks, 1973), p. 43. Carlyle captures this aspect of the Revolution in his depiction of "SANSCULLOTISM": "The age of Miracles has come back! 'Behold the World-Phoenix, in fire-consummation and fire-creation: wide are her fanning wings; loud is her death-melody, of battle-thunders and falling towns; skyward lashes the funeral flame, enveloping all things: it is the Death-Birth of a World!'" *The French Revolution* (New York: Modern Library, 1934), p. 168.

8. I use a phrase from a passage by Wordsworth in one of his notebooks. He describes a trancelike state in which "All melts away, and things that are without / Live in our minds as in their native home." See the discussion in Helen Darbishire, *The Poet Wordsworth* (Oxford: The Clarendon Press, 1950), p. 104.

9. *The Letters of William Blake*, ed. Geoffrey Keynes (Cambridge, Mass.: Harvard University Press, 1968), pp. 41–42.

10. *Blake: Prophet Against Empire*, rev. ed. (Princeton: Princeton University Press, 1969), p. 255.

11. *Childhood in Literature and Art* (Boston: Houghton, Mifflin, 1894), pp. 112, 182–83. Wordsworth utters this cry in *The Prelude*, when describing a boy who had somehow retained his innocence amid the indecent atmosphere of a London playhouse. The poet offers a prayer "that this fair creature, checked / By special privilege of Nature's love, / Should in his childhood be detained for ever!" (VII.374–76).

12. *Shelley's Prose*, ed. David Lee Clark (Albuquerque: University of New Mexico Press, 1954), p. 174.

13. Dorothy comments at some length on the distinction of child and incipient adult in another letter:

> Till a child is four years old he needs no other companions, than the flowers, the grass, the cattle, the sheep that scamper away from him when he makes a vain unexpecting chase after them, the pebbles upon the road, &c. &c. After the age of about four years he begins to want some other stimulus than the mere life that is in him; his efforts would be greater but he must have an object, he would run but he must run *races*, he would climb a wall but he has no motive to do it when he is alone; he must have some standard by which to compare his powers or he will have no pleasure in exercising them, and he becomes lifeless and inactive.
>
> (*Letters*, I, 222)

The child figure that interests De Quincey is not the "Child of Joy" but the maturing child represented in Dorothy's letter by Hartley Coleridge. His older sister, whose death at age nine he describes so memorably in *The Affliction of Childhood*, combined "the graces of childhood, and the graces of expanding thought." De Quincey claims that such children have a greater moral delicacy than adults, and "a more pathetic sense of the beauty which lies in justice." *Confessions of an English Opium-Eater*, ed. Malcolm Elwin (London: Macdonald, 1956), pp. 480, 492.

14. *Blake: Prophet Against Empire*, p. 393.

15. *The Friend,* ed. Barbara E. Rooke (London: Routledge & Kegan Paul, 1969), I, 124.

Chapter 12. Westward the Course of Empire

1. All citations of Byron in the text are from *The Complete Poetical Works of Lord Byron*, ed. Paul Elmer More (Boston and New York: Houghton Mifflin, 1905).

2. *Byron and the Ruins of Paradise* (Baltimore: The Johns Hopkins University Press, 1967). "The ruin is at once the remainder of past greatness, glory, even a kind of Eden on earth, and an assertion, all the more powerful for its immortal associations, that the paradisaical past is irretrievable. Further, in contrast to those splendid ruins, the structures of the modern world are dwarfed and awry, the flawed products of postlapsarian man" (p. 31).

3. Napoleon is called a "bastard Attila" in *Marino Faliero*, V.745. See the discussion in Carl Woodring, *Politics in English Romantic Poetry* (Cambridge, Mass.: Harvard University Press, 1970), pp. 175–80. Byron's attack on Lord Elgin appears in his poem *The Curse of Minerva*, wherein the goddess condemns not only the patron "whose noblest, *native* gusto is—to sell," but the state, "receiver of his pilfer'd prey" (172, 174).

4. From the poem, *America Independent* (1778). *The Poems of Philip Freneau*, ed. Fred Lewis Pattee (Princeton: The University Library, 1902), I, 280–81. Washington Irving, in the opening of *Bracebridge Hall*, repeats this sentiment with more regret than triumph. Crayon, the narrator, has found in England "signs of national old age, and empire's decay," which he contrasts to his memory of early America, "where history was, in a manner, anticipation; where every thing in art was new and progressive, and pointed to the future rather than to the past; where, in short, the works of man gave no ideas but those of young existence, and prospective improvement." *Works*, author's rev. ed. (New York, 1856), VI, 71.

5. *Lord Byron's Correspondence*, ed. John Murray (London: Murray, 1922), II, 148.

6. Cited and discussed in Leslie Marchand, *Byron: A Biography* (New York: Knopf, 1957), III, 1202.

7. *Poetical Works of Thomas Moore* (Boston, 1856), II, 23. Antonello Gerbi provides a full background to the belief in the inferiority of the Americas, with special attention to its most important advocates, Buffon, DePauw, and Hegel, in *The Dispute of the New World: The History of a Polemic, 1750–1900*, trans. Jeremy Moyle (Pittsburgh: University of Pittsburgh Press, 1973).

8. *The Travels of William Bartram*, ed. Mark Van Doren (Macy-Masius, 1928), pp. 143, 107.

9. *The New World*, ed. Stefan Lorant (New York: Duell, Sloan and Pearce, 1965), p. 7. See also Howard Mumford Jones, *O Strange New World* (New York: Viking, 1964), pp. 1–34.

10. *Atala and René*, trans. Walter J. Cobb (New York: Signet, 1962), pp. 58–59.

11. For *The Injured Islanders* passage see Lois Whitney, *Primitivism and the Idea of Progress* (Baltimore: The Johns Hopkins University Press, 1934), pp. 59–60. In his valuable book, *The American Adam* (Chicago: University of Chicago Press, 1966), R. W. B. Lewis describes the supercession of the Eden myth, in which the Indian figures prominently, by the doctrine of regeneration, the renewal of spirit through determined purpose and practical action. He cites Parkman's admiration for La Salle as a primary example of the civilizing virtues winning out over the love of wilderness.

12. All citations of Bryant's poetry in the text are from *The Poetical Works of William Cullen Bryant*, ed. Parke Godwin, 2 vols. (New York: Appleton, 1883).

13. *Democracy in America*, ed. Phillips Brady (New York: Knopf, 1953), I, 6–7.

Carlyle's description, in *The French Revolution* (New York: Modern Library, 1934), p. 7, makes the same point:

> The world is all so changed; so much that seemed vigorous has sunk decrepit, so much that was not is beginning to be!—Borne over the Atlantic, to the closing ear of Louis, King by the Grace of God, what sounds are these; muffled-ominous, new in our centuries? Boston Harbour is black with unexpected Tea: behold a Pennsylvania Congress gather; and ere long, on Bunker Hill, DEMOC-RACY announcing, in rifle-volleys death-winged, under her Star Banner, to the tune of Yankee-doodle-doo, that she is born, and, whirlwind-like, will envelop the whole world!

14. *The Writings of Henry David Thoreau* (Boston: Houghton, Mifflin, 1906), II, 266–67. In *The Imperial Self* (New York: Knopf, 1971), Quentin Anderson discusses the self-aggrandizement of the American spirit in the work of Emerson, Whitman, and Henry James. He uses the term "secular incarnation" to describe "the act not of identifying oneself with the fathers, but of catching up all their powers into the self, asserting that there need be no more generations, no more history, but simply the swelling diapason of the expanding self" (p. 58).

15. *The Works of Joel Barlow*, ed. William K. Bottorff and Arthur L. Ford (Gainesville, Fla.: Scholars' Facsimiles & Reprints, 1970), II, 758. For a full discussion of this mode see Ernest Lee Tuveson, *Redeemer Nation: The Idea of America's Millennial Role* (Chicago: University of Chicago Press, 1968), and Henry Nash Smith, *Virgin Land: The American West as Symbol and Myth* (Cambridge, Mass.: Harvard University Press, 1950). A useful bibliography can be found in Edward Halsey Foster, *The Civilized Wilderness* (New York: The Free Press, 1975), pp. 201–14.

16. *Prose Writings of William Cullen Bryant*, ed. Parke Godwin (New York: Appleton, 1884), VI, 405. Never the victim of a foolish consistency, Bryant could take the other side of the issue, as in his address, "The Mercantile Library," in which he praises American manufacture of "superabundant products" from its wealth of natural resources (pp. 270–73). For Moore's remark see *The Letters of Thomas Moore*, ed. Wilfred S. Dowden (Oxford: The Clarendon Press, 1964), I, 64.

17. *The Pioneers* (New York: Dodd, Mead, 1958), pp. 99–100. All citations in the text are to this edition.

18. *Prose Writings*, V, 308.

19. "A new field of enterprise was opened in America—the poets eye was not a prophetic one," Henry Crabb Robinson complained in 1826 to Dorothy Wordsworth about her brother. See Willard L. Sperry, *Wordsworth's Anti-Climax* (1935; rpt. New York: Russell & Russell, 1966), p. 48. Part of Wordsworth's conservative stance was a belief in the necessity of "large Estates continued from generation to generation in particular families" (*Letters*, III, 413). Cooper, who based Templeton on his ancestral home, Cooperstown, would have agreed.

20. *The American Democrat* (New York: Vintage Books, 1956), p. 138. Thomas Philbrick presents an excellent analysis of Temple as a leader and of the mixed nature of Templeton in "Cooper's *The Pioneers*: Origins and Structure," *PMLA*, 79 (1964), pp. 579–93.

21. Cited in Louis Legrand Noble, *The Life and Works of Thomas Cole*, ed. Elliot S. Vesell (Cambridge, Mass.: Harvard University Press, 1964), p. 167.

22. *Natural Supernaturalism* (New York: W. W. Norton, 1971), p. 380.

23. *Thomas Cole's Poetry*, ed. Marshall B. Tymn (York, Pa.: Liberty Cap Books, 1972), pp. 100–12. See also Cole's poem, *On Seeing that a favorite tree of the Author's had been cut down* (p. 67), in which Cole laments, "Vain is my plaint! All that I have must

die." About the same time, Thoreau noted in his journal, "Now I hear, half a mile off, the hollow sound of wood chopping, the work of short winter days begun, which is gradually laying bare and impoverishing our landscape. In two or three thicker woods which I have visited this season, I was driven away by this ominous sound." *The Journals of Henry David Thoreau*, ed. Bradford Torrey and Francis H. Alden, 14 vols. (New York: Dover, 1962), VIII, 942. An excellent survey of the ruins motif in early American literature, which, however, does not include Cole's verse, is Donald Ringe, *The Pictorial Mode: Space and Time in the Art of Bryant, Irving, and Cooper* (Lexington: University Press of Kentucky, 1971).

24. Howard S. Merritt, *Thomas Cole* (Rochester: Memorial Art Gallery, 1969), p. 16.

Chapter 13. Conclusion

1. *The Denial of Death* (New York: The Free Press, 1973), p. 281.

2. *The Standard Edition of the Complete Psychological Works of Sigmund Freud*, ed. James Strachey (London: The Hogarth Press, 1961), XXI, 95.

3. Quoted in Becker, *Denial of Death*, p. 256.

4. *Walden Two* (1948; rpt. New York: Macmillan, 1962), p. 54. This is a fundamental doctrine of graveyard philosophy. William Sherlock writes in *A Practical Discourse Concerning Death* (London, 1713): "All the fine Things you meet with, you rather look upon as Curiosities to be remarked in Story, or to be tried by way of Experiment, or to be used for present Necessity, than as such Things which are to be enjoyed, which you know they are not. And did we use the World thus, we should never grow over-fond of it" (pp. 11–12). See chapter six.

5. *The Christian Renaissance* (London: Methuen, 1962), p. 188.

6. "What made Wordsworth's poems a medicine for my state of mind, was that they expressed, not mere outward beauty, but states of feeling, and of thought coloured by feeling, under the excitement of beauty.... I needed to be made to feel that there was real permanent happiness in tranquil contemplation. Wordsworth taught me this, not only without turning away from, but with a greatly increased interest in the common feelings and common destiny of human beings." John Stuart Mill, *Autobiography*, ed. Jack Stillinger (London: Oxford University Press, 1971), p. 89. "With Wordsworth, it is his way of saying that has influenced me, consoled or made me cry—they come to the same thing.... I want to assert that, in my opinion, his idea of pedagogy is true and primary: it *is* the beauty of the world and simple human affections that develop great-souled and disinterested adults." Paul Goodman, "Wordsworth's Poems," *New York Times Book Review*, 12 January 1969, p. 20.

7. For the relations of Blake's characters and their Spectres see Peter F. Fisher, *The Valley of Vision: Blake as Prophet and Revolutionary* (Toronto: University of Toronto Press, 1961); Kathleen Raine, *Blake and Tradition* (Princeton: Princeton University Press, 1968), I, 249–68; and Janet Warner, "Blake's Figures of Despair: Man in his Spectre's Power," *William Blake: Essays in Honour of Sir Geoffrey Keynes*, ed. Morton D. Paley and Michael Phillips (Oxford: The Clarendon Press, 1973), pp. 208–24.

8. *Milton*, 30:2. His letter reads, "None can know the Spiritual Acts of my three years' Slumber on the banks of the Ocean... unless he should read My long Poem [*Milton*] descriptive of those Acts" (*Letters*, p. 67).

9. Gilchrist remarks, "His upper or bedroom windows commanded a glorious view of the far-stretching sea.... Often, in after years, Blake would speak with enthusiasm of the shifting lights on the sea he had watched from those windows." *Life of William Blake* (London, 1880), I, 158.

10. *Annotations to Watson's "Apology for the Bible,"* p. 14.

11. Blake's quarrels with his patron have received much attention as a paradigm of the artist's divided existence in the world of Experience. But these disputes were too limited in scope for Hayley to be compared in any meaningful way with either the Spectre or Satan in *Milton* and *Jerusalem*. Blake acknowledges in a letter to Hayley in 1805, "You, Dear Sir, are one who has my Particular Gratitude, having conducted me thro' Three that would have been the Darkest Years that ever Mortal Suffer'd, which were render'd thro' your means a Mild & Pleasant Slumber.... I *know* that if I had not been with You I must have perish'd" (*Letters*, p. 121).

12. In conversation with the author at the University of California at Los Angeles, 1964. In *Walden Two* it is the visiting professor who has never heard Bach's Mass, suggesting that the range and depth of experience is greater within the utopian community than outside it (p. 83).

13. *Prometheus Unbound*, IV.574–75.

Index